10/05

Deadly Cults

Deadly Cults

The Crimes of True Believers

ROBERT L. SNOW

PRAEGER

Westport, Connecticut
London

Library of Congress Cataloging-in-Publication Data

Snow, Robert L.
    Deadly cults : the crimes of true believers / Robert L. Snow.
      p. cm.
    Includes bibliographical references and index.
    ISBN 0–275–98052–9 (alk. paper)
    1. Crime—Religious aspects. 2. Cults. I. Title.
BL65.C7S66 2003
209′.024′364—dc22   2003058007

British Library Cataloguing in Publication Data is available.

Library of Congress Catalog Card Number: 2003058007
ISBN: 0–275–98052–9

First published in 2003

Praeger Publishers, 88 Post Road West, Westport, CT 06881
An imprint of Greenwood Publishing Group, Inc.
www.praeger.com

Printed in the United States of America

The paper used in this book complies with the
Permanent Paper Standard issued by the National
Information Standards Organization (Z39.48–1984).

10 9 8 7 6 5 4 3

Copyright Acknowledgments

The author and publisher gratefully acknowledge permission to reprint the
following material:

Excerpts from interviews with Maureen Dilley, Carol Giambalvo, Steven Hassan,
Lawrence Levy, Mitchell Mack, Cathleen Mann, Jim Martin, Nori Muster, Robert
Pardon, Erika Van Meir, and Mark Roggeman.

Every reasonable effort has been made to trace the owners of copyright materials
in this book, but in some instances this has proven impossible. The author and
publisher will be glad to receive information leading to more complete acknowledgments in subsequent printings of the book and in the meantime extend their
apologies for any omissions.

To Fred and Mike, brothers and friends

Contents

CHAPTER 1

Cults in Today's Society

According to reports in several Florida newspapers, on November 25, 1996, a teenage couple drove to a secluded graveyard in Eustis, Florida. After finding a quiet spot among the tombstones, the young man and woman sliced their arms and then drank each other's blood. This ceremony, part of Heather Wendorf's crossover ritual, initiated her into a vampire cult, a group where drinking each other's blood and engaging in group sex were common activities.

Six hours following Heather's initiation, the leader of the vampire cult, Rod Ferrell, surrounded by fellow cult members, savagely beat Heather's parents to death with a crowbar. Ferrell then branded the battered body of Heather's father with a V to symbolize his cult, which authorities say numbered approximately 30 members. The authorities believe the idea for committing these murders may have come about because Heather had reportedly told Ferrell that her home life was hell and she wanted to escape.

Following the murders, Ferrell, Heather, and three other members of the vampire cult fled from Eustis, driving a Ford Explorer belonging to the murder victims. Several days later, the cult members ended up, broke and hungry, in Baton Rouge, Louisiana. The police, alerted to the cult members' location when one of the young women belonging to the cult telephoned her mother in South Dakota to ask for money, arrested the five murder suspects in the parking lot of a Howard Johnson's motel in Baton Rouge. A judge eventually sent the five cult members back to Florida to stand trial.

The authorities in Murray, Kentucky, a town of 13,000 in the southwest part of the state, where the cult originated, first became aware of the existence of this vampire cult through the investigation of a break-in at a local animal shelter, where they found two puppies mutilated. One of the puppies had been stomped to death, while the other had had its legs pulled off. Members of the vampire cult, authorities later learned, had drunk the blood of the puppies. However, this wasn't the only blood they drank.

"They like to cut their arms and suck the blood," said Murray Police Sergeant Mike Jump. "In a ritual in a remote graveyard, they've been known to kill a small animal and suck the blood out of it, supposedly to give them more power."[1]

The police in Louisiana found that all five of the arrested cult members had self-inflicted cuts on their arms when apprehended.

While the existence of a vampire cult may have stunned most Murray residents, the identity of its leader didn't. Around the town of Murray, Rod Ferrell had been looked upon as a very strange individual for some time. Sporting shoulder-length black hair and always wearing a long black trench coat, Ferrell reportedly had often boasted to his friends that he was both a vampire and immortal. Heather also was no wallflower. After meeting Ferrell, she began dyeing her hair purple and wearing black fishnet stockings and a dog collar around her neck. Ferrell reportedly met Heather when he moved for a time from Kentucky to Florida, where he attended Eustis High School. According to her friends, Heather seemed to change radically after she met and began dating Ferrell.

"She was a real nice girl, but deep down you could tell she had some heavy problems," said a friend of Heather's. "She started dyeing her hair—purple mostly—and wearing all black clothes. Some people say she swore she was a vampire."[2]

A youth who dated Heather for several months said, "She enjoyed and got pleasure from drinking her blood and other people's blood."[3]

Rod Ferrell, according to his friends, adopted the vampire name Vassago soon after joining the cult and also apparently became driven by his belief in the power of the vampire cult. "Ferrell had become possessed with opening the Gates to Hell, which meant he would have to kill a large number of people in order to consume their souls," said one of the vampire cult members. "By doing this, Ferrell believed that he would obtain super powers."[4]

In February 1998, Rod Ferrell's trial for the murder of Heather Wendorf's parents began in Tavares, Florida. During the year he had spent in jail waiting for his trial to begin, Ferrell had claimed several times that the Wendorfs were murdered by a rival vampire cult, and at other times that he suffered from multiple personalities and blackouts. However, on February 5, 1998, Ferrell interrupted the opening statements of his trial and announced that he wanted to change his plea to guilty.

"He accepts responsibility and wants to live," his defense attorney said. "He's a young man, and he wants to live."[5]

The prosecutor, however, didn't see the plea change as in any way diverting him from his decision to seek the death penalty for Ferrell. "It doesn't carry any weight with the state of Florida," he said.[6]

During the sentencing hearing that followed his guilty plea, Ferrell claimed, as mitigating circumstances, that he had been sexually abused by his grandfather and his grandfather's friends during cult rituals that involved animal sacrifice. Ferrell told a psychiatrist, who testified about Ferrell's mental state, that his grandfather's cult was called the Black Hand and that the cult rituals, in addition to animal sacrifice, also involved sodomy and sadism.

"The goal of the cult was to release evil into the world and extinguish light," testified another mental health expert who had examined Ferrell.

The grandfather, who attended Ferrell's trial, naturally denied the charges. "You can walk down the street and be accused of anything," he said. "It's hearsay."[7]

Also during the sentencing hearing, jurors heard from Steven Murphy, the man who had initiated Ferrell into the vampire world. He told the court about the rules for being a vampire and about the crossover ritual necessary to become a vampire. "I took out a blade and cut my arm and he took from me," Murphy told jurors. "He cut himself and I took from him and we sat in meditation for a few hours."[8]

On the eve of his sentencing, however, a repentant Ferrell advised other teens not to follow in his path. "I want them to see that this is real life and that it has consequences. I didn't realize the impact and the consequences."[9]

On February 27, 1998, Circuit Court Judge Jerry Lockett, following the jury's recommendation, sentenced Ferrell to death for his role in the brutal murder of Heather Wendorf's parents. "I think you are a disturbed young man," the judge told him.[10] However, on November 9, 2000, the Florida Supreme Court intervened and reduced Ferrell's sentence to life imprisonment without the possibility of parole because he had committed the crime while only 16 years old. On March 4, 2003, Ferrell filed a motion to void his previous guilty plea. In court documents, he claims that his lawyers had pressured him into pleading guilty. He argues that if his lawyers had instead allowed the case to go to trial and introduced evidence about his severe mental problems and hallucinogenic drug use, he likely wouldn't have been convicted. No date has been set yet to hear this appeal.

Three other members of the vampire cult also received prison sentences for their part in the murders, ranging from 10 years to life imprisonment. In addition, Ferrell's mother, Sondra Gibson, age 35, pleaded guilty in Kentucky to "Criminal Attempt to First-Degree Unlawful Transaction with a Minor," for which she received five years of probation. The authorities discovered that she had written letters to a 14-year-old boy, attempting to entice him into having sex with her as a part of the ritual of initiation into the vampire cult.

"I longed to be near you...to become a vampire, a part of the family immortal and truly yours forever," she wrote to the 14-year-old. "You will then come for me and cross over, and I will be your bride for eternity and you my sire."[11]

Amazingly, given the sentences imposed on the other four cult members, two different grand juries cleared Heather Wendorf of any wrongdoing in the murder of her parents. They did this even though she had fled with the other four members of the vampire cult to Baton Rouge.

This story doesn't end, however, with the trials and sentences imposed by the courts. Even prison life apparently couldn't change some members of the vampire cult. In December 1998, prison guards discovered one of the members of the vampire cult, who was serving a 10-year prison sentence for her part in the Wendorf murders, in a prison bathroom sucking blood from the arm of another inmate.

Is the story just related simply an isolated incident? Just a secluded group of messed-up kids? Hardly.

In March 1998, authorities in Dallas, Texas, arrested four members of a vampire cult who, after smoking methamphetamine-laced marijuana during one of their rituals, went on a rampage of vandalism. The four cult members reportedly caused more than $300,000 in damage before the police arrested them.

"I expected it to be messed-up kids," said one of the victims of the rampage. "But this is really bad."[12] The vandalism included setting a fire in a church that destroyed an office and a fellowship hall, painting graffiti on walls, slicing tires, and pouring acid on cars.

According to the *Dallas Morning News*, as reported in a *St. Louis Post-Dispatch* article one of the arrested teenagers told the police that the four of them belonged to a vampire cult. Reportedly, all four members had self-inflicted cuts on their arms where they had sucked each other's blood.[13]

While the idea of a vampire cult may sound bizarre to many people, the truth is that many other types of cults, some just as bizarre, and some even more so, exist today. And while the two vampire cults talked about here demonstrate a high level of violence toward others, many cults can be just as dangerous to their own members. Readers have only to remember the 914 people who died in the Jim Jones Peoples Temple incident in Guyana in 1978, or the 1997 incident in which 39 members of the Heaven's Gate cult in California committed mass suicide. Although these examples may sound extreme, thousands of such cults are active today.

"Cults are just as prevalent today as they were in the 1960s and 1970s, but there are more smaller ones now," Dr. Margaret Thaler Singer, emeritus adjunct professor of psychology at the University of California and America's foremost authority on cults, told me in an interview. "They only get publicity though when they do something horrible, like Jonestown or Uganda" (incidents I will discuss in chapters 3 and 6).[14]

Determining the exact number of cults in existence today can be very difficult, however, because many are secretive and, as Dr. Singer points out, small, often with only a few members. Some that I will talk about, though, are more open and occasionally have tens of thousands of members. Although there is some disagreement about the exact number, experts such as Dr. Singer estimate the likely number of cults in the United States today at about 5,000. Madeleine Landau Tobias and Janja Lalich, in their book *Captive Hearts, Captive Minds,* agree on this number. The Cult Awareness Network, when the original organization was in operation, reportedly received more than 18,000 calls a year inquiring about cults.

Regardless of a cult's size, however, history has shown over and over that these groups are usually founded by charismatic, and always self-appointed, leaders who often attribute divine qualities to themselves. If the leaders don't claim to be God, they at least claim to be a personal representative who speaks for God. In addition, most cult leaders claim to have some type of supernatural or superhuman powers or abilities, or claim to have exclusive access to some universal truth or knowledge unknown to anyone else in the world. Because of this, cult leaders often feel that they are not bound by normal social, legal, or moral limitations of conduct.

As I will show throughout this book, due to the belief that their leaders have been appointed by or are God, cults often hold to what appear to contemporary society to be bizarre and unusual philosophies and theologies. In a cult, the members believe that whatever the leader says or proposes, no matter how bizarre, must be true because it comes directly from God. Of course, it must be remembered that a group can occasionally be labeled a cult not because of abusive or illegal actions but simply because the group's beliefs run counter to accepted theology. One person's cult can be another's religion.

Strong differences exist, however, between the very dangerous and destructive cults I will talk about in the following chapters and what are viewed by many as heretical religious sects. Many of today's accepted religious denominations were once considered heretical, including groups such as the Salvation Army, the Church of God, Christian Science, and others. The important distinction between these groups and cults is that while the accepted religious groups hold to beliefs that are often at odds with mainstream beliefs, they don't exhibit any of the characteristics of destructive cults that I will detail in this book. They are simply groups of fervent believers who disagree on some point of procedure or theology with church leaders.

A large part of religious history is made up of small groups of fervent, dissatisfied people who have broken away from larger religious organizations and formed their own groups. Over time, these breakaways often lose or modify their fervor and become simply other religious denominations. Our Constitution guarantees every citizen the right to practice his or her religion, as long as that practice doesn't harm others, which is the main distinction between religious sects and destructive cults. Just because a group holds to beliefs that appear to the mainstream population to be unusual, or even bizarre, doesn't make them bad, only different.

"One way to quickly cut through the smoke of the cult phenomenon is to avoid trying to make sense of their beliefs and instead look squarely at their actions," says Ken McCarthy in his article "On Cults, Computers, and Cash."[15]

That is exactly what I intend to do. I won't examine the validity of the religious or spiritual beliefs of any group. For the purpose of this book, I will partly use Dr. Michael D. Langone's description of a cult: "[A cult is] a group or movement exhibiting a great or excessive devotion or dedication to some person, idea, or thing, and employing unethically manipulative techniques of persuasion and control designed to advance the goals of the group's leaders, to the actual or possible detriment of members, their families, or the community."[16]

To expand on this definition, I will show throughout this book that cults, along with being centered around the veneration of a living being, use manipulative techniques in recruiting and fund-raising, use high-pressure thought reform techniques to indoctrinate their members (which I will talk about in depth in chapter 14), demand total and complete obedience from all cult members, and manipulate and use cult members (through free work, excessive donations, sexual favors, etc.) for the benefit of cult leaders.

My description of cults goes even a bit farther, though. I intend to look at cults from a law enforcement perspective. Therefore, for my definition of cults, these groups must also be involved in some type of criminal action, be it murder, sexual abuse, assault, kidnapping, arson, financial fraud, or some other offense. Otherwise, I believe, the differences between cults and legitimate breakaway religious movements become blurred. And while I have organized cults into various types, which I will discuss in chapters 3 to 11, in reality the lines between the various cult types are fuzzy at best. Often cults share many of the same traits, beliefs, and rituals, even though each claims to be unique.

Readers naturally may wonder why anyone would want to become involved with and/or stay involved with such a group. Why would anyone want to stay with a group that demands worship and devotion, along with unquestioned obedience, to a leader who is usually only looking out for his or her own good? Why would anyone want to be part of an organization that requires its members to cut all ties with family and former friends, demands sexual favors from its members, and directs its members to take part in fraudulent fund-raising, often for 12 or more hours a day? I will answer all these questions in the following chapters. Yet the fact remains that many people do become and stay involved with such groups. A number of cult experts, including Professor Singer, estimate that as many as 20 million people in the United States have been involved in cults at some time in their lives. A study of 1,000 randomly selected high school students in the San Francisco area discovered that 3 percent of these youths belonged to cults. Another study, this one involving two large metropolitan areas, found that between 2 and 5 percent of the adults interviewed belonged to cults.[17]

This high number of people involved in cults only increases the importance that the public recognize—as demonstrated in the two incidents at the beginning of this chapter involving vampire cults, and as I shall show throughout this book—that cults can be extremely dangerous organizations. A large part of this danger, the authorities find, comes from the fact that many cults teach their members that all people outside the cult, including the families of cult members, are the enemy and that they are all plotting against the cult. This view of the world can often lead cult members to believe that the continued existence of their group requires them to perform some type of dangerous and even deadly action against nonmembers. The poison gas attack carried out by the Japanese cult Aum Shinrikyo, which killed 12 and injured 5,500 innocent victims and which I will talk about in chapter 2, very clearly demonstrates this danger.

However, along with preaching this dangerous paranoia of outsiders, cult leaders also realize that for cults to continue to exist, cult members must be kept both obedient and subservient. Cult members must not be allowed to think independently or to question their leader's motives or actions. Instead, members must immediately do whatever their leader asks of them, no matter what. To accomplish this, many cults practice intense indoctrination and stern discipline, often accompanied by physical and/or sexual abuse. In a number of instances, as I will show, both cult members and the children of cult members have been physically and sexually abused to enforce compliance with the leader's will. Because of this, members of cults and the children of cult members are many times so psychologically damaged by their indoctrination and the time spent in the cult that it often takes intense mental health treatment once they are out of the cult before they are able to function normally again. And interestingly enough, contrary to the public's perception, it's not just losers or misfits who are drawn to cults.

"Often the public comes away with the idea that only wacky people get involved with these groups," said Janja Lalich of the Cult Recovery and Information Center in Alameda, California. "But they are often wonderful people with a real sense of idealism."[18]

Wide-eyed idealists are often joined in destructive cults by people with advanced academic degrees, individuals having large amounts of money, and even elected officials. According to an article in the *Los Angeles Times*, "Researchers say that cults tend to prefer sophisticated recruits, the better to woo them with fanciful pseudointellectual notions. A noted authority on deception, magician James 'Amazing' Randi, said that sophisticates are often easier to deceive than street-smart folks or, for that matter, kids."[19]

Janja Lalich adds, "Cult leaders and cult recruiters capture the hearts, minds, and souls of the best and brightest in our society. Cults are looking for active, productive, intelligent, energetic individuals who will perform for the cult by fund-raising, by recruiting more followers, by operating cult businesses and leading seminars."[20] Substantiating what Lalich says, a number of scientific studies have shown a positive correlation between the level of a person's education and the likelihood of cult membership.[21] However, it's not just the country's brightest youth that cults want. They want members from all age groups. At a cult recovery workshop sponsored several years ago by the American Family Foundation, the average age of the participant was 36.[22]

Putting it simply, one author on cult recruitment says, "The most likely person to be caught up in this type of behavior system is the one who says, 'I won't get caught. It will never happen to me. I am too intelligent for that sort of thing.'"[23] It often takes months or even years, once considerable psychological and often physical damage has been done, before these individuals realize how they were suckered.

Readers should not be left with the notion, however, that it's just individuals who suffer adverse effects from cults. The industry giant Procter & Gamble has suffered for years from bad publicity because of bogus claims that the company was involved in a devil-worshipping cult. Company representatives claim that Procter & Gamble has lost more than $500 million in sales because of these false rumors. Naturally, Procter & Gamble has done everything it can to quash these rumors, including suing those who spread them, and even going so far as to remove their trademark moon-and-stars emblem, alleged by many of the rumor-spreaders to be a satanic symbol.

"We want this thing to go away," said Procter & Gamble spokeswoman Elaine Matthews. "It's malicious. It's wrong. It's untrue.... If the company has a bad image, they're going to suffer."[24] Reportedly, Procter & Gamble has received more than 200,000 calls and letters in the last 15 years because of these rumors.

While the image problems suffered by Procter & Gamble may sound like simply a lot of gullible people listening to unsubstantiated rumors, this paranoia of cults runs extremely deep through our society. And while very often this fear is with good reason and based on fact, sometimes it's not. Occasionally, the immense damage done by some cults can make the public suspicious of any activity or group that is out of the ordinary.

In May of 2001, for example, a Minnesota lawmaker raised the eyebrows of his colleagues when he opposed the appearance of the Dalai Lama before the Minnesota State Legislature. In an e-mail to fellow legislators, he claimed that Buddhism was a cult. Buddhism, of course, is a world religion with hundreds of millions of believers and has been around since the sixth century B.C. In another example, several years ago in Georgia a group of local citizens banded together to oppose the use of a local recreation center for yoga classes. They were convinced that yoga led to devil worship.

"The people who are signed up for the class are just walking like cattle to a slaughter," said one religious leader in Georgia. "Half of yoga is a branch of Eastern mysticism, and it has strong occult influences."[25]

While these examples of vigilance may be a bit extreme, individuals still do need to be on the watch for cults moving in or already existing in their communities. Cults can tear families apart, strip their members financially, and, as I will show in the following chapters, often be involved in crimes such as murder, sexual and physical assault, financial fraud, child abuse, drug violations, arson, and kidnapping.

For readers who may wonder why it is important for them to know what makes a group a cult, since they are not themselves involved in either cults or small religious sects, the reason is cults can be dangerous, and not just to their own members but often to outsiders as well. Readers therefore need to be able to recognize the signs that groups in their communities are cults or that groups in their communities are starting to become cults. With this recognition, readers can then either avoid these groups or do something to stop them from regressing to the point where they become dangerous cults. The following case demonstrates this type of regression very clearly. It shows how what started out as simply a harmless Bible study group that met weekly to discuss Bible passages eventually regressed into a mind-controlling cult that cold-bloodedly killed two infants, one through intentional starvation and the other through neglect.

In the early 1970s, Roland Robidoux, a door-to-door salesman, heard a message on the radio about a religious group that would eventually become known as the Worldwide Church of God, a group that claimed theirs was the only true path to salvation. Although raised a Catholic, Roland felt so affected and moved by the claims of the church that he left the Catholic faith and joined the Worldwide Church of God.

In 1978, however, disliking the authoritarian stance of church leaders, Roland left the Worldwide Church of God and attempted to form his own church, which he called the Church of God of Mansfield (Massachusetts). When his new church failed, Roland moved to Attleboro, Massachusetts, a small town on the border with Rhode Island, and started a Bible study group. For a number of years early in its existence, this group simply spent time together studying and discussing Bible passages. However, by 1998, according to reports in several New England newspapers and a national television news channel, this group had been transformed into a cult that would call itself The Body and which would withdraw itself totally from society and even from family members who didn't hold to the cult's beliefs. People who knew the members of the cult when they began as a Bible study group all say they can't believe how radically these people changed.

The change actually took place through many small steps over many years, a process I will discuss at length in chapter 14. Little by little, Roland began to exert more and more authority over the group until finally any members who questioned him would find themselves accused by other group members of being controlled by Satan. Although Roland reportedly left the Worldwide Church of God because he disliked the authoritarianism of church leaders, he eventually instituted the same measures of absolute authority in his own group.

"He became the thing he hated," said Brian Weeks, who cofounded the Church of God of Mansfield with Roland. "All the things that he was originally disgruntled with, he became. The sole authority, not being questioned. He believed he had the truth."[26]

Members of his group, though obedient, found that in the 1990s Roland started becoming more and more susceptible to radical new ideas. One time he put the group on a high-protein diet, then on a vegetarian diet, and then on a diet of only organic food. However, after Roland read the book *Born in Zion*, by Carol Balizet, which advocates, among other things, reportedly withdrawing from the medical system and relying on prayer for healing, he seized on the ideas in this book with unstoppable enthusiasm.

"The book had a profound effect on the group," said Dennis Mingo, a former member of the cult. "Every week, they made little changes and became more and more radical."[27]

Fully immersed in the ideas presented in the book, Roland insisted that cult members, who by the late 1990s had begun believing they were the "Chosen Ones," completely divorce themselves from what he claimed were the seven systems of an impure society: education, medicine, government, banking, religion, entertainment, and science. A diary entry of one of the cult members read: "Of $4^1/_2$ billion inhabitants presently breathing, only a handful, a remnant, are being trained. The rest are tools of Satan to try to destroy God's anointed."[28] In support of the cult's belief that they were the Chosen Ones, anyone who left the cult or was put out of the group was afterward shunned by cult members and believed to be condemned to hell for eternity.

In keeping with Roland's new belief system, cult members withdrew their children from the local school system. In addition, Roland ordered members to throw away their checkbooks and deal only in cash, and also instructed those cult members who wore glasses no longer to wear them, even though some had serious vision problems. Roland claimed that God would heal them if they were faithful. Also in keeping with the new beliefs, members destroyed all books except the Bible; they no longer celebrated birthdays or conventional holidays; and all contact with individuals outside The Body, including family members, became severely curtailed. Along with this, cult members burned old photo albums because they saw them as symbols of vanity, and they no longer watched television, went to movies, or read newspapers. All information about the world came from Roland. But far more serious, Roland commanded all members of The Body to no longer have any formal medical treatment, including not even having a midwife present during childbirth. (Roland reportedly broke off all contact with his mother and two of his daughters because they sought some type of professional medical treatment.)

The only medicine cult members could use were certain herbal remedies and prayer. Because of this new rule, Jeremiah Corneau, a son born to cult members David and Rebecca Corneau, died soon after birth because his lungs had not been properly aspirated, a standard medical procedure in hospitals.

While some readers might think that parents in particular would object to such drastic measures, Roland told the group that he had received his instructions through direct revelations from God. Anyone who disobeyed one of his new rules disobeyed God.

However, it wasn't just Roland who experienced these direct revelations from God. Roland's daughter Michelle also claimed to have them, as did Roland's son Jacque, who in 1997 Roland "ordained" and promoted to coleader of The Body. Jacque, though at one time running a successful window-cleaning business, eventually abandoned the business so he could run the cult full time, afterward allowing the other cult members to support him.

In 1998, one of Jacque's revelations from God told him that the group was to travel to the "Promised Land," which Jacque said God told him was in Maine. Jacque said God instructed him to leave for the Promised Land immediately with no preparations, as God would provide for them during their trek. The group left carrying no food, water, change of clothing, diapers, or cash.

The convoy, however, soon began to have problems. Vehicles ran out of gas, and though cult members laid their hands on and prayed around the out-of-gas vehicles for hours, no new gasoline appeared. Eventually, cult members piled into the vehicles that still had gas and continued on until all the vehicles ran out of fuel. The cult members then remained on the side of the road for three days praying for gasoline, some of the children becoming so hungry they began vomiting. Finally, a family member who wasn't part of the cult found out where the group was and notified the police. The officers loaned the group enough money to get back to Massachusetts. While many noncult family members thought this episode would cause the cult to dissolve, it instead made it even stronger, a common phenomenon when dealing with unfulfilled prophecies, as I will discuss in a later chapter.

In March 1999, another revelation from God came, this one through Michelle Robidoux Mingo, Roland's daughter. She claimed that God told her that her sister-in-law Karen, Jacque's wife, was vain about her figure (Michelle, in her thirties, was stocky and matronly, while Karen, 24, was slim and attractive). On God's order, Michelle claimed, Karen was from then on to subsist on only a gallon of high-fat almond milk each day. Michelle also reportedly claimed that God had instructed her that Samuel, the 10-month-old son of Karen and Jacque, though already eating solid food, should from then on have no food or water but be fed only Karen's breast milk. Karen, however, was pregnant with another child and producing very little breast milk.

For the next 51 days, as the cult followed the instructions in Michelle's revelation, Samuel slowly starved to death. Whenever Karen attempted to protest, Jacque and Michelle would tell her she was listening to Satan and not to God.

"As their child is starving and they see his ribs sticking out and his eyes going in different directions, they walk past that starving child on their way to dinner," Bristol County District Attorney Paul Walsh would later say. "They starved their baby in a house full of food."[29]

Supporting Walsh's claim of indifference to Samuel's fate, Jacque wrote in a diary that he kept about his son's death, "Yet in all of this I see through God's eyes. Karen and I are the ones He is concerned with."[30]

Eventually, three days before his first birthday, Samuel died from severe malnutrition. The cult hid the infant's emaciated body, along with the body of Jeremiah Corneau, in the basement of one of the homes they occupied.

As might be expected, these events seriously disturbed the children of the cult members. "The older boys were very traumatized from having the dead bodies of their cousins 'kept in state' in the basement for months on end," Reverend Robert Pardon, who investigated the cult, told me in an interview. "Also, they had to carry the caskets around when the infants were finally buried."[31]

Four months after Samuel's death, members of the cult took the bodies of the two babies and left for the Promised Land. Putting the two infants in homemade caskets, they buried them in a remote part of the 200,000-acre Baxter State Park in Maine.

All might have gone well for the cult if they hadn't expelled one of their members, Dennis Mingo, Michelle's husband. Dennis had apparently begun questioning some of the cult leaders' decisions. After being expelled, Dennis went to the police, turning over the journal Jacque Robidoux had kept that detailed the slow death of his son Samuel. Although the cult at first closed ranks and refused to talk to the authorities, even though eight cult members went to jail for contempt of court, their solidarity began to break when the state started removing the cult members' children from their custody.

Eventually, the state of Massachusetts removed all the children of the cult members, 13 in all, after the juvenile court ruled that the cult members were unfit parents. Most of the children went to relatives not belonging to the cult. A large part of the reason the juvenile court ruled that the cult members were unfit parents was that, due to their belief that the legal system was a tool of an impure society, none of the cult members was represented by an attorney at the parental fitness hearing; instead, they all simply stood mute and refused to recognize the proceeding.

However, during a jail visit with David Corneau by Reverend Robert Pardon, who had been appointed guardian *ad litem* (a person appointed by the court to represent the best interests of children) of the cult members' children, Reverend Pardon brought along photos of David's three little girls. In defiance of cult rules, David took the pictures and kept them. Apparently missing his children and realizing what he was doing to them, David broke ranks with other members of the cult and soon began negotiating a deal with the prosecutor's office.

In October 2000, after arranging a grant of immunity for himself, his wife, and several other cult members, David Corneau led authorities to the spot in Baxter State Park where his son Jeremiah and Samuel Robidoux lay buried. The spot was so remote that the search team went there by floatplane, the nearest road being more than 5 miles away.

David Corneau, however, wasn't the only person to eventually break ranks with the cult's belief system. While previously maintaining that the legal system was part of an impure society that they wanted no dealings with, Jacque and Karen Robidoux, along with Michelle Mingo, eventually hired private attorneys. Karen also requested that her trial be separated from her husband's because her defense would be antagonistic to his. Even cult founder Roland Robidoux reportedly contacted Dateline NBC, another alleged tool of an impure society, and tried to sell the cult's story to them.

Jacque Robidoux first claimed at his trial that the court had no jurisdiction over him because he was a member of a sovereign nation not subject to American laws, but finally he tearfully told the jury that he didn't mean to hurt his son. He was only doing God's will.

However, jury member Jeffrey Jason said the jury didn't buy that. "What it came down to: Religion is no excuse for murder."[32]

On June 14, 2002, a jury found Jacque Robidoux guilty of first-degree murder. The judge sentenced him to life in prison without parole.

In another sign that the ranks of the cult had broken, on August 20, 2002, Karen Robidoux's attorney asked the court to postpone her trial, which had been set to begin September 3, 2002. He stated that he needed time to prepare a new defense for her: battered wife syndrome.

"It is apparent, based upon my investigation," attorney Joseph F. Krowski said, "that undue influence was exercised on her by members of her family which affected her decision-making process."[33]

An October 12, 2002, article in the *Boston Herald* quoted Reverend Robert Pardon's thoughts about Karen Robidoux: "This is clearly a case of thought reform and mind control."[34]

On October 1, 2003, a judge, finding Karen Robidoux competent to stand trial, released her on $100,000 bail.

As I have shown here, and will show further in the chapters that follow, cults can be very dangerous and destructive organizations. In the next chapter, I will show that, in accordance with the definition I presented here, cults regularly commit crimes and break the law. In addition, I will show that, along with being damaging and dangerous to their own members, cults can also be extraordinarily dangerous to the general public.

CHAPTER 2

The Danger of Cults

By a little after 8:00 A.M. on March 20, 1995, five containers of the extremely lethal nerve gas sarin, a chemical so lethal a single drop on the skin can kill, had been set up at five different locations within the Tokyo subway system. Suddenly, according to news reports from all over the world, as the unaware subway passengers boarded the cars or stood waiting for their trains, the containers began spewing deadly fumes. Before the Tokyo subway system, which handles over five million passengers a day, could be evacuated and the nerve gas neutralized, 12 people died and more than 5,500 needed medical attention, with at least 75 of these listed in critical condition. Tokyo citizens were outraged and flabbergasted, not only by such a cruel terrorist attack in a country that had mostly avoided such incidents in the past but even more so because the authorities eventually discovered that the attack had been carried out by members of what most citizens had viewed as a peaceful, religious group: Aum Shinrikyo (the true teaching of Aum).

"I thought Japan was a safe country," said a subway passenger after the attack. "It's really awful for us to see this kind of incident take place."[1]

In late March 1995, the police raided the headquarters of Aum Shinrikyo in the village of Kamikuishiki, about 70 miles southwest of Tokyo. There they discovered a complex full of secret passages and hidden rooms. They also found a secret laboratory, where the deadly nerve gas had been produced. However, along with the evidence of nerve gas production, the police additionally confiscated $7.9 million in cash and 22 pounds of gold. While searching the complex, the police also discovered more than 50 people in advanced stages of malnutrition who were wandering the complex aimlessly, and they freed 7 people who claimed that they had been held prisoner by the cult. Some weeks later, the police arrested the leader of the Aum Shinrikyo cult, a nearly blind former herbalist named Shoko Asahara, who had been forecasting a message of impending global doom for several years.

The 12 dead and 5,500 injured in the Tokyo subway attack, however, weren't the only victims of the Aum Shinrikyo cult. Police suspect that, before the subway attack, the cult had murdered at least two dozen other people. According to authorities, to get rid of the bodies of these victims, the cult used an industrial-sized microwave oven that could reduce bodies to dust and a cement-grinding machine that could pulverize bodies.

How did this all begin? How did a religious cult become involved in mass murder?

In 1989, Asahara, who claimed to have obtained enlightenment while on a trip to India, and who, before becoming a guru, had made his living as an herbalist, received notice from the Japanese government that Aum Shinrikyo had been officially recognized as a religion in Japan. This official recognition means that a group can operate without any government oversight or interference. Several years before, Asahara had attained a bit of fame as a religious figure when a Japanese occult magazine, *Twilight Zone*, published a photograph that claimed to show him levitating.

In the early 1990s, following recognition by the Japanese government as a religion, the Aum Shinrikyo cult quickly began gathering both recruits and generous donations. Soon communes run by Aum Shinrikyo began appearing all over Japan and quickly began filling up with young recruits. Aum Shinrikyo members, wearing white robes and standing on street corners and at subway entrances, would hand out invitations to free yoga classes. Those accepting the invitation, and who appeared to be good candidates for recruitment, were then shown videotapes of Asahara seemingly levitating, flying, and passing through walls. The recruits were promised that they too, with the proper training, could accomplish similar feats.

Interestingly, along with recruiting many of Japan's disaffected youth, the cult also attracted a number of highly educated individuals, including physicians, attorneys, chemists, and other scientists, among them even a virus and genetics researcher. It was through recruiting and indoctrinating these types of individuals, and then using their talents, that the cult managed to successfully manufacture and dispense the deadly nerve gas. By 1995, what had started out as a small religious group a decade before had grown to comprise more than 50,000 followers and reportedly more than $1 billion in assets.

However, since much of these assets had come from converts who turned over everything they owned to the cult, and who were also encouraged to give the cult other family property, family members of these cult converts naturally became concerned. They soon founded an organization called Parents of Aum Children. However, the cult didn't appreciate this type of organized opposition. An attorney who worked for the Parents of Aum Children, after a confrontation with Aum Shinrikyo officials, mysteriously disappeared, as did his wife and small child. An Aum Shinrikyo member later reportedly confessed to the police that an Aum Shinrikyo hit squad had entered the attorney's apartment, killed the three family members, and then buried their bodies, which the police later recovered.

During the early years of the cult, Asahara expounded its philosophy of Buddhism, which at first stated that followers must find the middle ground between excessive self-indulgence and harsh self-deprivation. Like most cult leaders, however, Asahara later exempted himself from any of these requirements. While the Aum Shinrikyo cult eventually required members to take a vow of chastity and adhere to strict dietary requirements, Asahara lived with his wife and indulged in fine food and other luxuries. In addition to setting down strict rules and requirements for cult members, the Aum Shinrikyo cult also created a special "action squad," headed by a former Japanese underworld figure who had joined the cult. This squad's purpose was to kidnap and bring back any cult members who tried to leave the group.

In 1990, before forming his action squad and before coming under police suspicion, Asahara and 24 Aum Shinrikyo members ran for election to Japan's parliament. They were soundly defeated. This greatly disturbed Asahara, who had always seen himself as a new Buddha who would be proclaimed by the world as its savior. This rejection by Japanese voters, many feel, is what shifted Asahara's thinking to that of a global doomsday prophet. In a speech given on the cult's radio program just days before the Tokyo subway attack, Asahara reportedly told the audience, "Wake up my disciples! With no regrets, with full courage, let's go to our death!"[2]

In 1992, in a self-published book, *Declaring Myself the Christ*, Asahara professed that in addition to his belief in Buddhism, he believed himself to be the reincarnation of Jesus Christ. He also began making his prophecies for Armageddon, which he forecast would begin in July 1999. Although most of humanity would perish in the end times, Asahara said that a small pocket of humanity, consisting of Aum Shinrikyo members, would survive to rebuild civilization.

At Asahara's direction, and in preparation for this doomsday, the cult began purchasing arms in Russia, where it had established six Aum Shinrikyo centers. The cult also bought a machine shop in Japan, which it converted to a weapons manufacturing plant. In addition, the cult purchased a 48,000-acre sheep farm in Australia, where the police suspect they carried out experiments while trying to manufacture the nerve gas sarin. Two dozen dead sheep found buried on the ranch contained residue of sarin.

Unfortunately, the sarin attack in the Tokyo subway system wasn't the first time nerve gas had been used by the cult. Almost a year earlier, in the summer of 1994, seven people died and 600 were injured by a sarin release in Matsumoto, Japan. Some believe that this was a test run by the cult, an attempt to judge the lethality of the nerve gas. However, at the time of the nerve gas release, no one suspected that the cult was involved; instead, police believed that a chemical salesman had accidentally mixed up the poison gas while attempting to manufacture fertilizer.

As 1995 began, Asahara predicted that many worldwide disasters, including earthquakes and nuclear attacks, would soon commence. An earthquake, on January 17, 1995, seemed to Asahara's followers proof positive that he was correct in his prophecy that the end of the world was coming soon.

Near the same time, as the Tokyo police began an investigation into the kidnapping of a cult critic that had allegedly been perpetrated by the cult action squad, police began hearing rumors about and then gathering evidence of the cult's chemical weapons manufacturing. When they had finally gathered enough evidence to show a significant threat, police set March 22, 1995, as the date when they would raid the Aum Shinrikyo headquarters and confiscate these chemical weapons. Lacking the equipment necessary for this sort of operation, however, and needing gas masks and protective clothing for the raid, the police contacted the Japanese army for assistance. However, as was later discovered, the Aum Shinrikyo cult had already penetrated the army and had several military members in its group. These army officials immediately reported the intelligence about the impending raid to the Aum Shinrikyo leadership.

Two days ahead of the raid, five two-man teams of cult members boarded crowded Tokyo subway trains during morning rush hour. They carried plastic bags of frozen sarin and sharp pointed umbrellas. The teams set the bags down near government hubs, punctured the bags with the umbrellas, and then hurriedly got away, afterward taking a sarin antidote. Some of the Aum Shinrikyo members later said that the attack had been meant to disrupt and paralyze the Japanese government, and consequently stop the planned raid on the Aum Shinrikyo headquarters. However, some high-ranking members of the cult disagreed and said that they believed Asahara ordered the attacks in the hope they would quicken the worldwide apocalypse he had prophesied.

"The attack was launched so that the guru's prophecy could come true," said Ikuo Hayashi, a doctor who admitted to planting one of the containers of sarin gas in the Tokyo subway.[3]

On May 16, 1995, in a simultaneous raid of 130 cult facilities that involved 2,000 police officers, authorities found Asahara hiding in a crawlspace at the cult headquarters. The police said he was carrying several hundred thousand dollars in cash on him when they apprehended him. The police had suspected he was hiding at the cult headquarters when they discovered that shipments of melons, a favorite food of Asahara, continued to be delivered to the compound.

Although Asahara's trial is still ongoing, on June 26, 2002, a court in Japan sentenced Tomomitso Niimi, a former leader in the Aum Shinrikyo cult, to death for his part in the subway poison gas attack and also for his part in 14 other cult murders, including the strangulation murder of a lawyer and his family. The murdered lawyer had publicly questioned the motives of the cult. Niimi, who claims he was only following the cult leader's orders and shouldn't be given the death penalty, joins several other Aum Shinrikyo leaders who have been sentenced to die. In September 2001, one of the cult members sentenced to death appealed his sentence. Like Niimi, he claims that when he committed the murders, he was under the mind control of Asahara and therefore not responsible. A court later denied this appeal. On October 10, 2002, another member of the cult who claims to have been brainwashed, Seiichi Endo, the man responsible for the actual manufacture of the sarin gas, became the ninth Aum Shinrikyo member to receive the death penalty. More than 100 other cult members have been convicted of other crimes and received lesser sentences.

Of course, many American readers, while appalled at the Tokyo subway attack, might say that this unfortunate incident is less frightening than most because it occurred halfway around the world. While that's true, it doesn't mean that the Aum Shinrikyo cult wasn't dangerous to Americans. The group had plans, cult members say, to release sarin at various locations in the United States.

"The guru has ordered us to release sarin in several places in America," said Dr. Ikuo Hayashi, a cardiac specialist before joining the cult.[4] Fortunately, the cult suspended these plans before they could be carried out. Dr. Hayashi eventually received a life sentence for his actions in the Tokyo subway incident.

While the cult may have canceled its plans to conduct terrorist attacks on American soil, it still made several attempts to commit the mass murder of Americans. Reportedly, trucks driven by cult members sprayed deadly botulinum germs around areas adjoining several U.S. military bases. Additionally, the cult attempted a similar attack using anthrax germs. Only the selection of germs, which, unknown to the cult scientists, proved too weak to cause disease, likely stopped a catastrophe that would have claimed many American lives.

As I will show several times in this book, just because cult leaders die or become incarcerated doesn't mean the cult will disappear. Often quite the opposite. Aum Shinrikyo, for example, is presently undergoing a revival. In January 2000, the new leadership of the Aum Shinrikyo cult denounced its former leader, Shoko Asahara, and changed the group's name to Aleph (the first letter of the Hebrew alphabet). In reparation, they paid 330 million yen ($2.8 million) to the victims of the gas attack.

However, on November 23, 2002, Japan's Public Security Investigation Agency announced that it had decided to file a request with the Public Security Examination Commission for permission to keep the cult now known as Aleph under surveillance for an additional three years. Its authority to monitor the group would otherwise expire in January 2003. The Public Security Investigation Agency said that it had filed this request because it believes the cult's former leader, Shoko Asahara, "continues to wield power over the cult and can order indiscriminate mass killings."[5]

In answer to claims that the group is still dangerous, the new leader of Aleph said, "Our current group has undergone reforms and abandoned the use of any type of violence. We are not a terrorist group."[6]

However, many Japanese citizens who live close to facilities owned by the cult don't feel assured by these words. "We live in constant fear; it's like living with terrorists," said cult neighbor Noriko Chiba. "Aum committed all these crimes in the past—how can you be sure they won't do it again?"[7]

As the cults talked about in the previous chapter demonstrate, and as I will show over and over in the following chapters, the Aum Shinrikyo cult isn't the only cult to have demonstrated a propensity for deadly violence. "The biggest terrorist threat is no longer from traditional terrorists, but from religious sects," says Bruce Hoffman of the Center for Terrorism. "[Palestinian terrorist] Abu Nidal may think in terms of killing 20 or 30 people. Religious sects are far less competent, but often have much grander ambitions."[8] While Hoffman made this quote before September 11, 2001, it can still apply to many types of cults. As I will show in the following chapters, a number of cults have been involved in mass murder. Many other cults, although perhaps not causing as large a number of casualties, can still be very deadly.

For example, according to news reports, a cult called the Church of the First Born Lamb of God reportedly had a religious text titled *The Book of the New Covenant*. This book called for the slaying of any defectors from the church. Unfortunately, this is exactly what occurred. In 1988, killers gunned down a married couple who had defected from the group, and then shot and killed the couple's eight-year-old child. Soon afterward, the same killers murdered yet another cult defector. The police arrested the killers, and eventually they and the cult leader, Aaron LeBaron, received lengthy prison sentences.

In Ohio, a local newspaper tells about how in 1989 Damon Lungren reportedly helped his father, Jeffrey Lungren, leader of a cult, kill Dennis and Cheryl Avery and their three children, ages 7, 13, and 15. Jeffrey Lungren, formerly a lay minister for the Reorganized Church of Jesus Christ of the Latter Day Saints, broke away from the church to form a cult, claiming that he was a prophet who spoke directly to God. Jeffrey Lungren later claimed that it was God who told him to kill the family.

On October 30, 2001, a judge in the state of Washington sentenced Chris Turgeon, the leader of a cult called the Gatekeepers, to 50 years in prison for the murder of Dan Jess. Jess had reportedly confronted Turgeon about bilking people out of their money. In 2000, Turgeon also received an 89-year prison sentence in California for attempted murder. Turgeon, however, claims that he isn't worried about the lengthy prison sentences because he has predicted that the world will end on March 22, 2004 anyway.

"It is the combination of individuals belonging to a group without rational ends, who are not in a bargaining relationship with the authorities, who are reckless as to their own survival and who possess the ability and inclination to use hitherto taboo methods of destruction, which make cults such a serious threat to society," says a report from an independent think tank.[9]

In addition to murder, though, cults have also occasionally resorted to kidnapping to keep their members from defecting. For example, after joining the Democratic Workers Party, a leftist cult, individuals found that getting out of the cult could be much more difficult than getting in. An article in *Redbook* about the cult states, "Those who tried to run away were often hunted down and dragged back to a 'safe house,' where they would be reindoctrinated under a kind of house arrest."[10]

Karl Kahler, a former member of The Way International, tells in his book *The Cult That Snapped* about how The Way International formed a special squad of men whose job it was to attempt to "rescue" The Way members who had been grabbed off the street by deprogrammers (individuals who would kidnap and confine cult members and then attempt to force them to see the fallacies of the cult they belonged to). The leadership of The Way International, however, reportedly disbanded the group after a year because most of the members didn't want to come back to the group even when "rescued." They just wanted to get away from both the deprogrammers and their "rescuers."

Occasionally, cults also kidnap people to get new members. According to *Time Asia*, a cult in China claims that Jesus Christ has returned to Earth in the form of a 30-year-old Chinese peasant woman, who has never been photographed and whose location is kept secret. The cult, called Lightning from the East, has been accused of kidnapping people and attempting to forcibly indoctrinate them into the cult. Individuals kidnapped by the cult claim to have been beaten, tortured, drugged, and sexually abused. When asked by reporters why the reborn Jesus, who supporters say has written a third book for the Bible, stays in hiding, a spokesperson for the cult said, "There's a time for secrecy and a time for openness, but she has her plan."[11]

While the many incidents of murder and other serious crimes involving noncult victims are certainly startling, the most common victims of cults are the cult members themselves, who are often physically abused, sexually abused, psychologically abused, or suffer ill effects from poor sanitation and diet. According to Rutgers University professor Benjamin Zablocki, cults are at high risk of becoming abusive to their members "because the members' adulation of charismatic leaders contributes to the leaders being corrupted by the power they seek and are accorded."[12]

Readers should keep in mind that much of the damage inflicted on people by cults happens because, as Professor Zablocki points out, cults are formed almost exclusively for the benefit of the leader. Because many cult leaders have been found to manifest a large number of personality deficiencies and have often been diagnosed as psychopaths, they usually feel no empathy for the people they harm. Most cult leaders care only about being worshipped and obeyed, and about living a life of luxury.

"Psychopaths are social predators who charm, manipulate, and ruthlessly plow their way through life, leaving a broad trail of broken hearts, shattered expectations, and empty wallets," says Dr. Robert D. Hare in his book *Without Conscience: The Disturbing World of the Psychopaths Among Us.* "Completely lacking in conscience and feelings for others, they selfishly take what they want and do as they please, violating social norms and expectations without the slightest sense of guilt or regret."[13]

Of all the types of harm that come from cults, however, the sexual abuse of cult members is a recurring theme that therapists hear over and over from cult members who have left groups and are attempting to recover. "Sexual abuse of women in cults is a pretty common story," says Lorna Goldberg, a cult expert and therapist. "Some groups demand celibacy, but either way cult leaders manipulate women sexually."[14] A complaint heard many times from former members of cults that demand celibacy is that this restriction didn't apply to the cult leader, who often demanded sex from the members.

Sexual abuse in cults, however, doesn't involve just females. It can also include males. And unfortunately, the sexual abuse of children within cults is much too common. It was well documented, for example, that Branch Davidian cult leader David Koresh regularly had sex with underage females. There are many, many other examples.

On October 4, 2002, according to the *Atlanta Journal-Constitution* and other newspapers, a grand jury in Georgia handed down a 197-count indictment against Dwight York, leader of a cult called the United Nuwaubian Nation of Moors. These charges involve the sexual molestation of 13 children in the group, both boys and girls, ranging in age from 4 to 14.

"This has been the most voluminous case, in terms of number of counts, number of victims, and the sheer scope of the investigation that I've ever been associated with," said District Attorney Fred Bright. "I want the trial jury to hear the whole scope of the child molestation that happened here in Putnam County."[15]

The approximately 1,000 members of the United Nuwaubian Nation of Moors live on a 476-acre plot in rural Putnam County, Georgia, while York, before his arrest, lived in a mansion nearby. With grandiosity typical of many cult leaders, York had reportedly planned to turn the commune into a nation separate from the United States called Egypt of the West. On October 25, 2002, York entered a plea of not guilty to all charges. However, his victims claim he told them that having sex with him was a religious ritual.

"If we do that, we would go to heaven with the angels and we would never die," one of his young victims said York told her before molesting her.[16]

Although York at first denied all the charges, claiming he was the victim of a conspiracy, on January 23, 2003, he entered into an agreement with the federal prosecutor and pleaded guilty. He would reportedly receive a sentence of 15 years in prison. He also agreed to forfeit $400,000 in cash confiscated when the police arrested him. However, in June 2003, a judge rejected the plea bargain and said York must stand trial.

In another case, this one in 1997 and reported by the Canadian news media, a court convicted the leader of the Kabalarian cult in British Columbia of two counts of rape, three counts of sexual assault, four counts of indecent assault, and three counts of gross indecency. The charges involved sexual misconduct with seven teenage girls. Ivon Shearing, the convicted cult leader, had preached that having sex with him was the only way to progress to higher levels of consciousness. He told other victims that the only way to exorcise the souls of dead people from their minds was by having sex with him. In July 2002, the supreme court of Canada ordered a retrial on two of the counts Shearing had been convicted of but let the remainder stand.

David Berg, the founder of the cult known as the Children of God (also known as the Family), told his followers: "We have a sexy God and a sexy religion with a very sexy leader with an extremely sexy young following. So if you don't like sex, you'd better get out while you can."[17] Berg reportedly encouraged the practice of "flirty fishing," or of having female cult members entice men into joining the cult by having sex with them.

As long as the sexual activity Berg was talking about was between consenting adults, it was no one's business. However, the philosophy of the group soon extended to young children. "A lot of the escape for children was sexual play," Daphne Sarran, whose mother was a former member of the Children of God, said in a *San Francisco Chronicle* article. "Everything was very sexualized....By the time I was 6, I was getting molested. I'd seen it happen to so many other children, it didn't really seem that strange."[18]

As the incidents described here show, many of the victims of cults are the children of cult members. The danger to the children of cult members can run from murder (hundreds of innocent children, for example, died in the Jonestown cult incident, which I will talk about in chapter 3, and in the cult murders in Uganda, which I will talk about in chapter 6) to sexual, physical, and psychological abuse. While adults joined the cult willingly, albeit often through deception, the children of cult members have no choice about joining or not and are often the ones who suffer the most from mistreatment. Yet they cannot leave and are often kept hidden away from outside sources that could see their plight and rescue them.

"The potential impact of cult involvement on the children of cult members is particularly marked because children are usually unable to defend themselves against the possibly destructive impact of their parents' cult affiliation," says Dr. David Halperin, professor of psychiatry at the Mount Sinai School of Medicine.[19]

Just as often as sexual abuse, or perhaps even more so, the children of cult members suffer physical abuse. Many times this abuse comes in the form of excessive punishment for some type of real or imagined misbehavior. Sometimes the discipline of children is seen as a test of the parents' commitment to the cult leader. To appease their leader, parents in cults often punish their children in bizarre and cruel ways. In one study of former cult members, 13 percent said that the punishment of children in the cult was sometimes life threatening or required a physician's care, while another 13 percent said that children in the cult were sometimes physically disabled or hurt to teach them a lesson.[20]

"I was beaten five to six times a day—on a good day," said Brenda Daeges, who grew up in a cult called the Apostles of the Infinite Love.[21]

In his book *The Children of Jonestown*, Kenneth Wooden says the following about child abuse at the Peoples Temple: "Physical abuse of the young was part of the routine at Peoples Temple. As Jones [the leader of the cult] began to exercise total control, children were beaten if they failed to call him Father or were otherwise disrespectful, or if they talked with peers who were not members of the Peoples Temple....Mild discipline gave way to making young girls strip almost nude in front of the full membership and then forcing them to take cold showers or jump into the cold swimming pool at Redwood Valley Church. Unequal boxing matches gave way to beatings with paddles, then electric shock, and finally something [Jones] called a 'blue-eyed monster,' which hurt and terrorized the younger ones in a darkened room."[22]

"Potential for the worst abuse is found in 'total situations' where the group is physically and socially isolated from the outside community," says Dr. Philip Zimbardo in an article in the *APA Monitor.* "The accompanying total milieu and informational control permits idiosyncratic and paranoid thinking to flourish and be shared without limits. The madness of any leader then becomes normalized as members embrace it."[23]

The cult called the Children of God also established "Teen Training Camps" to handle "disruptive" children born of cult members, children who wouldn't toe the doctrinal line of the cult. Many of the children who were sent to these camps said that they compared to concentration camps. The statement of one of the leaders of the cult acknowledged that these camps might have been a bit harsh: "Also, we apologize to any of you young people who may have been harshly and unlovingly disciplined in the past. We have heard a number of testimonies of past excessive corporal punishment, prolonged 'silence restriction' and/or isolation, as well as other means of discipline which some of you experienced, and we want to say that it pains us to hear such things. It was wrong, and we are truly sorry that any of you received such treatment."[24]

A court in Massachusetts recently made Reverend Robert Pardon guardian *ad litem* of over a dozen children removed from the members of a cult known as The Body, talked about in chapter 1. In an interview, I asked Reverend Pardon about the condition of the children when he received them. He told me, "All the children had been beaten severely. The younger ones had calluses on their rear ends from all the paddling. Emotionally, they were all expecting that the two children that died were going to be resurrected from the dead."[25]

Another extreme danger to children in cults is that cults, and especially religious cults, often disdain modern medicine and instead rely on faith healing, herbal cures, or some other unconventional method of treating illness and injury. While adults certainly have the right to choose whether they want to use conventional medical care or some alternative, children of cult members don't have this choice. Often, serious illnesses and injuries to the children of cult members go untreated or are treated in a manner that does more harm than good. For example, a medical study investigated 172 child fatalities in which the parents shunned conventional medicine for faith healing or some other unconventional means. The study, which even included the case of one family in which the father, before joining a cult, held a medical degree, found that 140 of these children would have had better than a 90 percent chance of survival if they had received regular medical treatment.[26]

"From a public health perspective, we are currently dealing with an epidemic of cult-related damage," says Dr. Louis Jolyon West, who has studied cults for more than 50 years.[27]

More often though, and just as damaging to the children, is the psychological harm that being the child of a cult member can bring. Cults seldom want their members who have children to follow customary parenting patterns. Spending too much time with their children reduces the amount of time parents have for working for the cult. Because of this, children in cults are often taken away from their parents and given to communal baby-sitters, many of whom are abusive, physically and emotionally, due to their lack of training or desire to raise children. In addition, the children of cult members many times find that the rules of cult life can be very strict.

"Children in such groups must often meet high standards of conduct," says Professor Dianne Casoni. "Since immaturity is sometimes inter-preted as maliciousness, children are often scolded and publicly rebuked. Moreover, the leader may feel jealous of the attention parents give to chil-dren, often expecting that attention be concentrated on him."[28]

Writer Barbara Grizzuti Harrison, in her 1984 article "Children and the Cult," tells what she found when she investigated reported psychological and physical abuse of children raised in a commune run by the Northeast Kingdom Community Church in Vermont. She wrote that during her investigation, she discovered that an adult had struck a 4-year-old 20 times for imagining that a block of wood was a truck, that the group "dis-ciplined" a 3-year-old until his neck bled, and that they "corrected" an 11-year-old by hitting him with a two-by-four.

"You understand why children can't fantasize," said a cult leader justi-fying the harsh discipline. "Because when the Lord calls our children, they have to be sure it's His voice, not the voice of another. They have to live in reality."

In her article, Harrison describes the children she meets in the cult com-mune: "The children standing nearby express no curiosity. They are with-out animation. They do not speak."[29] In addition, children of cult members often develop serious psychological problems because their entire childhood is spent in the closed and stifling atmosphere of the cult, where they are never exposed to any viewpoints or values other than those of the cult, which are many times completely opposite to the values of society at large.

Children who live with one parent in a cult and whose other parent is not in the cult can also suffer severe psychological stress. Religious cults in particular typically teach that everyone outside the cult is an agent of Satan. Consequently, children can become traumatized when the noncult parent comes for them. In addition, many cult leaders fear that the noncult parent could conceivably undermine the cult by exposing the child and possibly the other parent to outside sources of information that run counter to the teachings of the cult. Therefore, cult leaders many times attempt to stop noncult-parent visitation, often by hiding the children or even by sending them far away.

Psychologists and psychiatrists often find that, like the children, adult members of cults suffer not only physical and sexual abuse but also a number of psychological problems after spending time in a cult. These adult members often no longer have any friends other than cult members, and many of the thought-altering indoctrination techniques they underwent can negatively affect their ability to function in society after leaving the cult. Their time in the cult can lead to a condition known as post-cult trauma syndrome. Its symptoms include spontaneous crying, depression, feelings of isolation, panic attacks, disassociation, difficulty concentrating, and low self-esteem.

"I was a mental wreck," former cult member Maureen Dilley told me about her mental and emotional state after leaving a cult. "I believed I was crazy, and I had no friends or people to talk to."[30]

"For a year I would just sit and cry," another former cult member told me. One former cult member became so depressed after leaving a cult he told me he tried to commit suicide by stepping in front of a bus.[31]

The authors of the book *Cults and Psychological Abuse* state, "Clinical and research evidence suggests that many former members of abusive groups tend to blame themselves inappropriately for their problems, much as the group blamed them. Former members also tend to be depressed and anxious."[32]

In a study of 43 people who had left a cult in Sweden, 93 percent reported anxiety and panic attacks, 91 percent reported difficulty handling emotions, 74 percent reported difficulty making decisions, 63 percent had suicidal thoughts (with 23 percent actually attempting suicide), and nearly half had psychosis-like symptoms. While some readers might argue that these results only came about because these individuals had mental problems before joining the cult, the study showed that only 16 percent of them had such problems.[33]

A larger study, this one done in the United States and involving 353 former cult members who had belonged to 48 different cults, found that 75 percent of the ex-cult members reported serious depression; 52 percent reported suicidal tendencies; 42 percent reported an inability to break rhythms of chanting, meditation, and so on; and 15 percent reported hallucinations and delusions.[34] In another study of 308 members from 101 different cults, 83 percent reported serious anxiety, 67 percent reported depression, 61 percent reported despair and hopelessness, and 51 percent reported feeling as though they lived in an unreal world.[35]

Erika Van Meir is a mental health therapist who treats former cult members. When I asked her in an interview about the problems she saw, she told me the following:

With ex-members, I see trauma, intense fear, shame, guilt, loss of meaning (anomie), anger, loneliness, mental confusion, inability to concentrate, 'floating' (the feeling that a person is not really here, often triggered by something reminding the person of his or her cult experience), career and financial issues, and lots of relational issues (with some loved ones having been cut off due to group contact and other loved ones still being in the group).[36]

Of course, in addition to all of the damage previously mentioned, almost all destructive cults are involved in some type of financial fraud in their attempt to obtain all of the worldly possessions of their members. A cult in Korea called Heaven's Gathering, for example, scammed its members out of $35 million according to the court that sentenced its two founders to 10 years in prison. Actually, however, this amount is small compared with some of the larger cults that can claim assets in the billions.

Along with all of this damage, many cults also require their members to sever all outside relationships, and so being a cult member can destroy families and friendships. Once out of a cult, ex-members often find that family members or friends have died or have become so estranged that the previous relationship cannot be reestablished. Also, belonging to a cult usually requires that members give all of their worldly goods to the group, which can often include property jointly owned by others, such as bank accounts, ATM cards, and so on. It can many times take former cult members years to recover financially from cult membership, and these individuals may never be able to repair their relationship with family members whose property they fraudulently turned over to the cult. It can also be difficult to reestablish a close relationship with family members or friends whom the cult members have in the past loudly and often called corrupt and evil.

As I have shown in this chapter, and shall show throughout this book, cults can be very dangerous and destructive organizations to both members and nonmembers. In the following chapters, I will examine the many different types of cults, then show why people are attracted to cults, how they are recruited, and how cults indoctrinate new members. But most important, I will show that an informed and educated public has the power to combat and defeat the threat of cults.

CHAPTER 3

Religious Cults

The real "White Night" for the residents of Jonestown, Guyana, finally came on November 18, 1978. There had been many rehearsals in the preceding months, but now the loudspeakers in the compound blared over and over that this was not a drill. It was the real thing. Everyone was to report immediately to the pavilion.

Their leader, Jim Jones, worked up into a frenzy, said into a microphone that the 900 residents of Jonestown must be ready to willingly die with him. As the people of Jonestown crowded around the raised throne in the center of the pavilion, where their leader sat with a microphone and a tape recorder, Jones told them, "I'm speaking here not as the administrator, but I'm speaking as a prophet today.... When they start parachuting out of the air, they'll shoot our innocent babies.... The GDF (Guyanese Defense Force) will be here, I tell you. Get moving, get moving, get moving!"[1]

On a nearby table, nurses filled syringes with cyanide, which would soon be squirted into the mouths of babies and small children. Other workers began mixing cyanide and tranquilizers into a washtub full of red Fla-Vor-Aid drink. Obediently, most of the people began lining up to take their cup of the deadly poison, many of them much more zealously than one might have supposed, some singing, some dancing. Others crowded to get ahead of their neighbors. "Let's don't fight one another," Jones told the crowd. "Let's do it right."[2]

Reportedly, one woman in the crowd at first refused to drink the poison but apparently changed her mind when others around her shouted, "No, no, if Father says to do it, you should do it."[3] To back this up, a squad of

guards stood with weapons ready in case any organized dissent appeared. But little did.

Jones began speaking to the crowd, and he found that the magic of his charisma still worked, even in the face of certain death. Although there were a few protesters, the guards quickly silenced them. The majority, however, didn't act rebellious or disobedient at all. Many sang and danced. Some screamed in ecstasy.

"Take the potion like they used to take in ancient Greece, and step over quietly," Jones instructed the crowd, "because we are not committing suicide; it's a revolutionary act."[4]

The first to drink a cup of the poisoned Fla-Vor-Aid, a young woman carrying a small baby, afterward walked over and sat down on the ground. A few moments later, she gave several violent convulsions, screamed, and then died. The baby cried for a few moments and then died next to its mother.

"To me death is not a fearful thing," Jones said over the loudspeaker. "It's living that's cursed." The crowd applauded wildly. "Without me," Jones continued, "life has no meaning. I'm the best thing you'll have."[5]

The next morning, Guyanese troops, receiving reports of violence at Jonestown and expecting possible armed resistance, moved cautiously into the settlement. They came upon a grisly sight that would soon be broadcast on television all over the world and written about in thousands of newspapers. They discovered 914 corpses, 276 of them children. Most had died from drinking the cyanide-laced Fla-Vor-Aid. However, they found that Jones and his wife, instead of the poison, had died from gunshot wounds to the head. For years to come, the world would wonder what could have compelled more than 900 people to join Jones's cult and then follow him meekly and obediently into death.

Jim Jones's story began over 25 years before in Indianapolis, where for a time he served as an apprentice minister. Jones, however, soon left the vestiges of conformity behind. In 1953, he founded what would eventually become known as the Peoples Temple in a rented store in Indianapolis. A gifted speaker with considerable charisma, Jones soon began attracting large crowds to his storefront church. Most of the early parishioners were poor blacks, and Jones, in addition to having a son of his own, adopted a black child and two Asian children into what he called his "rainbow family," which also included his wife, Marceline, who was 21, he 17, when they married.

Because the Peoples Temple quickly and legitimately gained a reputation as a place where those down on their luck could obtain a hot meal and a bed, the church membership continued to grow in number, as did Jones's notoriety as a man committed to helping the poor and downtrodden. In 1961, because of a protest Jones organized for fair housing in Indi-

anapolis, the city appointed him as director of the Indianapolis Human Rights Commission.

As its reputation grew, the Peoples Temple finally started attracting not only the poor but also a sizable number of more financially well-off parishioners, who Jones found could be counted on for sizable donations. In addition to this, Jones expected all the poorer members to give every cent they could to the church, including welfare and Social Security checks. Consequently, the Peoples Temple suddenly began taking in large amounts of money. With this increased wealth, Jones bought himself diamond rings, flashy clothing, and expensive cars. He also surrounded himself with an ever-present circle of aides and bodyguards, who not only protected Jones but also singled out and silenced any grumblers or troublemakers in the crowd. Interestingly, although Jones's congregation was largely black, all his advisors and bodyguards were white.

Besides being known as a haven for the poor, a large part of the Peoples Temple's notoriety came from the claims that Jones was a prophet and that he could heal any disease with his touch. To perpetuate his reputation as being a man granted the power to heal, Jones regularly hired people to pretend to be sick or crippled and who, at his services, would miraculously rise from their sickbeds or wheelchairs, healed and whole again. Jones's confidants would also secretly circulate through the audience, surreptitiously transmitting to him the comments of various people, which Jones would then repeat from the pulpit, adding to the belief that he had supernatural powers.

Before long, however, city authorities became concerned about the activities of the Peoples Temple, particularly the nearly constant fundraising and the claims from Jones that he could cure any disease with his touch. Jones apparently saw this trouble coming, and in 1965 he announced to a startled congregation that God had visited him and told him that a nuclear war would soon destroy most of the world. Only two places would be spared: Belo Horizonte, Brazil (to which Jones had traveled once during a visit to missionaries) and Ukiah, California, a community 100 miles north of San Francisco, where Jones had also visited once.

Consequently, in 1965 Jones and, amazingly, more than a hundred of his congregation simply packed up and left Indianapolis, even though Indianapolis had been home to many of them for years. Forming a caravan with Jones's new Cadillac in the lead, the members of Jones's cult trekked across the country to Ukiah, where they founded the new Peoples Temple.

The newly founded church in Ukiah soon began to gather new members and, as with his old congregation in Indianapolis, Jones wanted to make sure his new congregation understood who he was. With the megalomania of most cult leaders, Jones wanted all attention focused on him. Reportedly, he could even become jealous of the attention his congregation paid to God. He would often throw the Bible to the floor and yell at

his parishioners that they were paying more attention to it than to him. He also insisted that everyone in the congregation, no matter what the person's age, call him Dad or Father. Later, when his cult was more firmly established, not calling Jones Dad or Father would merit extreme and certain punishment. As a further example of his megalomania, Jones reportedly saw himself as the personification of Christ. In one of his sermons, he preached, "Now Christ is in this body.... I am the Way, the Truth, and the Light. No one can come to the Father but through me."[6] Jones also believed that he was a black soul trapped in a white body, and that, besides being the reincarnation of Jesus, he had also had previous lives as Moses and Lenin.[7]

Apparently, however, not even God could curtail Jim Jones's ambition because, despite God's alleged warning to him about certain nuclear annihilation, Jones soon found Ukiah much too remote and rugged, so he moved 100 miles south to San Francisco, where he renovated an old Masonic Temple in the largely black Fillmore area. This became the new Peoples Temple, which eventually branched out to Los Angeles. As in Indianapolis, Jones's charisma, oratory skills, and fake healings soon began attracting huge crowds. All over San Francisco, posters and Peoples Temple members spoke of Jim Jones as a miraculous prophet and faith healer. Also, as in Indianapolis, the Peoples Temple reached out to the poor with free meals, beds for the homeless, and even a neighborhood health clinic. Consequently, large amounts of donations quickly began pouring into Jones's coffers, and he spent the money lavishly on himself. In addition, the Peoples Temple reportedly stashed more than $10 million in foreign banks.

Soon after arriving in San Francisco, Jones, always politically adept, joined a number of community boards and began working closely with local politicians. He also started using the large and ever-increasing membership of the Peoples Temple as a political tool. Jones became known as a man who could deliver a huge chunk of votes or several hundred ready workers to political candidates. Consequently, politicians began lining up looking for his support. In addition, Jones donated large amounts of money to various causes. All of this quickly labeled Jones as a major power broker in San Francisco, and, as a result, the city named him to the San Francisco Housing Authority Commission. Many politicians, including then Governor Jerry Brown, showed up at Peoples Temple events and services.

"It was raw politics," said long-time Peoples Temple attorney Timothy Stoen, who eventually broke with Jones and the Temple. "He was able to deliver what politicians want, which is power. And how do you get power? By votes. And how do you get votes? With people. Jim Jones could produce 3,000 people at a political event."[8]

Jones also used the vast wealth he accumulated in San Francisco very wisely. He donated large sums of money to causes and organizations favored by the news media and soon became their darling. He eventually won over so many journalists that even when the claims of serious misdeeds within the Peoples Temple began surfacing, the major news media outlets refused to investigate them.

As with all cult leaders, there was a dark, power-hungry side to Jones. He often demanded sexual abstinence from his followers, while he kept a harem (all white) for his own sexual appetites, which was rumored to run to both sexes. The police even arrested Jones for lewd conduct (with a male) in a San Francisco movie theater in 1973; however, the authorities kept it quiet. Whenever married couples who belonged to the Peoples Temple wanted to have sex, the act first had to be approved by Jones, who also kept children away from their parents as much as possible. Within his church, the traditional family unit was dissolved and replaced with the bigger family of the Peoples Temple, with Jim Jones as Father.

In addition to the requirements just mentioned, Jones also expected members of the Peoples Temple to give all their worldly goods to the organization, and often required them to attend mandatory meetings within the church, which many times lasted until the early morning hours. These meetings were reportedly for the purpose of listening and responding to complaints and problems with the Peoples Temple, but actually they became a method for spotting dissenters and others who might interfere with Jones's operation of the Peoples Temple. Jones had these individuals singled out and dealt with.

Jones's bodyguards often took dissidents and grumblers within the Peoples Temple away and beat them, while Jones had disobedient children paddled with wooden boards. Afterward, Jones required all those punished, both adult and children, to thank him and call him Father or Dad, which was also the required title in every sentence addressed to Jones.

Like most cult leaders, Jones tried to instill a paranoia within his flock about "outsiders." Because his efforts were so successful, Peoples Temple members soon began to see the world as "us against them." The temple had enemies everywhere, Jones would shout from the pulpit. Only Jones, as their Father, could protect the congregation from the certain doom that outsiders wished on them. As a part of this paranoia, Jones would often demand that everyone had to be willing to die for him and the Peoples Temple, and he would many times publicly point out people he didn't think were committed enough to him and the Peoples Temple. In his sermons, Jones would often talk about the mass death of the Peoples Temple congregation.

Not everyone who attended the Peoples Temple, though, became a committed follower of Jim Jones. A number of defectors from the Peoples

Temple eventually began to compare notes and loudly complain about both giving their life's savings to the church and Jones's physical and emotional mistreatment of temple members. The establishment news media outlets in San Francisco, however, many of which were long-time supporters of Jones and had published many laudatory articles about him and his church, didn't want to hear that they might have been duped, so they simply refused to investigate and report on the claims of abuse by former members of the Peoples Temple.

However, a journalist named Marshal Kilduff did listen to the stories from former members of the Peoples Temple, and as a result, he wrote an article exposing the fraud and abuse within the Peoples Temple. The magazine *New West* published Kilduff's exposé, despite threats of what would happen if they did, which included the burglary of their offices and a letter-writing campaign organized by Jim Jones to *New West* advertisers. Public officials in San Francisco, many of whom had been ardent Jones supporters, became red-faced when the article, which reported numerous instances of Jones's brutality, child abuse, sexual abuse and excesses, fraud, and extortion, ran in the August 1977 issue of *New West*.

Within two weeks of the article's publication, however, much to the relief of San Francisco officials, Jones resigned his post at the Housing Authority and moved his Peoples Temple and many of its members to the jungles of Guyana, a small former British colony, then a Marxist-controlled nation, on the coast of South America between Venezuela and Brazil. For some time, Jones had been searching for a location to which he could move the Peoples Temple, somewhere away from prying eyes and where he could have total and complete control over the congregation. Several sites had been investigated, but the small Marxist country of Guyana seemed perfect. The new Peoples Temple, whose stated goal was to become an agricultural mission that would grow food to feed the hungry, sat on 3,800 acres of dense jungle near the Venezuela border. The Marxist government of Guyana, reveling in the propaganda value of having a mostly black group wanting to flee the capitalist and imperialist United States, gave Jones a free hand to run his community with no interference.

In the following months, the members of the Peoples Temple toiled 12 to 14 hours a day, clearing the land and building the structures that would hold the residents of what would eventually become known as Jonestown. Meanwhile at home, the mainstream press in San Francisco, changing abruptly from their years of idolizing Jim Jones, began following the lead of the *New West* and started publishing their own articles about the many abuses Jim Jones had inflicted on the members of the Peoples Temple. Relatives of cult members living in Jonestown, aware that Jones had always spoken of mass suicide and who, they began to hear, was now apparently making this point more often and more fervently, started putting pressure on every politician they could to do something.

Always sensitive to public opinion, Jones struck back with publicity releases of his own. He insisted that the claims of abuse were being made by malcontents he had expelled from the Peoples Temple. He included in his press releases copies of "confessions" signed by these individuals. Jones's foresight had again paid off, because years before he had required every member of the Peoples Temple to sign a blank confession form as an act of faith and submission. Jones even hired the well-known attorney Mark Lane, a man famous for his Kennedy assassination theories, who held his own press conferences to denounce the "massive conspiracy to destroy the Peoples Temple and a massive conspiracy to destroy the Reverend Jim Jones."[9]

As a part of his publicity campaign, Jones tried to convey to the outside world, and especially to those Peoples Temple members still in the United States, a picture of a tropical heaven in Guyana, where smiling people worked and lived together in perfect happiness and harmony. Actually, however, he ran Jonestown more like a small country with a totalitarian government. On the arrival of a new resident in Jonestown, guards confiscated all personal items, including passports and prescription medicines. From that moment on, Jones ruled every aspect of the person's life in Jonestown, using a squad of thugs to enforce compliance. These guards, residents found, were always watching for any signs of dissent, which were often answered with severe beatings.

Jonestown housed the men, women, and children living there, no matter what their relationship, in separate dormitories, and rules forbade all sexual contact. The only family unit allowed in Jonestown was the Peoples Temple. This family, however, soon began facing serious problems. As food supplies spoiled in the tropical heat, a balanced diet quickly became only a dream, while personal hygiene also became nonexistent as sanitary conditions at the compound degenerated. Jones and his staff, on the other hand, enjoyed imported food, liquor, drugs, and sex with the persons of their choice.

Jones also required the residents of Jonestown, after sweating and toiling all day, to attend mass meetings held every night, which often lasted until the early morning hours. During these meetings, Jones, his face swollen and flush from drugs, would rant and scream from his throne-like seat, positioned on a raised platform in the center of the open camp pavilion. Jones would shout about how they were being conspired against by the outside world, and about how they had enemies everywhere. The residents had no choice but to believe Jones's version of the world because the only news of the outside world the residents of Jonestown had was the evening news reports that Jones delivered (Jones's staff censored correspondence to and from the outside). He would invent and tell the residents graphic stories of the United States as a country that was quickly deteriorating and where, Jones told them, a nationwide race war loomed, with the government herding black people into concentration camps.

As with most cults, Jones formulated rules for every aspect of life. Violators of any of his rules found their punishment swift, brutal, and public. Jones had adult residents who violated rules severely beaten and often forced them to strip naked and engage in sex acts in front of the others. Jones also had children, for offenses such as stealing food or expressing homesickness, locked for days in small boxes, held under water, or frightened with snakes. Afterward, Jones required all of those punished to say, "Thank you, Father."

In addition, Jones made it impossible for anyone who decided he or she didn't like living in Jonestown to leave. Passports had been confiscated, and to have even the extremely remote chance of escaping through the miles of dense jungle, a person would first have to get past the armed guards who always patrolled the camp. Also, a person's absence would immediately be detected when the escapee missed one of the three daily roll calls. As another security measure, Jones gave all outside visitors, though there were only a few, specially guided tours, during which they saw only the smiling faces of people who had been coached and rehearsed on what to say and do for the visitors.

White Night drills, or mass suicide practice drills, became common in Jonestown (43 held in 1978 alone), and they almost always occurred in the early morning hours. Jones, seated on his throne in the pavilion, would scream and rant about some imminent threat, about how the CIA or some other "evil" force was about to assault the town, and about how this invasion force would torture and kill the residents. During the drills, Jones required everyone to drink a fruit-flavored beverage that they had been told was poisoned. After a few minutes, when no one showed any ill effects, the loudspeaker would announce that this had just been a drill and that everyone could go back to bed. Jones likely figured that after the residents had done this enough times, doing the real thing would be easy.

A small bit of hope for the residents of Jonestown finally came with California Congressman Leo Ryan. In June 1978, a defector from Jonestown, Deborah Layton, described the settlement in Guyana to *San Francisco Chronicle* reporters as a hellhole with armed guards, public beatings and humiliations, and many suicide drills. In addition to this account, Ryan also heard many other disturbing reports of brutality and substandard living conditions from the relatives of the residents of Jonestown. As a consequence, Ryan used his position on the House Foreign Relations Committee to plan an inspection trip to Guyana. While the other Bay Area congressional members declined Ryan's request to go along, eight news media representatives decided to accompany him on the trip.

When he arrived in Georgetown, the capital of Guyana, Ryan immediately received a petition allegedly signed by 600 Jonestown residents, a document that demanded he return to the United States and leave them to their new home. Ryan, however, didn't believe the petition to be voluntary and still insisted on visiting Jonestown. Finally, Jim Jones, reluctantly and only at the insistence of his attorneys, agreed to allow Ryan to visit the settlement. Jones warned the residents of Jonestown, under the threat of the most severe punishment, to be on their very best behavior during Ryan's visit.

That evening, after Ryan arrived in Jonestown, Jones treated him and his party to an excellent dinner and hundreds of smiling faces. All the visitors began to wonder if perhaps they had just been listening to unsubstantiated rumors. Everything seemed to be fine and everyone seemed to be very happy in Jonestown. However, later that evening, a man secretly passed a note to NBC correspondent Don Harris that said: "Please help me get out of Jonestown!"[10]

The next day, Ryan and his party began seeing a different side of Jonestown. On looking around the compound, they found some of the barracks locked with the shades down. Insisting that they see everything, the visitors finally had the buildings unlocked. Inside, they found elderly residents, some of them ill, stacked in bunk beds in the suffocating heat. Suddenly, more of the residents began whispering and passing notes that said they also wanted to leave Jonestown. Finally, Edith Parks, an elderly resident of Jonestown and a person who had joined the Peoples Temple when it was still operating in Indianapolis, publicly approached Ryan and said, "I want to go with you. I want to leave Jonestown."[11] Fourteen other people then joined in and clamored that they too wanted to leave Jonestown with Ryan's party.

In response, Jones, becoming more erratic and agitated by the moment, tried to persuade the people to stay at Jonestown, and promised that he would let them leave later. But the people didn't believe him and said they wanted to leave with Ryan's party. A standoff developed and tensions mounted.

Suddenly, in the heat of the confrontation and without any warning, one of the camp guards grabbed Congressman Ryan from behind and put a knife to his throat, threatening to kill him. Two of Jones's attorneys, seemingly aghast at what was happening, struggled with the bodyguard and at last forced him to release Ryan. Finally, ending the standoff, Jones told Ryan to go and take with him the 15 people who wanted to leave.

However, as the truck containing Ryan's party and the 15 former Jonestown residents left the compound, one of Jones's top confidants, Larry Layton, brother of Peoples Temple defector Deborah Layton, suddenly jumped into the truck, saying that he too wanted to leave. The former residents panicked because they knew that Larry Layton was dangerous and very close to Jones, but Ryan tried to calm them down, assuring them that everything would be all right.

For Jones, as a cult leader, the ultimate disaster had just occurred. The defection of 15 people, some of whom had joined his church nearly 25 years before in Indianapolis, was, he knew, a heavy blow to his status as a god in Jonestown. Jones was already well aware that his proposed agricultural community was an economic failure simply because the majority of the residents were either too elderly or too young to undertake the strenuous work necessary to convert Jonestown into a productive settlement. And now he found his oldest supporters deserting him. Within the space of just a few minutes, he had been publicly discredited as a messiah, prophet, and unquestioned leader. Jones knew that something had to be done quickly to reestablish his position and credibility.

What was done occurred at the airstrip in Port Kaituma, the closest settlement to Jonestown. Earlier, two aircraft had been summoned from Georgetown to transport the Ryan party and the Jonestown defectors. Once the two airplanes arrived, Ryan began supervising the boarding of the people. Suddenly however, a tractor pulling a flatbed trailer drove up, and three of Jones's bodyguards, armed with automatic weapons, jumped off and began firing. The gunfire immediately wounded several of the people trying to board the airplanes, and then the guards quickly killed three reporters as they tried to photograph what was happening. The gunmen also riddled Congressman Leo Ryan with bullets, afterward shooting him point blank in the face. On board one of the small airplanes, Larry Layton, whose job it was to kill the pilot and effectively ground the airplane, produced a revolver and shot and wounded two of the defectors, but not the pilot, before having the gun wrestled away from him. All in all, five people died at the airstrip, and 11 others were wounded. As the airplanes hurriedly took off amidst the gunfire, survivors who hadn't made it onto one of the airplanes fled and hid in the jungle.

"I survived that night on Guyanese rum," said Jackie Spier, then Leo Ryan's legal assistant and eventually a California state senator. She had been shot five times by the Jonestown guards. "One hundred and fifty proof, really potent stuff. We took turns taking swigs."[12]

Back at the compound, a nearly hysterical Jones, who had become so addicted to drugs in the last few years that his behavior had become more and more erratic, cried to his attorneys that three of his guards had gone after the Ryan party with guns, and he feared what they might do. Shortly afterward, the loudspeakers in Jonestown began blasting another White Night alert. The loudspeakers instructed everyone to come to the pavilion wearing their very best clothing. Realizing this wasn't just another drill, a few Jonestown residents fled and hid in the jungle. However, 914 of them didn't.

While the preceding incidents involving the Peoples Temple, which are detailed in such books as James J. Boyle's *Killer Cults* and Catherine Wessinger's *How the Millennium Comes Violently,* may seem to be extreme examples of the dangers and destructiveness of a religious cult, they are by no means isolated cases. Although the number of fatalities may be close to unmatched in modern history (the cult tragedy in Uganda in 2000, which I will discuss in a later chapter, had even more deaths), the likelihood that the actions of a religious cult will result in the deaths of nonmembers, or the likelihood that belonging to a religious cult will result in a member's death, is certainly much more common than most might suppose. One has only to recall the circumstances surrounding the demise of the Branch Davidian cult, a cult that centered on David Koresh's claim of a special relationship with God. In Waco, Texas, in 1993, four federal agents and more than 80 members of David Koresh's cult, including nearly two dozen children, perished.

More recently, in August 1996, both the leader and a follower of the Jesus-Amen cult in San Francisco received prison sentences for their part in the beating death of a 25-year-old woman. According to reports in the *San Francisco Chronicle,* the victim reportedly had originally complained of insomnia, but cult members decided that her real problem was demonic possession, and as a consequence they decided to attempt to rid her of the demons. The exorcism ceremony they attempted, which lasted six hours, involved more than 100 kicks and punches to the victim, who was restrained by cult members and had a towel stuffed in her mouth to stifle her screams. The victim suffered 14 broken ribs and severe injuries to her head, which subsequently led to her death. Even after the victim died, the members of the Jesus-Amen cult stayed and prayed over the woman's dead body for four days before finally notifying her relatives. The cult leader stated from jail that she believes the cause of the woman's death was not the six hours of beating but rather the demons that possessed her.

"There was no evil intent here," said the cult leader's lawyer. "They're just true believers who got carried away."[13]

Even religious cults that profess to believe in and practice peace, love, and honesty are not always as peaceful and honest as they try to present themselves. "I saw the human rights abuses," said Jim Polly, a former adherent of the Hare Krishna movement, whose followers, with their shaved heads and saffron robes, were once common features in airports and on street corners, where they would sing, chant, and beg from passersby. "They were using us. They were living off us. I got fed up. When I saw how the people were treated at the commune and the deplorable conditions they lived under, I left."[14]

There were worse problems in the Hare Krishna movement, however, than just exploitation. In 1996, for example, the leader of the West Virginia temple of the Hare Krishna cult, a man named Kirtanananda, began a 12-year prison sentence for racketeering. A court convicted another member of the West Virginia Hare Krishna temple of murder.

"What happened in West Virginia was our biggest devastation in North America," said Bruce Dickmeyer, director of the Hare Krishna temple in Detroit. "But finally there is a sense of closure on that, because Kirtanananda is gone, and most of those problems have been resolved."[15]

However, the problems had actually only begun for the Hare Krishna movement. New complaints of criminal acts within the cult began surfacing in 2001. During the 1960s, 1970s, and 1980s, the children of those in the cult had typically been separated from their parents and sent to various boarding schools that the movement operated. This was done so that the parents could work for the cult unhindered by the need to raise their children. A researcher of the Hare Krishna movement stated that he found there used to be an old saying about expectant mothers in the cult: "Dump the load and hit the road."[16]

As it turned out, individuals poorly prepared to deal with children often ran these boarding schools. When accusations of widespread physical and sexual abuse in many of the cult's boarding schools arose, leaders of the Hare Krishna movement hired Professor E. Burke Rochford of Middlebury College in Vermont to investigate the claims. Unfortunately, Dr. Rochford found, many of the claims proved to be true.[17] Boys and girls alike suffered repeated sexual abuse as children, while others told of being beaten, slammed to the floor, and being forced to undergo inhumane punishments, such as being stuffed into a closed trash barrel for days. In addition, a number of former boarding school children reported suffering serious psychological abuse during their stay there.

"They would terrorize us with brainwashing," said Brigite Rittenour in a June 2002 interview. "They taught us that people outside the movement were evil, that they ate meat and would eat us."[18] Rittenour, who is one of dozens of people suing the Hare Krishna movement, also reported being sexual abused as a child while living in one of the cult's boarding schools. But along with being sexually abused, she alleges that the cult forced her to marry a 37-year-old man when she was only 14.

In response to the multitude of lawsuits filed against the cult, Hare Krishna leaders have announced that they will likely file for bankruptcy protection in several of their temple areas. Interestingly, one of the main pieces of evidence used by those suing the Hare Krishna movement is Professor Rochford's report confirming the abuse, which leaders made public in an attempt to deal with the problem.

The problems of the Hare Krishna movement, however, weren't confined to their boarding schools or even to the United States. In 1987, according to news reports, which included a June 21, 1988 article in the *London Times*, a long-time and very close disciple of James Immel, the head of the Hare Krishna movement in Europe, beheaded Immel because he said he was disgusted by Immel's drug use and sex orgies. The disciple was still holding Immel's head when the police arrived. The tenets of the Hare Krishna movement forbid alcohol, drugs, gambling, and sex.

As this example illustrates, it sometimes takes years for devoted members of a religious cult to finally recognize that the leader they have idolized and venerated for so long is actually corrupt, controlling, and far from the godlike image the leader has tried to portray. A member of the Siddha Yoga cult, for example, said, "At the time I idealized everything about Gurumayi (the leader). We all found ingenious ways of making her perfect no matter what, and making her bizarre and cruel behavior 'for our own good.'"[19]

In later chapters, I will discuss the dynamics of what can make cult members see their leader as godlike, despite abundant evidence to the contrary. Suffice it to say here that, despite what happened in Jonestown, a number of people still venerate Jim Jones and believe him worthy of sainthood.

Beyond the few cults I have mentioned so far, literally thousands of other cults exist in our country and around the world. However, of all the types of cults in existence today, religious cults are by far the most numerous. This is because many people consider them to be simply offshoots of traditional religions. This perception comes about because religious cults usually include in their teachings elements of traditional religious beliefs that prospective candidates have been familiar with all their lives (some religious cults, for example, combine and intertwine various aspects of Christianity, Buddhism, Hinduism, Islam, and other faiths into their theology).

But far different from regular, orthodox religions, religious cults, using my definition, can be fairly easy to spot because, along with being involved in some type of criminal activity, they offer their members a certain ticket to heaven as part of a group especially appointed and chosen by God. Along with this, religious cults often teach that everyone outside the group is working for Satan and consequently condemned to hell for eternity. In addition, religious cults offer their members ready and complete answers to all life's seemingly unanswerable questions. Although they usually encompass the teachings of some traditional religious faith, or often the combination of the teachings of several religious faiths, almost all religious cults center their veneration on a living leader who claims to be God, to have special access to God, special access to teachings or knowledge unknown to the rest of the world, or to possess some type of supernatural powers.

"He was a man who I thought spoke directly to God," said Jim Martin, associate editor of *Ex-Cultworld* magazine, speaking about Victor Paul Wierwille, founder and leader of a cult called The Way International. "At the time, I thought his words were revelations from God."[20]

"He was the second coming of the Messiah," said Mitchell Mack, Jr., talking about his feelings concerning Reverend Sun Myung Moon while a member of the Unification Church, also known as the Moonies, which I will talk about later in this chapter.[21]

However, as another sign that a group may be a cult, along with being involved in criminal acts, few cult leaders, particularly those who claim to be on a first-name basis with God, have substantial theological credentials. "Many of these ministers are self-ordained or ordained by groups with low academic standards," said Cynthia Kisser, former executive director of the original Cult Awareness Network. "They rely on personal charisma or direct revelation from God. There is much less accountability than in larger churches."[22]

As an example of this, in 1968, an itinerant preacher named David Berg founded the cult known as the Children of God, which I talked about in the previous chapter. This cult, which in the turbulent 1970s attracted many disaffected youths, believed in and practiced sexual excesses, including spouse swapping and the circulation of pornography. For a number of years, the cult sponsored a "Hookers for Christ" campaign, in which female members of the cult, known as "God's Whores," were sent out to pick up men in bars and nightclubs and then sexually seduce them in order to recruit the men into the cult. Although these practices are no longer widely used by the cult, many of the present-day members of this cult are the offspring of these liaisons. In addition, and as I discussed in the previous chapter, child abuse, both sexual and physical, was extremely common in the Children of God.

Along with hundreds of small religious cults in our country, there also exist several large religious cults that can claim thousands of members. I've already talked about the Hare Krishna cult, officially known as the International Society for Krishna Consciousness. While many adherents of the Hare Krishna movement may be simply devoted and true believers, this group, as I have shown here, has been involved in considerable criminal activity. An Indian businessman named A. C. Bhaktivedanta Swami Prabhupada brought this organization to the United States in 1966. It is an offshoot of the Hindu religion, which recognizes many gods. Hare Krishna adherents, however, believe that Lord Krishna is the Supreme God and that all other gods are only minor manifestations of him. At its height in the 1960s and 1970s, the movement had 30 temples in various cities in the United States and about 5,000 adherents living in these temples. Today, the number of people living in Hare Krishna temples has declined drastically, but as more and more Asian Indians move to this country, it is expected that the overall membership will increase.

Another large religious cult that can claim thousands of members in the United States is the Holy Spirit Association for the Unification of World Christians, or the Unification Church for short; its members are known as the Moonies. This cult, established by North Korean business-man Sun Myung Moon, reportedly wants to unite all Christians world-wide into one fellowship. In the early 1980s, however, a federal court convicted Reverend Moon of tax evasion and conspiracy in connection with the Unification Church, and he spent more than a year in a federal prison. In addition, many former members of the Unification Church claim that they were used in fraudulent fund-raising by the group. Despite this, Moon has stated that he is the messiah sent by God to finish Jesus's work and to correct some of Jesus's mistakes. As the Unification Church's holy text, the *Divine Principle,* states, "God has sent his messen-ger to resolve fundamental questions of life and the universe. His name is Sun Myung Moon."[23]

As an example of Moon's megalomania, a trait typical of most cult lead-ers, in July 2002, the Unification Church purchased full-page advertise-ments in numerous large newspapers around the world. Included in this advertisement were "testimonials" confirming that Moon is indeed the true savior appointed by God. The advertisement claimed that these testi-monials had come from the spirit world. The individuals giving written testimonials in this advertisement for Moon included Jesus and numerous historical Christian figures, Confucius, Buddha, Muhammad, the Gods of Hinduism, and several deceased communist leaders, including Karl Marx and Joseph Stalin, who said he was giving his testimonial from hell. The advertisement closed with a letter from God himself confirming that Moon is indeed his son and messenger.

Moon claims that in 1935, while in prayer on a mountainside in Korea, Jesus appeared to him and asked him to complete the mission he had started. Moon states that he believes one of Jesus's greatest mistakes was that he never married. And yet, while glorifying marriage, the Unification Church forbids romantic liaisons unless they are approved of and blessed by the church. In June 2002, I attended the national conference of the American Family Foundation, the country's leading cult information organization. At a seminar there I heard two women speak who had been raised by at least one parent who belonged to Reverend Moon's church. In one of the women's cases, Reverend Moon had approved of both her par-ents; therefore, in the eyes of the Unification Church, she was a "blessed child." Reverend Moon, however, had not approved of both parents of the other woman, so she was seen as an "unblessed child," even though her mother had belonged to and sworn allegiance to the Unification Church (her father had not belonged to the Unification Church). The differences in the treatment of the two children while being raised by the Unification Church were appallingly similar to the segregation of the early twentieth century. The "unblessed child" told the seminar attendees that she often found herself shunned by church members and was not allowed to attend certain social functions.

However, according to Unification Church doctrine, even approved couples can only have sex in church-approved positions. Moon claims that Adam and Eve brought about mankind's fall by having sex before they were spiritually ready. As a part of the Unification Church doctrine, church officials often arrange marriages for couples who many times meet their future spouses for the first time at the marriage ceremony. In September 2002, Moon married 250 such couples at New York City's Manhattan Center.

Along with arranged marriages, Reverend Moon has also laid down rules for the role of women in his church. At a meeting in March 2001 in Oakland, California, he said that every woman should bear a child, and if she did not, he stated, "I'm sorry to say, you're disqualified as a woman."[23] Moon has also stated, "If a woman deliberately avoids having children, she is a substandard animal."[25]

One of Moon's top American aides who defected from the Unification Church warned that Moon has told Unification Church leaders, "When we take power in America, we will have to amend the Constitution and make it a capital offense for anyone to have sexual relations with anyone other than the person assigned to him."[26]

This quote is not an idle boast. The Unification Church has long been involved in the political side of America. Along with supporting conservative candidates—including former President George H. W. Bush who, according to an article in the March 10, 2001, issue of *The Consortium,* has spoken at events sponsored by the Unification Church—the church also founded the right-wing newspaper the *Washington Times* and purchased the news organization *United Press International* (UPI). In one of his speeches, Moon said, "When it comes to our age, we must have an automatic theocracy to rule the world. So we cannot separate the political field from the religious.... Separation between religion and politics is what Satan likes most."[27] In addition to founding and constantly funding the profitless *Washington Times,* which Ronald Reagan once called his favorite newspaper, the Unification Church also funnels a considerable amount of money into politically far-right causes.

Another former Unification Church official also gives a warning about Moon's intentions. "It's like the sheep's skin the wolf wore when he went to see Little Red Riding Hood," said Ford Greene, an attorney and former Moonie. "Moon is a malevolent exploiter of people's idealism. All of this about unifying world religion is a bunch of flowery sweet talk, when his real goal is a world government with Moon himself as the head."[28]

Religious cults, however, don't have to be large and well known like the Hare Krishnas and the Moonies to be involved in criminal activity. According to newspaper accounts, on December 20, 1986, a federal judge sentenced William Lewis, leader of a cult called the House of Judah, to three years in prison for conspiring to enslave the children of cult members and for causing the death of a young boy. The authorities in southern Michigan removed 66 children, ranging in age from 2 months to 16 years old, from the religious cult's compound after a 12-year-old boy died from a beating administered when he refused to do his chores. The leader of the House of Judah claimed that the Bible gave him the authority to impose strict discipline on both children and adults in the group.[29]

As another example, a November 23, 1984, article in the *New York Times* tells how the authorities in Portland, Oregon, filed child abuse charges against the leader of a commune run by a religious cult called the Good Shepherd Tabernacle. The children told the police of being confined with ropes and handcuffs in dark rooms, being hung by ropes from ceiling hooks, and being denied food, water, and toilet facilities. The children also complained of regular beatings as a part of their life in the commune.[30]

Not all religious cults, however, commit murder, physically and sexually abuse their members, or are bent on world domination. Yet they can still be extremely destructive to their members financially. Many religious cults use fraudulent promises to persuade their members to empty their bank accounts, sell all their worldly goods, and then give this money to the cult. Many of these cults also persuade new members to quit their jobs and to sever personal and family relationships. The isolated and impoverished cult members are then convinced to follow a self-proclaimed messiah who, after taking all their money, fraudulently promises them a major part in a world-shattering event. Of course, the event never takes place, and the members, once they realize they have been swindled and leave the cult, are left to try to reassemble the pieces of their shattered lives. Such an event occurred several years ago in Garland, Texas.

In 1997, according to several Texas newspapers and a half dozen prime-time television news accounts, a group of 160 Taiwanese citizens, belonging to a cult called God's Salvation Church, which combined aspects of Christianity, Buddhism, and science fiction, began settling in Garland, Texas, a suburb of Dallas. The leader of the group, Hon-Ming Chen, a 42-year-old sociology professor, claimed that he, in a past life, was Joseph, the father of Jesus. Also in his group, Chen asserted, were two young boys who were the reincarnations of Jesus and Buddha. As reported in the December 24, 1997, issue of the *Houston Chronicle,* Chen proclaimed to the press that on March 31, 1998, at 10:00 A.M., God would descend from heaven and appear at 3513 Ridgedale Drive in Garland. God would appear in Chen's physical form and then split into hundreds of Chen clones (in order for Him to be able to speak to everyone at one time). God's reason for appearing, according to Chen, was to save Chen's group and other worthy individuals from the nuclear holocaust that would sweep the world in 1999. But before this appearance by God, Chen said, the earth would be shrouded in darkness and, on March 25, 1998, God would appear worldwide on television channel 18 to explain his plan.

Chen also told that press that, on March 31, when God came to Earth in person, he would travel in a special "Godplane," and at the same time, aircraft previously lost in other dimensions would suddenly reappear. When asked why he came to Garland, Texas, Chen said that golden balls of light had floated down from the sky and told him to come to Garland. He also said that he believed God picked Garland because if a person said it quickly enough it sounded like "God's Land."

While all of this may sound like a man seemingly suffering from psychotic delusions, the individuals who followed Chen to America were not uneducated or unsophisticated people. The group, who had been convinced to sever professional and family ties in order to follow Chen, included other college professors, high-ranking government employees, and other professionals. Most of Chen's followers had been fairly affluent in Taiwan, and with the money they raised from selling their homes and all their possessions, the cult bought 20 expensive pieces of property in Garland.

"They all came down here this past summer and bought up all the houses with cash," said Garland resident Tawania Winchell. "It's a trip."[31]

Early in 1998, Chen and 30 members of his group traveled to Gary, Indiana. He told reporters that Gary was one of the chosen loading docks, where God's flying saucers would land to transport true believers to another dimension so they could escape the nuclear annihilation.

"After the Great Tribulation happens in 1999, God's flying saucers will carry off survivors that come here," Chen said. "There will be other loading docks, but Lake Street Beach will be the headquarters."[32]

As late March approached, the residents of Garland began to worry about what the cult members, who always wore white clothing and even white cowboy hats, might do when Chen's prophecy didn't come true. Residents especially worried about the possibility of a mass suicide.

"As soon as groups commit to a date, it can get dangerous," said Professor Robert Smith, who teaches a course on apocalyptic beliefs at the Graduate Theological Union in Berkeley, California. "When they get disappointed, they either have to make revisions to the prophecy or compel it to happen."[33]

On March 26, 1998, when God had not appeared around the world on television channel 18, as predicted, and when darkness didn't shroud the earth, as predicted, an obviously disappointed Chen appeared and attempted to explain what had happened. "Even though the image doesn't show on television," he said, "I don't have any reason to doubt the existence of God in the universe."[34]

When asked about what would become of his followers, Chen replied, "Tomorrow they have the freedom to go where they want....I would recommend anyone not believe what I said anymore." He also added, "You can now take what we have preached as nonsense."[35] Unfortunately, this was little solace to people who had liquidated their property, forsaken careers, and severed personal relationships to follow Chen to America.

A week later, however, even though God had not appeared as predicted, a much more confident Chen, apparently having recovered from his earlier disappointment, announced that his group was moving to Michigan. He claimed that he had been ordered to go there and await further instructions from God, who Chen said would soon begin gathering worthy souls in order to save them from the certain nuclear holocaust of 1999. God, he said, would still rescue these people in flying saucers and then shuttle them to Gary, Indiana, for transport to another dimension.

A year later, however, only 30 of the original 160 members of Chen's group remained with him, the rest returning home and attempting to resurrect their lives. Fortunately, the mass suicide fears of Garland residents had not come true. Although I could find no information about what happened to the 130 individuals who returned to Taiwan, one can only imagine the difficulties they likely faced trying to resurrect the business and family relationships they had severed to follow Chen. In addition, they also likely faced extreme difficulties attempting to rebuild their finances after emptying their bank accounts and selling all their property. I will discuss in later chapters the dynamics of what can cause seemingly rational people to accept irrational claims such as those Chen made, an act that clearly can have devastating effects on a cult member's life. First, however, I will look at other types of cults that often make even more irrational claims than many of the religious cults do yet still attract many followers.

CHAPTER 4

Occult Cults

Interest in the occult—the belief in the power of supernatural spells and incantations, the belief in communication and interaction with supernatural beings, and so on—has always been popular in our country, as noted by the many movies and books devoted to it every year. A June 2001 Gallup poll, for instance, found that 42 percent of Americans believe in haunted houses, 38 percent in ghosts, 28 percent in the ability to communicate with the dead, 26 percent in witches, and 15 percent in the ability to "channel" with a spirit being.[1] However, the following incident, which was reported in the *Houston Chronicle* and the book *Killer Cults* by James J. Boyle, illustrates very clearly that cults based on occult beliefs can have grisly outcomes.

The magic of human sacrifice, cult members believed, would protect them and their drug-dealing business from both the police and rival gangs. With this mystical protection, bullets couldn't touch them, police officers couldn't arrest them. Therefore, the authorities report, to keep their magical protection intact, an occult-based cult killed and mutilated at least 13 young men in the south Texas/Mexico border area. One of the sacrificial victims was Mark James Kilroy, a 21-year-old University of Texas pre-med student.

During spring break in 1989, Mark decided to accompany several of his friends to South Padre Island, a popular resort area off the tip of south Texas. Hitting the beaches by day and the bars by night, Mark and his friends partied hard. Several times during Mark's trip to South Padre Island, he and his friends crossed the border into the Mexican town of

Matamoros, where cheaper prices often brought crowds across the Rio Grande. One night, however, after Mark and three of his friends had joined the long lines of people waiting to go through customs coming from Matamoros back into the United States, a Mexican man approached Mark and began talking to him. His three friends, in different lines, didn't think much about it until they were through the lines and didn't see Mark. Worried, the three friends went in search of Mark but couldn't find him anywhere.

Finally, the next morning, when Mark still hadn't returned, the now frantic friends called Mark's parents, who notified the police. What no one suspected at the time was that Mark had been kidnapped after cult members, under orders to bring back a blond-haired male, had selected him as the next human sacrifice that the cult believed would give them magical protection.

After the police began their investigation into Mark's disappearance, members of his family traveled to the south Texas area and began an investigation of their own, walking the streets of South Padre Island and Matamoros and handing out flyers that offered a substantial reward for information about Mark. The family also kept constant pressure on the police, who gave the case as much attention as they could but naturally had many other cases that also needed attention.

"Once Mr. Kilroy showed up, he was there every day for the next 30 days," said George Gavito, a former police lieutenant. "He wouldn't leave....I think that's what kept us all going."[2]

The leader of the occult cult that had kidnapped Mark, Adolfo de Jesus Constanzo, had been involved in occult worship for many years. As a young child, Constanzo had been introduced to Santeria, an occult mixture of Roman Catholicism and voodoo, and had worked for a time as a Santeria mystic. Santeria came into existence as a religion when the new masters of West African slaves brought to the New World attempted to forcibly convert these slaves to Catholicism. The slaves, rather than simply converting, blended their own religion with the Catholic faith, and it became Santeria. Constanzo brought this belief in the occult-based Santeria with him when he formed his drug-dealing cult, setting up its headquarters at Rancho Santa Elena, just outside Matamoros, Mexico.

As a part of the "protection ritual," Constanzo and his high priestess, a woman named Sara Maria Aldrete Villareal, drew circles of blood around cult members that Constanzo and Villareal insisted would protect the members from any harm. Although at first the cult used animal sacrifices for the blood, the cult leaders soon became convinced that, for the protection shields to be maximally effective, they needed human blood. Thus young men began disappearing around Matamoros. They would be brought to the cult's ranch, ritually beheaded, and bled into a large cauldron. The cult then used their blood in its rituals.

The murderous cult's rituals finally came to an end when Mexican police on drug interdiction patrol chased a pickup truck that they had witnessed acting suspiciously. After running off the road into a ditch, the truck's occupants jumped out and raced on foot to a warehouse, with the police right behind. Inside the warehouse, the pursuing police officers found that the fleeing men had stopped running, and were instead now just standing inside a reddish brown circle and laughing at them. The men truly believed, and told the police so, that Constanzo's blood shield would protect them. They believed the police couldn't touch them. When the startled and amazed men found that the blood shield didn't work after all, they broke down and told the police everything about the cult. Working on the information provided by the men, the police discovered the remains of several butchered human beings inside the warehouse, while outside, in a corral, they found the buried remains of 13 beheaded and mutilated young men, including the body of Mark Kilroy.

Later, when the police closed in on Constanzo, who had fled to Mexico City, he ordered one of his cult members to kill him rather than be taken by the police. In May 1994, a judge sentenced the cult high priestess, Sara Maria Aldrete Villareal, to a 62-year prison sentence for her part in the cult rituals, while four other cult members received 67-year prison sentences.

In their son's memory, Mark Kilroy's parents founded the Mark Kilroy Foundation, which, among other things, sponsors drug awareness programs in schools. The foundation still operates today.

As many parents know, teenagers often go through a phase during which they rebel against established authority. While this usually involves harmless acts that the teens hope will shock adults, occasionally it can also involve more serious acts. Although parents probably shouldn't be alarmed by most teenage rebelliousness, on the other hand, becoming involved in some acts of rebellion, such as a deep immersion in the occult, can occasionally lead to extremely serious consequences. Signs that parents and others should look for indicating a teenager has gone beyond simple rebellion and is possibly deeply immersed in the occult are discussed in a later chapter.

Young people's involvement in the occult often stems from their perception that the world is a place over which they have little control. They see the world as being run by powers that care little for them. Because of this, many teenagers find themselves drawn to the occult, which they feel gives them some power and control in a technological world they feel they don't fit into. Of course, the feeling of power offered by the occult is only an illusion, and often the belief system comes crashing down when adherents attempt to use this power to manipulate objects or to control people who don't believe in the occult. Although the results of these failed attempts at power are usually harmless, the example of the vampire cults in chapter 1 illustrates how deadly they can be.

"The simplified Machiavellianism of the Temple of Set [an organization that promotes occult beliefs]," says Dr. David A. Halperin, a psychiatrist at the Mount Sinai School of Medicine, "may appeal to adolescents who see the world around them as being dominated by force, immorality, and unreason."[3]

A number of people concerned about youth involvement in the occult fear that the popularity of movies such as *Harry Potter* and the newly re-released *The Exorcist* will spark even more interest in the occult. Most of this, however, is simply harmless entertainment unless individuals twist ideas from the movies into occult beliefs that harm others. While most adherents of the occult can legitimately claim that theirs is a peaceful belief system, there are always those who can use the same beliefs to build a deadly and destructive cult. An incident that occurred several years ago in Greene County, Tennessee, vividly illustrates how seemingly harmless engagement in alternative belief systems can turn deadly.

According to an article in *Campus Life* and a report on *CNN*, Natasha Cornett didn't have what most would consider a traditional wedding. She wore black, while her bridesmaids wore dog collars that were chained together. According to her mother, Natasha, who didn't finish high school, had always had a strong interest in witchcraft and the occult.[4] The acts that Natasha and five other members of an occult cult committed on a gravel road in eastern Tennessee became a notorious crime that would be talked about all across the state.

On April 4, 1997, Natasha and members of her occult cult held a séance and bloodletting ritual in a motel room. A cousin of one of the cult members said that when he knocked on the door, he found that all the occupants, including the males, wore black clothing and facial makeup. On April 6, 1997, six members of the cult, ranging in age from 14 to 20, left their homes around Paintsville, Kentucky, in an old Chevrolet Citation owned by the mother of cult member Joe Risner. In the car, the six individuals, known around their hometown as an odd lot that usually wore only black and did extensive body piercing and self-mutilation with razor blades, carried two books with them: *The Book of Black Magic* and the *Complete Book of Magic and Witchcraft*.

"We were trying to find answers," Crystal Sturgill, a member of the cult, told a reporter for *Campus Life*. "We all had been to church. It didn't provide answers. We were interested in Wicca, books on witches and spells. We were anarchists."[5]

The six cult members passed the morning of April 6 burglarizing homes, obtaining guns, and buying drugs. They then decided to head for New Orleans. Joe's car, however, kept overheating, so the cult members allegedly tried unsuccessfully to hot-wire and steal a car from a used-car lot. Finally, they pulled the overheating Chevrolet into a rest stop near Baileyton, Tennessee, still looking for a vehicle to steal. There they encountered a family on their way home from a religious gathering: Vidar Lillelid; his wife, Delfina; and their two children, Tabitha, age 6, and Peter, age 2. Vidar and his wife had moved from Miami to Tennessee because they had become concerned about the crime level in Florida and wanted to raise their children in a safer environment.

"They decided things were a little on the rough side in Miami," said a friend of the Lillelids, "and they wanted to move to get away from the violence, among other reasons."[6]

The cult members, still needing a new car, decided to take the Lillelid's Dodge van. Forcing the family into the van at gunpoint, they drove to a nearby gravel road, where the cult members shot and killed Vidar, Delfina, and Tabitha with .25-caliber and 9-mm. pistols. They also shot Peter, but he would survive his wounds, though losing an eye. Abandoning Joe's overheating car on the gravel road, the cult members left in their new vehicle, but before doing so, they ran over the Lillelid family with the van.

Two days later, at the Arizona/Mexico border, authorities arrested the cult members still driving the murdered family's van. Although two cult members fought extradition, eventually the authorities returned all six of them to Tennessee to stand trial.

On April 13, 1998, a judge sentenced the six cult members to life in prison without the possibility of parole. Earlier, to escape the possibility of the death penalty, all six cult members pleaded guilty to first-degree murder. Since then, the six cult members have appealed their guilty pleas. However, the courts have denied all of their appeals, the latest on April 2, 2002. Peter Lillelid, fitted with an artificial eye, went to live with an aunt and uncle in Sweden.

Besides Santerians and offshoot groups engaged in criminal forms of witchcraft, there presently exist many other groups of individuals who believe in and practice occult worship. There are, for example, the Rosicrucians, believers in Eckankar, practitioners of voodoo, and others. When I attended a recent national conference about cults, I sat in on an interesting presentation about the Waldorf School System, which runs a number of schools in the United States, mostly in the West. According to the speakers, these schools, while representing themselves to be artistically directed schools, actually teach a "magical" view of the universe, which relies more on occult teachings than on science. Because these schools remain in existence and sign up new students every year (though some parents who register their children at the schools may be unaware of the underlying belief system), obviously a number of people are attracted to and agree with this view of the world. Still, as I have previously stated, most of these groups pose no danger but are simply legitimate, alternate belief systems.

However, there are also some occult practices with a dark side. On October 8, 2002, the police in Newark, New Jersey, raided a temple of the Palo Mayombe sect. Like Santeria, this is a West African religion brought to the New World by slaves. In the temple, the police discovered three human skulls, apparently stolen from graveyards, in cauldrons sitting on altars. Authorities say this is the second time in two months that the police have found stolen human remains in a Palo Mayombe temple.

While, as I have stated, most occult practices are harmless, occasionally, as the incidents in Tennessee and South Texas illustrate, cults can twist some of these beliefs into dangerous activities that present a serious threat both to their members and to the public. Another such example occurred several years ago in Wisconsin.

In July 1997, according to reports in the *Minneapolis-St. Paul Star Tribune,* the police found Mark Steven Foster, a pharmacist from Minneapolis, shot to death along a rural Wisconsin road near Wascott. Next to the body, the police recovered a .44-caliber bullet casing fired by the murder weapon, a Ruger carbine. In the victim's shoe, the police discovered a clue to who the murderer was: a scrap of paper with a man's name on it. A week before he died, Foster had called a friend and said that he was being threatened by a man he was planning to meet soon late at night. However, the police found that the man Foster was to meet had a verifiable alibi. When the police investigated further and discovered who the real killer was, they also uncovered a cult of voodoo practitioners, with Foster as the high priest.

"In the 19 years I have been with the department," said Douglas County Sheriff Larry McDonald, "this is probably the most bizarre case I've ever experienced."[7]

Mark Steven Foster wasn't always just an obscure pharmacist. In the early 1990s, Foster had been an entrepreneur on the rise in Minneapolis. A company he owned had developed a new product called the CD-ROM. At one time, Foster's company had more CD-ROMs for sale than any other company in the nation. Because of this, Foster found himself propelled from a simple pharmacist to a fast-rising star in the software industry.

"He was so far out front," said Tom McGrew, a former vice president of Compton's News Media. "It took a long time for everyone else to catch up to thinking about it, to understanding what he was doing."[8]

For a time, Foster lived the high life, with limousines and trips to Europe. But the precarious world of computer software soon caught up with him when he spent too much of the profits on himself rather than reinvesting them. In addition, other software companies soon began improving the CD-ROM, making Foster's product obsolete, and much of what his firm offered was eventually freely available on the Internet. After a while, with huge mounting debts and no income, Foster found himself forced to close the company he had started and seek a job again as a pharmacist in Minneapolis. On top of all this, the IRS decided to audit him. His world suddenly came apart. Foster, however, had a solution.

Somewhere along his travels as a successful entrepreneur, Foster had picked up an interest in the occult, particularly voodoo. For some reason he became convinced that he could perform supernatural voodoo acts. Consequently, he formed a voodoo-based cult, with him as the leader. Depressed about his business failings and his inability to support his family as he previous had, Foster decided to use voodoo magic as a way to remedy the situation. First, he took out a $300,000 life insurance policy on himself, then he had one of his cult members shoot and kill him. Foster, however, didn't expect to die.

"The apparently arranged death had a dual purpose," said an investigator for the Douglas County Sheriff's office. "Foster's apparent belief—through the voodoo—that he could leave the current body he was occupying and have his soul and powers transferred to the person who killed him. And also for the money he could leave his family. We believe he also did it for the life insurance money his family would receive. He had a $300,000 policy."[9]

Unfortunately, the person who killed him was incarcerated for murder when the police sorted out the case and found out what really happened.

This sort of faith in occult magic, faith enough to have someone kill you, is incomprehensible to most rational people, but, as Foster demonstrated, and as I will show throughout this book, cult leaders can not only often convince rational people to subscribe to irrational beliefs, but the cult leaders themselves many times also subscribe totally to them. In the next chapter, I will discuss Satanism, another occult belief that is just as dangerous, and perhaps even more so, than the cults discussed in this chapter.

CHAPTER 5

Satanic Cults

According to reports that appeared in newspapers all over the country, 16-year-old Luke Woodham, before leaving for school on October 1, 1997, armed himself with a butcher knife. He then stabbed his mother, 50-year-old Mary Woodham, seven times, leaving her to die on the floor of her brick ranch home in Pearl, Mississippi, a suburb of Jackson.

The pathologist who performed the autopsy on Mary, Dr. Steven Hayne, said that, in addition to her other wounds, he found 11 defensive slash wounds on Mary's arms, evidence that she had vigorously attempted to defend herself against the knife attack by her son. Dr. Hayne also stated that Mary had likely lived for 20 to 40 minutes after the attack, dying only after blood finally filled up her chest cavity. After his arrest, Luke allegedly told police he got a cut on his hand "stabbing my mother." He also told the police that "my mother never loved me."[1]

Following this attack on his mother, Luke drove the family car to Pearl High School, where he was a junior. Under the blue trench coat he wore that day, Luke carried a hunting rifle. At the school, Luke confronted and then shot and killed his ex-girlfriend, Christina Menefee, and a friend of hers, 17-year-old Lydia Kay Dew, as the two girls waited for classes to begin. Luke then went on a shooting rampage at the high school, wounding seven other students.

Because he had poor eyesight and wore thick glasses, Luke apparently mistook some of the people he fired at. Shooting victim Jeffrey Safley recalled, "He looked at me—Luke has poor eyesight—and said, 'I didn't realize it was you. I thought you were Kyle.'"[2] Luke apparently meant Kyle Foster, the mayor's son, who the police believe Luke wanted to kill for the shock value. The mayor's son, however, had been late for school that day.

An assistant principal at Pearl High School, Joel Myrick, finally stopped the rampage. Racing out and grabbing a .45-caliber pistol he kept in his vehicle at the school, Myrick chased Luke down and held him on the ground for the police. "I think he's a coward," Myrick said. "I had my weapon pointed at his face, and he didn't want to die."[3]

What at first appeared to be just a disturbed young man going on a shooting rampage for unknown reasons soon turned into something much darker when stories of a satanic cult and devil worship at Pearl High School suddenly began surfacing. Luke, the police eventually discovered, had been involved with a half dozen other youths in a satanic cult called the Kroth, which was reportedly led by another Pearl, Mississippi, youth named Grant Boyette. Described by Pearl High School students as brainy loners who often dressed in dark clothing, the cult members reportedly took part in animal sacrifices and held an intense fascination for Adolph Hitler and the German philosopher Friedrich Nietzsche.

"He (Boyette) made us take an oath to swear allegiance to Satan," Luke wrote in his diary.[4]

"They all talked about Hitler," a Pearl High School student said. "They'd all say they wanted to take over the world like Hitler." Another student said that one member of the cult "talked a lot about how he loved the devil."[5]

Reporters investigating stories about a devil-worshipping church north of the school found the bones of small animals scattered around the area. The county district attorney, John Kitchens, said that his investigation "has led us to believe that there is satanic activity occurring in this county."[6]

At his trial the following year, a weeping Luke Woodham told the court about being possessed by demons and how a friend of his, Grant Boyette, had ordered him to commit the killings. He said Boyette allegedly warned him, "We cannot move forward until all our enemies are gone."[7]

Luke also told the court, "I remember I woke up that morning and I'd seen the demons that I always saw when Grant told me to do something. They said I was nothing and I would never be anything if I didn't get to that school and kill those people."[8] The police eventually arrested 18-year-old Boyette, whom members of the cult called Father, and charged him as an accessory to the murders.

In addition, at Luke's trial, the jury learned that the police investigation uncovered evidence that the cult had drawn up detailed plans for an assault on Pearl High School, which called for the cult members to lay siege to the school, cut the telephone lines, set off fire bombs, and then kill selected people at the school. The cult members afterward planned to flee first to Louisiana and then to Mexico, where they would eventually board a boat to Cuba. The cult members had also reportedly planned to smear poison on doorknobs that would be used by one cult member's father, who had caught several of them using his credit card to purchase $9,000 worth of computer equipment.

The jury also listened to excerpts from Luke Woodham's diary, in which he recounted the torture killing of his family's dog. The diary excerpt read, "On Saturday of last week, I made my first kill. The victim was a loved one, my dear dog, Sparkle....I'll never forget the sound of her breaking under my might. I hit her so hard I knocked the fur off her neck....It was true beauty."[9] A neighbor testified that he witnessed Luke and a friend beating the dog.

Also in his diary, Luke wrote, "Satan would give me anything I want...money, power, sex, women, revenge."[10]

On June 5, 1998, it took the jury less than three hours to convict Luke Woodham of the murder of his mother. Several weeks later, in another trial, a court convicted Luke of murdering two students and wounding seven others during his shooting rampage at Pearl High School. Luke received three consecutive sentences of life imprisonment for the murders, plus 140 years for the seven shootings. On February 13, 2000, Grant Boyette, who prosecutors had called the "mastermind" of the cult, pleaded guilty to Conspiracy to Prevent a Principal from Doing His Job. A judge sentenced Boyette to Regimented Inmate Discipline, a boot camp–style program, followed by five years of supervised probation.

An isolated case of a disturbed young man fascinated by Satanism and devil worship? Hardly.

In February 1999, according to the *Indianapolis Star*, 36-year-old Jay Scott Ballinger of Yorktown, Indiana, became a suspect in as many as 50 church arsons in 11 states. The police became suspicious when Ballinger waited two days before seeking medical treatment for severe burns to his face, chest, legs, and hands. When he finally went for treatment, he told the hospital personnel that he'd been injured in a bonfire. The hospital contacted the police who suspected that he had actually received the injuries while committing a church arson in Ohio. The police believed that as Ballinger splashed gasoline around inside the church, a pilot light caused the gasoline fumes to ignite prematurely.

Eventually, Ballinger admitted to the police that between 1994 and 1998, he had set fire to between 30 and 50 churches in 11 states. A firefighter died fighting one of the church fires Ballinger set in Georgia.

"This is by far—by far—the largest number (of arsons) attributed to one person or group of people that I know of," said FBI spokesman Tron Brekke.[11]

Along with the arsons, Ballinger also admitted to being involved in satanic worship. At an Indiana church that Ballinger, his girlfriend, and another man set on fire, they painted an upside-down cross on the steps of the church as a part of a satanic ritual. At another church arson, they painted the name Satan and the number 6.

As might be expected, Ballinger was no stranger to the police. In 1994, they arrested him for giving alcohol to minors. Parents had earlier complained to the police that Ballinger was attempting to recruit local youths into a satanic cult. When the police went to Ballinger's home, they found considerable satanic literature and 50 contracts signed in blood by local youths. The contracts stated that the youths gave their souls to Satan in exchange for promises of power, money, and sex.

"I give my body and soul to Lucifer for eternity," the contracts read. "I promise in blood to do all types of evil in the service of our Lord, until the end of time."[12]

In November 2000, after pleading guilty in federal court to burning 26 churches in eight states, Ballinger, who liked to call himself a "missionary of Lucifer," received a prison sentence of $42\frac{1}{2}$ years.[13] In early 2001, the state of Georgia sentenced him to life without parole for setting the fire that killed the firefighter.

Ballinger's girlfriend, an exotic dancer named Angela Wood, received a 16-year prison sentence for assisting him in the arsons. On January 11, 2002, because of Wood's testimony against Ballinger and her assistance to the authorities during the investigation, Federal Judge Sarah Evans Barker reduced Wood's sentence to 12 years. Another member of Ballinger's satanic cult received a sentence of 2 years, 3 months in prison for his part in the church arsons.

Satanic worship, readers will find, is much more widespread than the public might suppose. According to news reports from Donna, Texas, for example, authorities suspect satanic gangs in the murder and mutilation of a 12-year-old boy. Local law enforcement officers found his body missing both arms, a foot, and his scalp. The police theorize that satanic worshippers used him in a sacrifice. The Santa Monica, California, police arrested a 24-year-old man who, along with two other satanic cult members, strangled a 13-year-old girl to death as part of a satanic ritual. In Fall River, Massachusetts, the police uncovered a satanic cult responsible for the ritual murders of three young women, who the cult members killed as a sacrifice to Satan. The state of Illinois put Andrew Kokoraleis to death by lethal injection for his part in a satanic cult that authorities discovered was responsible for as many as 18 rapes, murders, and mutilations of young women.

Unbelievably, considering the number of crimes connected to the practice of Satanism, the Kentucky Department of Corrections, in August 2002, suspended formal satanic worship services that had been being held for some time at the Green River Correctional Complex. Apparently, inmates had been allowed to perform satanic rituals at the prison as part of the prison's religious services program.

"We honestly didn't know it was on the religious calendar," said prison system spokesperson Lisa Carnahan.[14]

Satanic cults, however, are by no means confined only to the United States. In August 1999, according to news reports, a court in Finland sentenced a 24-year-old man to life in prison for a murder that occurred during a satanic ritual. Two other members of the cult also received prison sentences. Reportedly, after suffocating the victim, the cult members ate parts of the victim's body, sexually abused the corpse, and then sawed the body into small pieces. In Argentina in April 2000, the police reported that they had arrested two daughters, ages 21 and 29, who had stabbed their 50-year-old father more than 100 times and ate parts of his face. The daughters allegedly belonged to a satanic cult known as the Alchemy Center for Transmutation. In September 1999 in Australia, the police arrested two women who had attacked a 59-year-old woman with a knife. The police found certificates the two women carried that stated they were satanic devotees.

"Their relationship centered on the development of a pervasive and insidious system of beliefs situated around a satanic concept," said the prosecutor of the case in Australia.[15]

In Greece, three individuals admitted to leading a 20-member satanic cult that murdered at least two women during satanic rituals. An article in the *Wall Street Journal* reported that in Norway, arson destroyed more than 20 churches. Norwegian authorities have attributed these arsons to a satanic cult that has issued a proclamation stating, "Kill the Christians. Burn their churches. Destroy their homes. Torture their children."[16]

A January 2003 report in the British newspaper the *Telegraph* tells of the investigation of an apparent satanic cult in Germany. Horst Roos, a prosecutor in Germany, stated, "These proceedings are dealing with a level of violence which is hardly imaginable." A person connected to the cult claimed, "Women were habitually raped by men while children were brutally murdered before being eaten."[17]

As can be seen by the examples presented here, the danger of satanic cults cannot be overstated. While some readers may claim that such cults are often just naturally rebellious youths dabbling in something they know their parents and society will consider ghastly, far too often, satanic worship turns much more dangerous and deadly than simply harmless teenage rebellion.

Although for many youths, Satanism may be simply a way for a previously unpopular person to suddenly look "cool," far too often, an unbalanced member of a satanic cult can be overwhelmed by the teachings of the cult and commit unthinkable acts. Such was the case for a young man named Sean Sellers who, according to newspaper accounts, killed a store clerk and then his own parents "for Satan" and wound up being the youngest person on Oklahoma's death row. The state of Oklahoma executed him in 1998. Another teenage dabbler in Satanism, Ricky Kasso, killed a friend during a satanic ritual and then committed suicide after being arrested. In Fort Lauderdale, a 17-year-old youth reportedly stabbed an acquaintance he had met through a mutual interest in satanic Web sites. The two met in a deserted woods to perform a satanic ritual that got out of hand.

"These are kids on the fringe, outsiders," says Linda Maxwell, a social worker who has investigated satanic cults. "They often have problems at home and suffer from low self-esteem. Often the other kids are afraid of them, so it gives them identity, strength, and a sense of power."[18]

Luke Woodham, whose crimes were described earlier in this chapter, told a reporter for ABC's *Prime Time Live*, "My whole life...I just felt outcasted, alone. Finally, I found some people who wanted to be my friends. I was just trying to find hope in a hopeless world, man."[19]

Teenagers like Luke Woodham who want to dabble in Satanism don't have to look very far to find information about it. Along with the many heavy-metal music videos that depict and glorify Satanism and the fantasy role-playing games that involve Satanism, there are also many satanic Web sites on the Internet. The popular search engine Google, for example, listed in late 2003 159,000 sites for the keyword *Satanism*. One of these sites is the Church of Satan, the largest known satanic organization. Anton LaVey, the actor who portrayed Satan in the 1968 movie *Rosemary's Baby*, and who eventually became known as the Black Pope, founded the Church of Satan in 1966 in San Francisco. In an article that appeared in the *Toronto Star*, LaVey claimed that the Church of Satan, at its height, had 10,000 members worldwide.[20] As a part of his satanic ministry, LaVey wrote the *Satanic Bible* in 1969, which has become a guidebook for those interested in Satanism. This book has sold hundreds of thousands of copies and has been translated into dozens of languages. Other sacred texts for Satanists include *The Satanic Witch, The Satanic Rituals, The Devil's Notebook,* and *Satan Speaks*.

According to the Church of Satan teachings, Satan represents indulgence rather than abstinence. Reportedly, LaVey believed that religion's suppression of man's indulgence in carnal pleasures caused most of the mindless violence we see in society. The Church of Satan believes that individuals should be able to indulge in any pleasures they want, provided no harm comes to anyone else from this indulgence. The Church of Satan doesn't believe in an afterlife or a spiritual God; therefore, self-gratification is a virtue. Along with satanic virtues, however, there are nine satanic sins, which are stupidity, pretentiousness, solipsism, self-deceit, herd conformity, lack of perspective, forgetfulness of past orthodoxies, counterproductive pride, and lack of aesthetics.

Anton LaVey died of pulmonary edema on October 29, 1997, ironically enough at St. Mary's Hospital in San Francisco. His daughter, Karla LaVey, high priestess of the Church of Satan (though others claim LaVey's long-time companion, Blanche Barton, is the high priestess), had her father cremated in a secret ceremony because of her fear of disruption by nonSatanists.

Another daughter of LaVey, Zeena Schreck, reportedly left the Church of Satan and joined a rival satanic cult, the Temple of Set, whose members worship an Egyptian god who they believe was a precursor to Satan of the Bible. Since LaVey's death, the Church of Satan has declined considerably in popularity. According to an article in the January 25, 1999, issue of the *San Francisco Chronicle*, LaVey's two daughters and Blanche Barton finally settled a bitter legal battle they had been having since LaVey's death over the leadership of the church and the ownership of LaVey's assets.

Actually, the content of the Church of Satan Web site is pretty tame compared with what many other satanic Web sites contain. Most of the content of other satanic Web sites is intentionally and very crudely blasphemous of Christianity. Much of it is simply incoherent rambling masquerading as intellectual or religious writing. The sites are so blatantly, crudely, and violently anti-Christian—such as one that tells about Christ being sodomized on the cross and another that describes the rape of Mary—they are likely written by people who have a vehement repulsion and lack of respect for personal belief systems. However, because a youth's indulgence in something like Satanism often begins as a simple act of rebellion against established authority, young people may find in these sites just the repudiation of society they are looking for. And for someone not intellectually aware, the writing may take on a mystical quality. Unfortunately, however, much of the writing also involves suggestions of violence.

Juvenile dabbling in Satanism aside, there exists a much larger problem in our country involving satanic cults—the satanic ritual abuse of children. There have been literally hundreds of cases reported to the police and social welfare agencies in the United States in which children claim they have been sexually and physically abused by adults during satanic rituals. There have also been a large number of adults who, while undergoing psychotherapy, have suddenly been able to recall childhood memories of being sexually and physically abused by adults during satanic rituals, which many therapists then attribute as the root cause for the person's mental or emotional problems.

However, the problem with these claims, according to FBI agent Kenneth Lanning, an expert in the field of ritual abuse, is that there is very little corroborating evidence of these ritual molestations. Consequently, two camps have formed with totally opposing viewpoints concerning the claims of abuse. The one camp insists that since there is very little corroborating evidence, the claims are likely just fantasies or stories.

They insist that children who tell of ritual abuse have invented these tales from incidents they've seen in movies or perhaps from viewing the heavy-metal rock videos of older siblings. As for the adults who suddenly recover memories of childhood satanic abuse, they point out that most of these "memories" are from individuals who have a life history of mental problems (though a person could reverse this argument and insist that the childhood satanic abuse was what caused the mental problems).

The other side of the dispute believes that there exists a huge underground network of Satanists in this country, who regularly molest and even kill children during satanic rituals. They base their argument on the fact that the stories told by child victims and adults with recovered memories are amazingly similar all over the country, including the statement that the satanic cults often contain very powerful and influential people. And these proponents claim, because the network contains very powerful and influential people, this explains why its members have not been exposed or prosecuted.

As a police officer with more than 30 years of experience, my feelings about this lie somewhere in between these two camps. The incidents related so far in this chapter clearly show that satanic murders do occur; however, I don't believe they occur in the thousands or even hundreds. Do satanic molestations of children also occur? Yes, they do. As a police captain, I have seen scattered reports of satanic abuse, but again, not at a huge rate. The idea that there are hundreds of groups of Satanists molesting and murdering children without leaving any evidence flies in the face of everything I've experienced during my years as a police officer. However, no matter what the rate, large or small, any satanic abuse at all of children or other innocent victims is too much.

Kenneth V. Lanning, a special agent for the FBI, wrote a paper for the Behavioral Science Unit of the National Center for the Analysis of Violent Crime at the FBI titled "Investigator's Guide to Allegations of 'Ritual' Child Abuse." In this paper, Lanning states, "Many people do not understand how difficult it is to commit a conspiracy crime involving numerous co-conspirators.... The more people involved in the crime, the harder it is to get away with it. Why? People get angry and jealous. They come to resent the fact that another conspirator is getting 'more' than they."[21]

I feel Special Agent Lanning is absolutely correct. As I've seen repeatedly, in any large criminal conspiracy, a disgruntled conspirator will eventually tell about the crime. This is how the police solve many of their cases and makes the belief in a huge underground network of Satanists very unlikely.

In his paper, Special Agent Lanning also agrees with my assessment that although there may be small pockets of satanic child abuse in the United States, the records available to us do not support the claims of it being widespread. However, he also states the following: "In spite of any skepticism, allegations of ritual abuse should be aggressively and thoroughly investigated...Some of what the victims allege may be true and accurate, some may be misperceived or distorted, some may be screened or symbolic, and some may be 'contaminated' or false. The problem and challenge, especially for law enforcement, is to determine which is which."[22]

I agree wholeheartedly with Special Agent Lanning's statement. However, even with a small number of ritual abuse cases, the police often find that it is still difficult to prosecute many of them because people simply don't want to accept or believe that these kinds of acts occur.

"Another major obstacle to determining the extent of ritualistic abuse is the skepticism with which such allegations are met," says Dr. Susan J. Kelley. "The more horrible and bizarre the child's allegation, the less likely it is that the child victim will be believed."[23]

As a police officer, I have found that disbelief in abuse is true for almost any kind of child molestation, ritualistic or not. As I note in my book *Family Abuse*, in the worst cases of child abuse, juries often refuse to believe that adults would do such things to children, no matter how much proof the police have. However, I have also discovered during my career that there is no accusation against any person that is too bizarre or too outlandish to be true.

Regardless of the extent of ritualistic abuse, the fact remains that many people in the United States, particularly teens going through a typical period of adolescent rebellion, will seek out philosophies and beliefs to which they know society is opposed, and Satanism and satanic cults often become the ultimate rebellion. Although this can be just a harmless, passing phase for a young person, it can also, as the incidents in this chapter have demonstrated, be deadly.

In the next chapter, I will discuss a concern that affected not just young people but also a large percentage of the adults in the world: the approach of the new millennium. While most people, myself included, felt a bit anxious about the possible Y2K problem, others felt anxious about something much larger. Many people felt that the new millennium would usher in with it huge, world-shattering changes. As a result, many millennial cults formed, and, as I will show, some had disastrous results.

CHAPTER 6

Millennial Cults

According to reports in several Denver, Colorado, newspapers, during the night of September 30, 1998, dozens of people, including a number of young children, suddenly disappeared from Denver. Most of the missing adults had been well educated and financially secure (one person even a millionaire). Authorities later discovered that in the months before their disappearance, the missing people had been quietly selling their houses, cars, and other possessions.

Denver authorities learned that all the missing people were members of a group called Concerned Christians, a very tight-knit cult led by a man named Monte Kim Miller who, interestingly enough, until just a few years before had been a crusader preaching against the danger of cults. Miller had formed Concerned Christians in the 1980s as an attempt to combat the evil of both cults and the New Age movement. However, in the mid-1990s, Miller, for some unknown reason, did an about-face and formed his own cult. Like most cult leaders, Miller maintained extremely tight control over every aspect of cult members' lives and expected unquestioned obedience from them.

"Kim Miller has total control over their minds," said the father of two cult members.[1] Others report that Miller's control is so absolute that cult members must ask him what to wear each day.

There is, of course, always a dark side to this much control. "He has the potential to turn very dangerous," said Mark Roggeman, a Denver police officer and specialist in cults. "His followers do whatever he says, and if they disobey him he can turn very angry."[2] Miller's control is reported to be so absolute that one cult member allegedly told her daughter that if

Miller told her to shoot her, she would. The family of one cult member went to court to stop any more transfers of money or property to Miller, claiming that Miller was defrauding members.

As previously mentioned, though Miller started out as an anticult crusader, educating people in the Denver area about the danger of cults, people who had been close to him said that in the mid-1990s, Miller began to act strangely—for example, claiming that God occasionally possessed his body and spoke through him. At an October 1996 meeting with several people who were becoming increasingly disturbed about Miller's control of the members of Concerned Christians, Miller reportedly pretended to go into a trance and then said in a loud, booming voice, "I am the Lord your God! I know you are here to deceive me, and you need to bow down to me, and if you don't, you will die!"[3]

While the individuals at this meeting were more stunned than convinced by Miller's actions that God spoke through him, cult members took his words very seriously. "They just sincerely believe that it's the Lord speaking," said Rachel Powell, a friend of one of the cult members, "and they don't want to disobey God—that's how seriously they take it."[4]

Miller also decreed to his followers that he is one of the "witnesses" told about in chapter 11 of the book of Revelation. According to the families of cult members, Miller stated that he was destined to die in the streets of Jerusalem during the last days of 1999 and three days later would arise from the dead, as foretold in the Bible. Miller, however, also prophesied that an earthquake would destroy Denver on October 10, 1998, and this was the reason the members of Concerned Christians quickly left the Denver area on September 30. At the time of the cult members' disappearance, the authorities suspected they had likely gone to Israel to fulfill Miller's prophecy about his death and resurrection.

As far back as September 1996, Miller had told a local television station, "Jesus Christ died on the cross and we have a duty to die. The Lord's judgment has been with the Earth for 2,000 years and now judgment is ready to begin."[5]

Bill Honsberger, a Colorado evangelist who knew Miller before he became a cult leader, said that Miller preached that his followers "must take up the cross and be willing to die for God." Honsberger added, "But you stand up for God by being loyal to him. It's the same mentality as Jones [cult leader Jim Jones, who persuaded 913 people to commit suicide in Guyana in 1978], but the manipulation is even more glaring. He has incredible control."[6]

Professor Richard Landes, director of the Center for Millennial Studies at Boston University, called Miller "a classic case of millennial megalomania."[7]

After the group's disappearance in September 1998, reporters checking Miller's home in Denver found it vacant with newspapers stacked up on the porch. His leaving the Denver area didn't really surprise authorities, though. The previous year, Miller and his wife had declared bankruptcy, listing among their debts more than $100,000 in back taxes and several thousand dollars owed to Christian radio stations that had aired his messages.

For the families of cult members, however, the biggest fear was not what had happened to Miller but what would happen to the cult members. "My fear is that like Jim Jones and David Koresh, his litmus test for his followers is that they sacrifice themselves for him, for his ego more than anything else," said the father of one of the cult members.[8] A sister of one of the cult members talked to her sister on the telephone a week after the cult had disappeared from Denver. "She said she couldn't tell us what they were doing and that I was asking too many questions," the sister said.[9] Nicolette Weaver, a young girl who had been a member of Concerned Christians for 10 years but dropped out when Miller began acting strangely, said that her mother, who was still in the cult, told her not to call anymore because she was not spiritually enlightened.

The earlier stated belief that the cult had likely gone to Israel eventually proved true. On January 3, 1999, after raiding two expensive homes the cult had rented in Jerusalem, Israeli authorities arrested 14 members of the cult, 8 adults and 6 children. Israeli police officials stated they had information that Concerned Christians had planned to commit violent acts on the streets of Jerusalem in late 1999 in their belief that it would hasten the return of Jesus. The police, however, didn't find Monte Kim Miller among this group.

"They planned to carry out violent and extreme acts on the streets of Jerusalem at the end of 1999 to start the process of bringing Jesus back to life," said Brigadier General Elihu Ben-Onn, an Israeli national police spokesman.[10] Reportedly, cult members had planned to open fire on the Israeli police. The Bible, in the book of Revelation, proclaims that a war will erupt in the "end times," and authorities believe the cult apparently wanted to provoke this war.

The authorities eventually deported the 14 cult members back to Denver, Colorado, even though cult members had requested that they be sent to Greece because they believed the United States would be destroyed soon. The whereabouts of Monte Kim Miller and the other members of the cult were unknown at this time, though rumor placed Miller in London. Cult experts like Professor Richard Landes didn't expect the cult to simply give up on their millennial plans because of this setback but believed that it would probably make members believe even more devoutly in Miller and his prophecies.

"This could just make them more dependent on their leader, make him up the ante, and spiral into more paranoia and potential violence," Landes said.[11]

Experts also didn't expect the cult to disband because of this setback.
"What keeps a cultic group together is maintaining an 'us vs. them'
mentality," said Janja Lalich of the Cult Recovery and Information Center.
"What could do more to convince you the world is out to get you than
having the Israeli police raid your house?"[12]

In February 1999, reporters discovered at least 30 members of Concerned Christians living in villas in the resort town of Rafina on the
Aegean Sea in Greece. Most of the cult members who had been deported
from Israel to the United States in January 1999 were believed to then be
living in Rafina. In December 1999, Greek police began rounding up the
cult members, most of whom had expired resident permits. Neighbors of
the cult had complained that the members had been preaching to everyone they met that the world would end soon. The Greek government
quickly deported the detained cult members back to New York.

December 31, 1999, became January 1, 2000, under relatively calm conditions. The world didn't end, Jesus didn't reappear, and Monte Kim
Miller didn't die in the streets of Jerusalem in order to be resurrected three
days later.

Of course, the first question most readers will ask is, Why should we be
concerned about millennial cults? The new millennium is here and nothing earthshaking has happened. Didn't all these cults just disappear? I
have asked this question of many cult experts, and they all say the same
thing: No, the millennial cults haven't disappeared. These experts also
warn that the reason we should still be concerned about millennial cults is
because many of them have resurfaced, sometimes with new names,
sometimes as the same cult, but usually with a new date for the end of the
world. Most important, though, is that their doomsday philosophies
always carry with them the threat of death to their members and others, as
I will show in an incident later in this chapter.

As I stated, cult experts I spoke with told me that most millennial cults
haven't disappeared. True to these experts' predictions, I found that members of Concerned Christians and their leader, Monte Kim Miller, didn't
simply pack up and go home when the millennium passed and none of
Miller's predictions came true. Instead, the membership of the cult has
stayed together and is still a very cohesive group.

In May 2001, Miller, silent since his failed millennial end-of-the-world
prophecy, spoke out on the cult's Web site. On it, he claimed that he never
prophesied the destruction of Denver in an earthquake, even though this
was the reason most cult members sold their homes and businesses and
then quickly left the city. Miller used the Web site to state his position in
the world: "I am the prophet of the Lord, the direct spokesman for the
Lord."[13]

In early February of 2002, Miller again posted a message on the group's Web site, now giving, as the cult experts had told me he likely would, a new prediction for the end of the world. "I am the prophet of the last days," Miller wrote, "and on February 15, 2002, the 777th day of God's 7th millennium with fallen man, I am the 'heaven on earth' manifestation of the sounding of the Seventh Angel, warning you of the Lord's intentions that the kingdoms of this world are to become the kingdoms of the Lord Jesus Christ."[14]

Of course, the deadline has passed for this last prediction and still nothing earthshaking has occurred. What will happen next with this cult? "He is so controlling, they would do anything he said," said Nicolette Weaver. "He has been prophesying the end of the world for so long. When it doesn't happen, he will have to find some way for their world to end."[15]

In July 2002, I contacted Denver police officer Mark Roggeman, who has tracked the Concerned Christians cult for many years. I asked him if he believes Miller is dangerous and what he felt Miller's next move would be now that all his prophecies have failed to come true.

"Whether he is dangerous or not is the million dollar question," Officer Roggeman told me. "Somehow he has to spin his prophecies to make it appear to his followers that he did not make a mistake. Considering the fact that his followers sold everything they had and quit their jobs believing Miller about the end of the world, it concerns me that they are still following him without question."[16]

Hal Mansfield of the Religious Movement Resource Center said about Miller, "The problem here is Miller has become more isolated. He probably started believing his own PR. I think he's so far out there it's impossible to gauge what will happen now."[17]

Millennial cult leaders, however, aren't the only ones trying to find a new spin for previously made prophecies of doom. When January 1, 2000, came around without significant changes to the world, many noncult doom forecasters began trying to soften the predictions they had made pre-2000.

"We regret having talked about it," said Jerry Jenkins, one of the authors of the hugely successful *Left Behind* book series.[18]

Reverend Jerry Falwell, who in 1999 had reportedly predicted doom in the new millennium, told a reporter for the *Washington Post*, "I don't anticipate any major problems."[19]

"The end times people are backing down," says author Damian Thompson, who wrote a book about modern doomsday groups. "They're extremely nervous about having December 31st, 1999, pinned on them forever."[20]

Some noncult millennium doom forecasters, however, didn't try to soften their warnings when January 1, 2000, appeared and the world didn't end. Some of these people simply came up with new dates. Robert "Bobby Bible" Engel of California had raised considerable commotion around the Chapel of the Ascension in Jerusalem in 1999 as he preached millennium doom while wearing a long flowing robe. When questioned by a reporter in January 2000, he said, "Now we're looking at the Jewish New Year, which on our calendar is September 30th. You know, if we keep guessing like this, we're eventually going to get it right."[21]

In his book *A.D. 1000: Living on the Brink of Apocalypse,* Richard Erdoes states that at the end of the first millennium, many Christians "knelt trembling in their churches, waiting for the last trumpet to sound."[22] During the previous year, he reports, numerous believers had sold all their belongings to finance a pilgrimage to Jerusalem, where they expected the Last Judgment to occur. When the year 999 began, people started to worry. Debts were forgiven, old grudges were forgotten, and people began to prepare for huge events to occur. Of course, nothing huge on the cosmic scale happened in 1000, and soon life soon returned to normal.

Over his throne in Jonestown, cult leader Jim Jones had hung a sign that read, "Those who cannot remember the past are condemned to repeat it." These words, penned by philosopher George Santayana, were unfortunately the basis for the formation of a large number of millennial cults in the last decade of the twentieth century. Despite what happened, or rather didn't happen, in the year 1000, the individuals belonging to millennial cults still believed that the year 2000 would bring with it the certainty of huge and very ominous changes for mankind.

"Millennial thinking is preoccupied with an arbitrary number of zeros on the cosmic odometer," says E. C. Krupp in an article in *Sky & Telescope* magazine, "and those who engage in it sense danger in round numbers."[23]

Much as the people in 999 did, a large number of people in 1999 migrated to Jerusalem in the belief that it would be the epicenter of millennial events. Many of these people settled around the Mount of Olives, where the Bible tells us Jesus ascended to Heaven and where He was expected to return in 2000. As might be expected, many of these people said that God had spoken to them and told them to come to the Mount of Olives to await Jesus's return.

"Time is short," said Brother David, one of the pilgrims who in 1999 also said God had told him to come to the Mount of Olives. "We see the signs. A lot of people have been asking us how close we are to the end. We are that close. And God is challenging us as believers. We are not to waste our time."[24] Fearing that these individuals would possibly perpetrate violent acts in the belief that it would hasten the end times, Israeli police rounded up and deported, in addition to the Concerned Christians, several dozen other millennium doom predictors in late 1999.

Most of the millennial cults that sprang up in the last decade of the twentieth century took the prophecies given in Revelation as the basis for their belief that something momentous would happen in the year 2000. However, the book of Revelation is written in such cryptic language that millennial cult leaders were able to make the words fit any prophecy or belief system they wanted.

"Because of its highly cryptic language," says Philip Lamy in his book *Millennium Rage*, "Revelation has no single, indisputable meaning, and its ambiguity has left it open to numerous interpretations, imbuing it with the power and persistence of myth."[25]

An article in the *Minneapolis-St. Paul Star Tribune* adds this about the book of Revelation: "Another reason for the prophecies' endurance and potency is that they are endlessly adaptable. The Mantle of the Beast has been hung on everyone from the Pope to Hitler to Henry Kissinger. Until the collapse of the Soviet Union, the evil empire served to personify the Anti-Christ; Saddam Hussein filled in for a while, as did radical Islamic clerics."[26]

To make the book of Revelation fit their personal prophecies and belief system, all millennial cult leaders had to do was insert current events into the language, and then to the cult's members this seemed to be divine proof that the cult leader was right. "Prophetic popularizers are always inserting current events into an archaic belief system," says Paul Boyer, professor of history at the University of Wisconsin. "They insist that at this moment all of the jigsaw puzzle pieces are falling into place."[27]

Besides Christian interpretations that the year 2000 would bring with it something world-shaking, a number of other groups and individuals also saw 2000 as a turning point in human history. The Japanese group Sukyo Mahikari predicted that mankind would be annihilated by fire in 2000, Edgar Cayce predicted that the earth's axis would shift, students of Nostradamus forecast an assortment of catastrophes, Philip Berg of the Kabbalah Learning Center reportedly predicted that a great ball of fire would hit the earth, and on and on.[28]

Of course, the Y2K problem (the concern that computers worldwide would malfunction when their clocks turned to 2000 because the computers wouldn't be able to recognize 00 as being 2000 rather than 1900) only added fuel to the dark prophecies of the millennial cults. Predictors of doom saw the Y2K problem as further proof that the year 2000 was the beginning of the prophesied end times.

Larry Spargimino, author of the book *Y2K = 666?*, says this about millennial beliefs and the end times: "There are a lot of things that are going to go into the end-times events, but with Y2K, it's being hastened. Y2K is a contributing, moving force that is pulling events in prophecy together quicker than we could have imagined."[29]

The Y2K problem, even though it obviously didn't become the huge, world-stopping crisis many feared it would, still figured large into millennial thought because it appeared to be modern-day proof of nearly 2,000-

year-old prophecies. Many millennial cult leaders pointed to the Y2K problem as proof that the year 2000 was something magical and important.

Many people took the Y2K threat and the predictions of doom that would accompany the approaching millennium so seriously that they sold their homes and moved to "safe areas." For example, the Web site for a millennium survival community in Arizona said, "At Heritage West 2000, 500 families of the New Millennium can grow their own food and food for their neighbors to purchase or barter. They will harvest electrical power from the sun and wind."[30] In Minnesota, a group founded a "Christian Y2K Relocation Site" called "God's Wilderness."

Adding to all this millennial fear and apprehension was the belief of many in the conspiracy-minded militia movement that the year 2000 was the target date for the military takeover of the United States by a shadowy and feared organization called the New World Order. "It just so happens that the New World Order has the answer—it's called Force 2000," said John Trochmann, one of the founders of the Militia of Montana.[31] "When the troops come in, they'll come in such force it'll be incredible!" Trochmann warned. "In forty-eight hours, they can have one hundred million troops here. They'll come out of the ground! They'll come from submarines! They'll come from airdrops! They'll come from everywhere!"[32] (For more information about the militia movement, see my book *Terrorists Among Us—The Militia Threat*.)

The militia movement and others aside, most of the people who saw religious overtones in the predictions of doom for the year 2000 obviously didn't know of the many problems and mistakes calendar makers have experienced over the centuries. Because of these mistakes and problems, many biblical scholars believe that Jesus was actually born between 7 and 4 B.C. For example, Augustus Caesar gave his famous order that all the world should be taxed in 7 B.C., while a triple planetary conjunction occurred in 6 B.C., which would have created what appeared to be a new, very bright star. Consequently, the 2000 years since Jesus's birth had already passed by 2000. However, most millennial cult leaders simply ignored this information because it didn't fit in with their dire predictions for the end of the world. So, in 1999, what did cult experts believe would happen as 1999 became 2000?

"Every cult has this sense of urgency," says Marcia Rudin of the International Cult Education Program in New York. "But when you add in millennialism, it really increases the danger that something drastic can happen."[33]

Hal Mansfield, an expert on alternative religions, adds this warning: "This is only the beginning as the year 2000 approaches. We're in for a helluva ride with these millennial groups."[34]

After reading Mansfield's prediction, most people would probably smile and say, "What ride? Y2K was a flop, the arrival of the new millennium was unspectacular, and all of the millennium doom predictors likely just went to bed disappointed when January 1, 2000, rolled around and nothing significant had happened." Very true, but while we know the preceding statement applied to most of the world, it didn't apply to everyone. For more than a thousand members of a millennial cult in Uganda, rather than simply being disappointed, tragedy struck when 2000 rolled around and nothing earthshaking happened. As I relate in the following section, the change to the new millennium for this group brought about, instead of the return of Jesus and salvation for the cult members, a grisly mass murder by cult leaders who couldn't face up to the fact that on January 1, 2000, the world had remained the same.

According to reports that appeared in practically every news outlet in the world, in 1989, a former Ugandan prostitute and beer merchant named Credonia Mwerinde claimed that while in a cave near the Uganda village of Ngakishenyi the Virgin Mary appeared to her and instructed her to begin a crusade to bring people back to living according to the Ten Commandments. Her claims of divine direction reached the ears of many people in Uganda, including Joseph Kibwetere, a schoolteacher and lay worker in the Catholic Church. Known by all as a pious man, Joseph had become a supervisor for the region's Catholic churches and had even founded a private Catholic school of his own.

"He was a godly man," said Matthias Igusha, a former student of Joseph's. "You could tell by his practice: going to church, tending to the sick."[35]

After hearing of Credonia's claims of revelations from the Virgin Mary, Joseph attended one of her talks and felt moved by what he saw as her deep commitment to religion. After the talk, Credonia and two other women, Ursula Komuhangi and Angela Mugisha, approached Joseph and told him that the Virgin Mary had instructed them to seek him out, that because of his piety, prayers, and good works he had been anointed to help them spread the word of God. Many people suspected that the three women were actually just looking for a male figurehead to lead their movement because male leadership is needed for any group to be taken seriously in Uganda.

Joseph, apparently taken with the women and their message, invited them to come live with him and his family. However, once Credonia and the other two women moved in, they began taking over. Almost immediately they started setting down rules and punishing those who didn't follow them.

"When the people came here," Joseph's son Juvenar recalled, "they started mistreating us, the family members, the children, and the mother, saying the Virgin Mary had told them to do things, to keep us without food and to punish us."[36]

However, because Joseph would not do anything about the three women's conduct despite many complaints from his family, Joseph's family finally revolted and said they weren't going to stand for the mistreatment any longer. As a result, in 1992, Joseph and the three women moved out, leaving Joseph's wife of 40 years and more than a dozen children behind. Not long after this, the organization that had begun as a religious movement began transforming into a cult and eventually named itself the Movement for the Restoration of the Ten Commandments. After moving from Joseph's home, the group set up its main headquarters in Kanungu, a small trading center 200 miles southwest of Kampala, the capital of Uganda.

Although Joseph remained the public head of the cult, few people believed that he really ran it. "Kibwetere could not give orders as such," said a former cult member. "He was put there as the leader, but the whole program was Mwerinde, that woman."[37]

The preaching of the cult, its promise of salvation and a better life for those who joined, reached the ears of many residents of Uganda. The cult also published and distributed thousands of copies of a booklet titled "A Timely Message from Heaven: The End of the Present Times." The booklet contained the many messages the cult leaders claimed they had received from the Virgin Mary. It also contained dire predictions for the future: famine, war, pestilence, and death, except for those who belonged to the cult. Uganda, the booklet stated, had been chosen by God as the new Israel.

Soon, people from all over Uganda began flocking to the cult. As most prospective cult members were disaffected Catholics, Joseph and other cult leaders even managed to recruit two ex-Catholic priests and several ex-nuns into the cult. One of the ex-priests recruited into the cult, Dominic Kataribabo, had been educated in the United States. Also included in the cult membership were local government officials, including Geraldine Tumusime, the elected official for women to the local government. Cult leaders also managed to recruit a half dozen police officers, whose membership in the cult, many believe, kept authorities from interfering with the cult's activities. Although Uganda, after the overthrow of Idi Amin, had established a policy of religious tolerance, religious groups still had to register with the government, which is supposed to monitor them. However, possibly because police officers were involved in the cult, the government didn't monitor the activities of the Movement for the Restoration of the Ten Commandments.

Before interested individuals could join the Movement for the Restoration of the Ten Commandments, cult leaders demanded that they sell all their worldly belongings and give the money to the cult. One woman Credonia attempted to recruit into the cult stated that she was told she would be accepted only if all her worldly goods were worth at least 250,000 Ugandan shillings, or about $175, a large sum in financially strapped

Uganda.[38] A Catholic priest who belonged to the cult for three years before leaving said Credonia was "obsessed with the desire to obtain the property of her followers."[39]

New members quickly found that life inside the cult was extremely strict and austere. Sleep for cult members was short and usually interrupted. Cult members often ate only once a day, while sex, even between married couples, was forbidden, as was medical care, wearing makeup, using soap, smoking, and drinking. AIDS, the cult leaders preached, was God's punishment for drinking beer.

The cult leaders, to maintain their hold over their followers, increased cult members' dependency by creating uncertainty. Many times, they took children away from their parents, and occasionally separated married couples. Cult leaders also forbade talking, so cult members could only communicate through hand signals. The leaders said this rule became necessary because conversations lead many people into telling lies about their neighbors. Cult experts, however, believe this rule was likely instituted to stop any challenge or questioning of the cult leadership. Violations of this rule against talking brought quick and harsh punishment. Reportedly, a young girl had her legs wrapped in burning banana leaves for talking.

As a part of the mysticism of the cult, Credonia claimed that she regularly received visits from the Virgin Mary. Finally, however, these visits began to carry an ominous message. Credonia said the Virgin Mary told her that God was extremely displeased with the world and would destroy it on December 31, 1999. Cult leaders though told the members that the Virgin Mary had said they would be the only ones who would survive.

However, when January 1, 2000 came around and the world survived, grumbling began in the group. Cult members who had sold all their worldly goods started demanding that the cult leaders return their money. Authorities believe that, in response to the rising discontent within the cult, soon after January 1, 2000, the systematic murder of cult members began. The police, however, wouldn't begin their investigation until more than 500 cult members perished in a suspicious fire on March 17, 2000.

"These leaders had a lot of money from members who sold their properties to join the cult," said police spokesperson Asuman Mugenyi. "There were people wanting their money back, and we think the leaders decided to get rid of them."[40]

Because of the disappointment of December 31, 1999, cult leaders, wanting to maintain their control over the group, assured members that the world was still going to end soon but that the new date was now March 17, 2000. On that day, they instructed, all cult members were to put on their ceremonial green-and-white robes and report to the chapel. After receiving this announcement, and in anticipation of the world ending, cult members slaughtered and ate three bulls and drank 70 cases of Coca-Cola.

However, once the cult members assembled inside the chapel on March 17, someone bolted shut the windows and doors from the outside. Inside the chapel, cult leaders had positioned containers of highly flammable sulfuric acid and had also spread around large quantities of gasoline. Several days earlier, former Catholic priest Dominic Kataribabo had purchased the sulfuric acid, telling a suspicious salesman that he needed it to recharge batteries at the chapel. When the fire began, apparently set by cult leaders, it spread rapidly, and escape from the inferno became impossible.

"The intense heat, exemplified by the way the heads exploded and brains liquefied suggest that it was all over very quickly," said a senior police official.[41]

At first the police believed that, reminiscent of Jonestown in Guyana, these people had committed mass suicide, but a closer study of body positions pointed instead to murder. Bodies, the police found, tended to be piled up around the doors and windows as cult members had apparently tried frantically to escape the inferno.

Then a few days later, and for the next several weeks, authorities began discovering more bodies of cult members in various spots around Uganda; these individuals had also been murdered. First, on March 21, 2000, authorities discovered six bodies buried in a latrine on cult property. It appeared the bodies had been there for at least several weeks. The murder victims had been severely beaten and their faces had been doused with battery acid. Then on March 24, 2000, the police found 153 bodies, including 59 children, buried on property owned by the cult. Again, these people had been murdered at least several weeks before the fire in the cult chapel. On March 27, 2000, the police found 80 more bodies in a sugarcane field owned by Dominic Kataribabo, the U.S.-educated former Catholic priest. These people had been dead for at least a month. The next day, buried under a newly poured concrete floor in a home owned by Kataribabo, the police found 81 more murder victims. These individuals appeared to have been buried before the ones found in the sugarcane field. On March 30, 2000, the authorities found 53 more bodies on the property of a man described as a fervent cult member. Finally, on April 27, 2000, the police uncovered another mass grave, this one holding 55 bodies under the floor of a garage rented by Kataribabo. Later, forensic tests showed that the majority of the victims dug up in the various locations around Uganda had been poisoned.

What stumped investigators though was who had done all this extensive transporting of bodies, digging of graves, and burying of corpses. "That is physically hard work," said ABC News correspondent Sheila MacVicar. "It could hardly have been carried out by a 64-year-old former priest, a 68-year-old former businessman and a 50-year-old ex-prostitute. There must have been many others involved, perhaps even people who were paid to do the work."[42] Were these individuals then murdered with the others in the chapel? No one really knows.

Without a doubt this is one of history's worst cult tragedies, and the total number of cult members murdered will likely never been known. Although Ugandan authorities eventually changed their original estimate of more than 1,000 victims to no less than 800, Chris Tuhuirwe, author of *The Kanungu Cult Saga: Suicide, Murder or Salvation?*, states that he and his colleagues have the names of more than 1,000 people murdered by cult leaders. Police spokesperson Asuman Mugenyi acknowledged that Tuhuirwe might be correct since the authorities do not have a precise death toll "because we did not go deep to check the exact numbers. Some suspected mass graves were left out. But the number was no less than 800."[43]

On April 6, 2000, Uganda authorities issued arrest warrants for six leaders of the Movement for the Restoration of the Ten Commandments. However, it is believed by many that the six perished in the fire on March 17, even though someone, who is likely still alive, bolted the chapel doors and windows shut.

Joseph Kibwetere's wife still keeps a picture of him on the mantel in their home with a printed copy of his favorite prayer: "Oh Lord God: Help me keep my big mouth shut until I know what I'm talking about."[44]

Regardless of whether the total number of deaths in this cult tragedy exceeds the number of deaths in the Jonestown cult tragedy, the fact remains that the cult leaders in Uganda murdered many, many innocent people, including hundreds of children, when the millennial doomsday they had prophesied didn't materialize. The people who joined this cult believed that the leaders would show them the way to salvation. Instead, when the fraud the cult leaders were perpetrating became obvious, rather than delivering salvation, the cult leaders resorted to murder.

What this incident in Uganda vividly demonstrates is that any cult, even those that claim benevolent purposes, can become deadly. As I stated at the beginning of this chapter and as demonstrated by the Concerned Christians, the millennial cults didn't dissolve on January 1, 2000. They simply readjusted the date for the end of the world. The Movement for the Restoration of the Ten Commandments, incidentally, also didn't dissolve. In December 2000, it resurfaced in Kenya, believed to be under the leadership of cult members who had escaped the many episodes of murder. The resurrected cult has changed its name to Choma, which is Swahili for burn, and has also set a new date for the end of the world.

In the next chapter, I will look at another phenomenon from the latter part of the twentieth century, the New Age movement. While most people perceive this movement as simply an innocuous collection of beliefs, cult leaders, as I will show, have been able to subvert the New Age to their own designs.

CHAPTER 7

New Age Cults

Reports in *Newsweek* and *Psychology Today* tell that when police divers pulled suicide victim Frederick Lenz out of the waters of Conscience Bay off the shores of Long Island in April 1998, what they saw startled them. They found that while Lenz wore a suit and tie, around his neck he also wore a dog collar with a rabies tag attached.

In Lenz's $2 million estate that bordered on Conscience Bay, the police discovered an unconscious woman in one of the guest rooms. In another room, they found two heavily sedated dogs. The woman, in an apparent suicide attempt, had swallowed a fistful of Valium, which had also been given to the dogs. The attempted suicide victim, who was one of Lenz's devoted followers, and the dogs all survived. A note found next to the woman said, "We all tried to go to the other world last night, and only Rama made it."[1]

Lenz's suicide caught most of those who knew him as the New Age guru called Zen Master Rama completely unprepared. He seemed to them to have everything to live for. To most he appeared to be a successful businessman, a best-selling author, and a sought-after guru who touted his own materialistically oriented brand of Buddhism. A *Newsweek* article called him the "Yuppie Guru."[2] In a 1991 interview, Lenz said, "I'm just a fun New Age guy."[3]

However, there also existed a dark side to Lenz's life. Shortly before his death, he had been accused by a number of people of being an exploitative cult leader and had also been accused of sexually abusing numerous female members of his cult. In addition, several former cult members had filed lawsuits against him, accusing Lenz of fraudulently manipulating them into turning over large sums of money to him. After Lenz's death, those close to him estimated his estate at around $18 million.

Lenz began on the road to becoming a New Age guru and cult leader soon after graduating from high school, where he had been known as "Crazy Fred, the cut-rate philosopher." Moving to the Haight-Ashbury district of San Francisco during the height of the hippie era, Lenz became deeply immersed in the lifestyle. This ended, however, when a court convicted him of selling marijuana and sentenced him to a year at a work camp. While living in San Francisco, Lenz became interested in the teachings of Guru Sri Chinmoy, whose philosophy combined traditional Buddhism with physical fitness.

Even though Lenz, after his conviction, left San Francisco and eventually moved to Connecticut to go to college, he continued his relationship with Chinmoy, who operated an ashram near the campus of the University of Connecticut, where Lenz attended classes. All through college and at graduate school at the University of New York at Stony Brook, where Lenz earned a doctorate in English literature, Lenz continued to recruit for Chinmoy. Eventually, however, Chinmoy became fed up with Lenz's constant womanizing and finally, to teach Lenz humility, sent him to San Diego under orders to open a Laundromat there.

Lenz instead separated himself from Chinmoy's influence and decided to formulate his own belief system, independent of his former guru. Switching to Zen doctrine, Lenz took the name Zen Master Rama and began recruiting people in southern California to his new brand of Buddhism that, rather than favoring a simple life with few possessions, touted instead a Buddhist-flavored materialism. Lenz's belief system, while different in many ways, included some traditional Buddhist aspects, including meditation and a belief in reincarnation. Lenz claimed he had, in previous lives, been a temple elder in Atlantis, a Tibetan lama, a Zen master in seventeenth-century Japan, and a teacher of the occult in Egypt. Lenz promised prospective cult members that he could give them the quick path to Nirvana. He claimed his techniques were so powerful that one hour with him was the same as 100 years of meditating. He also claimed to be one of the 12 enlightened beings on Earth (the only one of the other 11 he would identify was his dog Vayu).

Unlike traditional Buddhism, the new version that Lenz touted held that the sign of a member's spiritual growth became his or her material success. The more money individuals attained, the higher a spiritual plane they were on. Lenz disdained what he saw as the "begging bowl" mentality of traditional Buddhism.

"Material success, if it's part of a balanced approach to life, is very healthy," said Lenz. "I don't consider poverty to be spiritual."[4]

Lenz believed completely in practicing what he preached about material success. He soon began drawing large numbers of members into his cult, some of whom paid Lenz up to $5,000 a month for the honor of studying under him one or two nights. However, Lenz didn't attract these new members by street-corner recruiting or even by word of mouth. He did it through elaborate and expensive advertising. Lenz took out ads in publications such as *Vanity Fair,* the *Los Angeles Times,* and the *New York Times.* He had his face printed on posters that hung all over Times Square in New York City. In 1987 alone, Lenz reportedly spent more than $500,000 on advertising himself and his abilities as a guru.

His investment in advertising quickly paid off. Soon after his advertising blitz, Lenz found dozens of people with money flocking to his meetings, wanting to learn how they could partake of spiritual enlightenment and brazen capitalism at the same time. Many of his followers, even after his death, still believe that they owe much of their success to Lenz and his teachings, even though they found them hugely expensive. However, as with many cult leaders, besides asking for large sums of money from his followers, Lenz also began demanding sex from many of his female cult members.

"He considered his sperm to be liquid enlightenment and we should be honored to have it in our bodies," said one of his female followers. "I'm embarrassed to admit that I fell for that."[5] Reportedly, many of Lenz's other female followers also "fell for it."

By the mid-1980s, Lenz began to see the impact that computers were going to have on our society, and he switched much of his energy, and the energies of his followers, to computer programming. To manage his efforts, he founded a company named Advanced Systems, Inc. Like many other of his efforts, Lenz did very well in the computer software business.

Unfortunately, despite his considerable success as a spiritual leader, software developer, and writer (one of his books hit number 11 on the *New York Times* best-seller list, though reviewers universally panned it), Lenz began suffering psychological problems. During the 1980s, he reportedly started using LSD and encouraged cult members to use it. Because of his extensive drug use, Lenz became increasingly paranoid and delusional. He started believing that everyone, even his closest cult members, wanted him dead. About this time, and feeding this delusion, a number of his followers who had become disillusioned with him began complaining about his behavior toward them and breaking away from the cult. One of his students, Donald Cole, even stabbed himself to death because of Lenz's treatment of him. He had told others that he didn't feel he was meeting Lenz's standards. "Bye, Rama," his suicide note said. "See you next time."[6]

Lenz's stature as a leading New Age guru began to suffer as more and more accusations of abuse arose. In addition, the bad press he received due to the complaints of former cult members began to seriously affect Lenz's mental well-being. For years he had been considered a near God to many people, and now suddenly he seemed surrounded by individuals complaining about him and even suing him.

"He almost went completely bald because of depression when the allegations came out," said one of the members of his inner circle that stayed loyal to him. "He had these huge periods of depression because everyone was after him."[7]

As the complaints continued and grew, they further fed Lenz's paranoia and he became more and more withdrawn. He finally secluded himself on his Long Island estate, where people close to him found his behavior becoming more and more bizarre. He didn't like change or small denomination bills because he said they were "low vibed" and had "bad energy." He feared being poisoned, he feared bad energy from people around him, and he feared spiders because he thought they might actually be entities. Lenz finally became so fearful he slept with a gun under the bed. He had his house alarmed so tightly, friends said, that no one could move around the house at night without setting off the alarm system.

Finally, the only things Lenz trusted and loved were his dogs. He even dedicated one of his books to his favorite dog, Vayu, who Lenz claimed was one of Earth's 12 enlightened beings. Many of the people who knew Lenz intimately believe that Vayu's death in 1998 was likely what drove him to suicide. Already depressed over his lost stature and the many lawsuits by former students and cult members, Vayu's death may have been all Lenz could stand. According to the woman who lived with Lenz at the time of Lenz's death, Vayu's body lay on the couch for two days after he died because Lenz couldn't accept the dog's death.

On the night of April 12, 1998, Lenz and his female companion downed large quantities of Valium (according to the coroner, Lenz took more than 150 of them). The woman didn't die, but Lenz, who wandered out of the house and into Conscience Bay, did, wearing Vayu's collar around his neck.

In his will, Lenz stated that if he took no steps during his life to establish a foundation to handle his $18 million estate, then it should all go to the National Audubon Society, of which Lenz was a member. While the executor of Lenz's estate believes that his assets should go to a foundation formed after Lenz's death, the National Audubon Society has filed papers in court arguing that since Lenz was a cult leader and an obvious phony, his assets should go where they would do the most good: the National Audubon Society.

"The sincerity and extent of Lenz's belief in Buddhism is disputed," said the affidavit filed by the National Audubon Society. "He lectured about something called 'American Buddhism' which, by all accounts, was a belief system consistent with his lavish lifestyle."[8] Attached to the National Audubon Society's legal documents was a three-inch thick folder of news articles critical of Lenz.

Mainstream Buddhists also have little regard or respect for Lenz and his teachings. "I've never seen a serious reference to this man in all my reading of Buddhist literature and discussion," said Melvin McLeod, editor of the international Buddhist magazine *Shambhala Sun*. "He's not someone American Buddhism in any way recognizes, to my knowledge."[9]

The final disposition of Lenz's estate, however, promises to be a long and interesting court battle. In May 1999, two women, both claiming to be Lenz's wife, filed papers in court saying they believe they are entitled to at least part of his estate. However, in the first paragraph of his will, Lenz stated that he was not married and wanted to disinherit his family.[10]

Interestingly, in late 2003, well after his death, Lenz's official Web site was still operating. On February 9, 2001, former students of Lenz celebrated his birthday by hosting an outing to Bandelier National Monument in New Mexico.

The New Age is not a single concept or philosophy but actually a large collection of concepts. Few individuals can say that they are total New Age adherents because the New Age movement contains so many separate disciplines and belief systems. "The New Age Movement...is too 'fuzzy' and disparate to constitute a great conspiracy, as some have claimed," says Dr. Michael D. Langone. "Nor is it a cult, although cults exist within the New Age Movement."[11]

The New Age movement, like Wicca and traditional religious beliefs, is simply a spiritual belief system with no illegal or evil purposes. But as the examples of Frederick Lenz and others presented in this chapter will show, the New Age movement can be used as the basis around which a leader can form a cult by my definition. And potential New Age cult leaders have a large choice of philosophies around which to form a cult because the New Age movement contains such varied concepts as the belief in spiritualism, channeling, reincarnation, meditation, crystal and pyramid power, astrology, Eastern mysticism, psychic healing, and much more. A *New York Times* article describes the New Age as follows: "Drawing on humanistic psychology, Asian religions, occult practices, and subterranean religious traditions in the West, as well as the shamanism and nature worship, the movement has assembled a smorgasbord of concepts and techniques for achieving personal peace and stretching human capabilities."[12]

As reported in the *Cultic Studies Journal*, a panel of experts from the American Family Foundation and the Committee for the Scientific Investigation of Claims of the Paranormal describe the New Age in this way: "An eclectic collection of psychological and spiritual techniques that are rooted in Eastern mysticism, lack scientific evaluative data, and are promoted zealously by followers of diverse idealized leaders claiming transformative visions."[13]

Despite these "lukewarm" descriptions, a large number of people believe in or are interested in New Age concepts. The American Booksellers Association, for example, states that Americans purchased almost $10 million worth of New Age books in 1995, and according to *Forbes* magazine, $2 billion is spent each year on New Age paraphernalia.[14] There is even an entire town in Florida, called Cassadaga, that promotes itself as a New Age center, while Lily Dale, New York, boasts that it is the largest and oldest community of mediums in the United States.

Although not all New Agers hold the same beliefs because of the New Age movement's diverse believe system, many New Agers do agree that they believe our planet will soon be reborn and rejuvenated by human beings who are much more spiritually enlightened. How this will happen though is a bit fuzzy. Many New Agers saw the beginning of the new millennium as the starting point for this changeover. For example, a New Age Web site says, "Planet Earth and Humanity are about to undergo major changes as part of a significant step-up in their evolutionary development....Deep down, many of us harbor a fundamental feeling that there will be, and has to be, a significant change to our whole way of life before the new Millennium begins."[15]

Yet even though many of the concepts and beliefs of the New Age may be fuzzy and ill defined, the movement has made some major inroads into modern society. Many courses in stress management and leadership attended by executives from major corporations, for example, teach meditation and other Eastern religious and mystical concepts. Corporate executives, therefore, should screen "stress management" and "leadership training" courses very closely before sending employees or attending. Some have been found to be simply recruiting vehicles for New Age cults, as were Frederick Lenz's seminars. According to a *London Times* study, "Management training, self-improvement and prosperity courses offered to professionals and companies in Britain by American consultants are using disturbing New Age methods that can do more harm than good."[16]

Another example of a New Age concept that has gone mainstream is transcendental meditation. Brought into the public awareness by the Beatle's promotion of it, transcendental meditation has now grown so large and prestigious that it has its own corporate structure, a medical center in Washington, D.C., an accredited university, and even its own town, Vedic, Iowa, which was incorporated in 2001 (in 2002, the town of Vedic actually began issuing its own currency). Two miles south of Vedic lies the Maharishi University of Management, which offers degrees up to the doctorate level, and is accredited by the North Central Association of Colleges and Schools.

The Web site for the Maharishi University of Management claims, "Utilizing the managing intelligence of Nature for professional success and personal fulfillment in Business, Computer Science, Engineering, Arts, Humanities, and Sciences. Our consciousness-based approach to education develops alertness and creativity. You become more awake as your awareness expands."[17]

While none of this sounds, or is, illegal or terribly dangerous, an incident in Oregon with a cult that practiced and promoted a philosophy based on New Age concepts shows that cults can twist and use any belief system to attract members to its group. More importantly, however, the following incident shows how some cults will use whatever means they have to, including bioterrorism, to take and keep control.

According to an article in the *Columbia Journalism Review,* along with newspaper accounts, in 1981, a former citizen of India, spiritual guru Chandra Mohan Jain, who had renamed himself Bhagwan Shree Rajneesh, purchased the 65,000-acre Big Muddy Ranch southeast of the small town of Antelope in Wasco County, northern Oregon. At its height, Rajneesh's movement, now known as Osho, had 600 meditation centers and more than 200,000 members worldwide. His intentions in Oregon were to establish an international headquarters for his movement and to start a commune where his disciples could practice his theology, which was an assortment of beliefs taken from the Hindu, Buddhist, and Christian religions, along with a bit of pop psychology and New Age concepts. His theology included a type of meditation called "dynamic meditation," in which he encouraged the participants to jump up and dance around, shouting whatever came into their minds. Rajneesh's bible, which he called *The Orange Book,* tells readers, "Explode! Go totally mad.... Jump up and down shouting the mantra.... Each time you land on the flats of your feet, let the sound hammer deep into the sex center."[18]

Rajneesh also preached that sexual energy was the body's primary energy and that denying the expression of this energy was the cause of many bodily and psychological ailments. In his commune, he discouraged marriage and also encouraged people to stay together only as long as they loved each other. Any children born of these unions, according to his dictates, would not have parents but belong to everyone.

Soon after the commune opened, several thousand people came to learn from Rajneesh and almost a thousand stayed to live there. More than half of those who stayed were women, 66 percent of whom had college degrees. However, like most cults, life within the compound soon became very strict and regulated. A visitor to the commune in 1984 wrote that life there was "'authoritarian' and that it displayed a preoccupation with total control...regimented and regulated even in minutiae."[19]

To maintain discipline and control within the commune, the cult formed its own security staff, and soon guards with assault rifles patrolled the area. One of Rajneesh's top lieutenants, in an attempt to keep security tight, also set up an illegal wiretapping system that recorded all telephone messages coming in, going out, or transmitted within the commune.

While life for the commune's residents soon became strictly regulated, life for Rajneesh certainly didn't appear to be one of self-denial. At one time, Rajneesh owned 96 Rolls Royces and over $1 million in jewelry, while often boasting that he'd had more sex partners than anyone in history.

Soon though, conflicts over land use and other issues began arising between the residents of the commune and the people living in nearby Antelope and the rest of Wasco County. However, the voting block the cult maintained because of the large number of residents living in the commune allowed the cult to take over the local government of Antelope, and also allowed the cult to put its own people in key government spots in Antelope, such as the city council and school board. Once the cult took over, they even changed the name of the town to Rajneeshpuram. Still, this was not enough. To really have their way, the cult knew they needed to control the entire county. However, the population of Wasco County in 1984 exceeded 21,000, far outnumbering the voting-age population of the commune. So the cult conspired to illegally win the upcoming election for county commissioners and sheriff, whose offices, once taken over, they could use to run the county any way they wanted.

First, the cult attempted to bolster their voting block by busing in several thousand homeless people and trying to register them as voters. When this plan didn't work after officials made the cult aware they would investigate all new voters, the cult decided to take more drastic measures. They purchased a strain of *S. typhimurium* bacteria from a commercial supplier of biological products. This bacterium causes salmonella, a serious gastrointestinal disease. Using its own laboratory at the commune, the cult then began growing more of the bacteria.

The cult's plan was to introduce the bacteria into the county's water supply and thereby incapacitate a large number of voters on election day, consequently allowing the cult's voting block to control the election. They first tested the bacteria by introducing it into glasses of water given to two county commissioners who visited the commune and also by sprinkling some on produce in several area grocery stores.

When these tests didn't bring about the results the cult had hoped for, in September 1984, members of the cult performed another test, secretly contaminating the salad bars and coffee creamers in 10 area restaurants. As a result, 751 people in Wasco County came down with salmonella, the victims ranging in age from newborn to 87 years old. However, the huge influx of health workers and investigators this outbreak of disease brought into the county frightened the cult away from their original election day plan.

"They apparently didn't expect it to be such a huge success," said Leslie L. Zaitz, a reporter for *The Oregonian*. "The attention attracted by the salad bar escapade brought hordes of health officials and investigators into The

Dalles (Wasco County seat). It dashed the cult's plans to do worse on Election Day."[20]

Many of the residents of Wasco County, long suspicious of the cult and intimidated by its armed guards and strange ways, immediately suspected that the cult had something to do with the salmonella outbreak. "People were so horrified and scared," said Wasco County resident Laura Bentley. "People wouldn't go out, they wouldn't go out alone. People were becoming prisoners."[21]

While the cult was not officially blamed at first for the salmonella outbreak, trouble still soon began for them. A federal grand jury returned a 35-count indictment against Rajneesh and seven others for conspiracy to evade immigration laws. The cult had allegedly been fabricating sham marriages between U.S. citizens and foreign followers of Rajneesh so that the foreigners could stay in the United States. Following this indictment, investigations by several government agencies turned up evidence of many more crimes. At the time of the salmonella outbreak, despite the suspicions of local residents, investigators had officially attributed it to poor food handling. However, on October 2, 1985, officials discovered a vial of *S. typhimurium* bacteria in a laboratory at the Rajneesh Medical Center on the compound grounds. The bacteria the police found matched exactly the bacteria recovered from individuals sickened after eating at area restaurants. The police also uncovered the vast illegal wiretapping operation the cult had used, including 3,000 cassette tapes of recorded conversations. In addition, they discovered a plot by cult members to murder the U.S. Attorney for Oregon Charles Turner. Members of the cult, police learned, had already purchased weapons to commit the murder and had been charting Turner's movements.

Apparently receiving advance warning of the coming arrests, most of the cult leaders either fled the United States or attempted to, including Rajneesh, whose jet, while reportedly in route to Bermuda in October 1985, was intercepted and stopped at Charlotte, North Carolina. Eventually extradited back to Oregon, Rajneesh entered into a plea bargain in November 1985 and received a suspended 10-year prison sentence. He also agreed to pay a hefty fine and court costs and to leave the United States within five days. Rajneesh died in India of heart failure in 1990.

The United States extradited other leaders of the cult from various foreign countries, the latest in December 2002. Except for this last extradited cult member, most have served their prison sentences and now live outside the United States.

"The Rajneeshees committed the most significant crimes of their kind in the history of the United States," said former Oregon Attorney General Dave Frohnmayer. "The largest single incident of fraudulent marriages, the most massive scheme of wiretapping and bugging, and the largest mass poisoning."[22]

After Rajneesh and other leaders of the cult had abandoned the community they founded in Oregon, it eventually became the property of an insurance company. In 1991, Montana millionaire Dennis Washington purchased the 65,000-acre compound and gave it to a Christian youth organization, which in 1999 founded the Wild Horse Canyon Youth Camp. The 88,000-square-foot meeting hall of Rajneesh now contains basketball courts, climbing walls, and a skate park. The commune's former 140-room hotel now serves as a camper dormitory.

The point to this chapter is not to debate the worth of the New Age movement or the validity of its concepts. The point is to show how cult leaders like Frederick Lenz and Bhagwan Shree Rajneesh can use some of its concepts, twist them to fit a belief system that prospective members will accept, and then become the belief system's guru, consequently gaining total control over members attracted to the new movement. The reason New Age concepts make such an excellent basis for forming cults around is that they are largely unproven and unprovable concepts that many people believe in anyway. For example, a recent Gallup poll of teenagers found that approximately one-third of churchgoing Christian teenagers believe in reincarnation,[23] while other Gallup polls show that 54 percent of the American public believes in psychic or spiritual healing, 50 percent in extrasensory perception (ESP), 36 percent in telepathy, 32 percent in clairvoyance, and 15 percent in channeling.[24]

"We have a spiritual crisis in this country," says Joe Szimhart of the Cult Awareness Network. "New Age gurus are feeding off it. It seems that anyone can sell metaphysical snake oil and get away with it."[25]

As this quote points out, and as I shall continue to show throughout this book, cult leaders can reshape any spiritual belief system to make it fit their particular needs and then use the new belief system to attract and hold cult members. Although some belief systems expounded by cults may seem totally outlandish to most people, cult leaders can make the outlandish seem very believable and acceptable to cult members, as I will show in the next chapter regarding the belief in UFOs.

CHAPTER 8

UFO Cults

Born the son of a Presbyterian minister, Marshall Herff Applewhite, for a large part of his life, also planned to become a Presbyterian minister. However, in the end he died a cult leader whose persuasive powers and belief system, though considered bizarre and almost psychotic by most people, nevertheless persuaded 38 other people to join him in 1997 in a mass suicide—an incident that would be talked about and reported in thousands of publications around the world. In between, Applewhite led a life of confusion, self-doubt, sexual frustration, and unfulfilled predictions.

In 1948, after graduating from Corpus Christi High School, Applewhite enrolled in Austin College with the idea of pursuing a career in the ministry, as his father had done. His roommate at Austin College described Applewhite as very smart and popular.

"Herff wasn't weird or strange or anything like that," roommate John Alexander added. "You just wonder what makes a person do such a radical change."[1]

After graduation from Austin College, Applewhite continued his career pursuit, enrolling at the Union Theological Seminary in Richmond, Virginia. However, Applewhite also loved music and reportedly possessed an excellent singing voice. After one semester at the seminary, he dropped out and became the director of music at the First Presbyterian Church in Gastonia, North Carolina. During this time Applewhite also met and wed Ann Frances Pearce. Soon after his marriage, Applewhite found himself drafted into the Army, where he served in the Signal Corps and received an honorable discharge two years later.

For a while in the 1950s and 1960s, Applewhite held musical positions at the University of Alabama at Tuscaloosa and at the University of St. Thomas in Houston. In Houston's arts community, Applewhite became known as a talented vocalist who often sang with the Houston Grand Opera. During the early 1960s, he moved to New York City for a year in an attempt to find work on the stage, but after achieving little success he returned to teaching music. During this time, though still married, Applewhite reportedly had homosexual relationships with several men. In February 1968, after 16 years of marriage and two children, the Applewhites divorced.

In 1971, Applewhite reportedly checked himself into a mental hospital in an attempt to be cured of his homosexuality, though he told family members he'd had a heart attack. He apparently went there seeking help because he had been fired recently from his position as music professor due to a homosexual relationship with a student. Earlier, in 1964, he had been fired for the same reason from another teaching position. During his stay at the hospital he met Bonnie Lu Nettles, a registered nurse who dabbled in astrology and claimed to channel a nineteenth-century monk named Brother Francis. How they met depends on whether she or Applewhite tells the story. Regardless, they immediately felt an attraction and afterward became inseparable. Nettles and her husband at the time had been going through a period of marital difficulties, and after she and Applewhite met, Nettles broke all ties with her husband, and she and Applewhite began a relationship that continued until Nettles's death in 1985.

For most of the 14 years of their relationship, which by all reports was nonsexual, Applewhite and Nettles wandered across the United States, often living in tents at campgrounds while either working menial jobs or begging at churches. Because of their meager and often desperate financial condition, Applewhite and Nettles, who regularly skipped out on food and motel bills, also took some liberties with other people's credit cards and with rental cars. The police arrested the pair in Harlingen, Texas, for credit card fraud. Although the police dropped the charges a few days later, a court extradited Applewhite to St. Louis, where he served six months in jail for vehicle theft. This charge came from his failure to return a rental car, a Mercury Comet, for nine months. Nettles waited patiently for him to be released from jail.

During the early part of their relationship, Applewhite and Nettles, also known as "The Two" and "Bo and Peep," began to formulate their belief system and recruit members into a cult that in the 1990s would be known as Heaven's Gate. Their theology began as a mixture of Christianity and bad science fiction. At first, Applewhite and Nettles believed they were the "two witnesses" talked about in chapter 11 of the book of Revelation. They told cult members that they would be killed by unbelievers and then brought back to life three and a half days later in a cloud of light. To fulfill the prophecy in Revelation, Applewhite once reportedly asked recruits, "Would you be willing to bear arms for this cause? . . . If they saw you carrying guns, then that would give them cause to bear arms against us....It might take that to get us killed."[2]

They also believed and taught their recruits that 2,000 years ago, beings of a dimension known as the Level Above Human sent a representative (Jesus) to teach people how to enter the Kingdom of God. He didn't finish the task though, due to his premature death at the hands of demonic forces. According to the cult leaders' developing theology, beings of the Level Above Human dispatched two more representatives (Applewhite and Nettles) in the 1970s to resume Jesus's job. On the cult's Web site, Applewhite wrote, "Our mission is exactly the same. I am in the same position in today's society as was the One that was in Jesus then."[3]

As time passed, Applewhite and Nettles began to modify their belief system and ultimately became convinced that they were actually alien entities that had arrived on Earth in staged spacecraft crashes. According to their evolving belief system, the personalities of the aliens had been placed into the bodies of an unsuspecting Applewhite and Nettles, whose personalities they then replaced. As such, Applewhite and Nettles claimed they belonged to and came from a dimension they called the Level Above Human, and they believed that they would eventually be taken back to that level by aliens in a flying saucer. As a part of their belief system, they held that to ascend to the Level Above Human (where there was no sexual orientation), all base human drives, such as the desire for sex, drugs, and alcohol, had to be stifled and overcome.

During the time they were developing and redesigning their philosophy, Applewhite and Nettles also continued recruiting members into their cult, which went by the name Total Overcomers Anonymous for a number of years before changing to Heaven's Gate. They would hold recruitment meetings in school auditoriums, on college campuses, in motels, and in private homes—anywhere they could find an audience. In the 1970s, in an attempt to spread their message, Applewhite and Nettles cooperated with two men named Hayden Hewes and Brad Steiger, who wrote a book titled *UFO Missionaries Extraordinary.*

"We did voice stress (lie detection) tests," Steiger said. "They believed what they were saying."[4]

A colleague of Applewhite while he taught at the University of Alabama said of him, "He was sort of into what we would now call 'New Age.' He was not a con artist out to enrich himself from suckers. He actually seemed to believe this stuff."[5]

Applewhite and Nettles apparently continued to believe in the message they preached—even though their predictions about their belief system continually failed. One time, in 1994, cult members waited without success at the end of the Santa Monica pier for a spacecraft supposedly in route to pick them up. Several other times, the cult also assembled to wait for a reported pick up by a flying saucer, only to be disappointed. Often, the group would go out into the desert and wait all night, hoping to be picked up.

Although the spaceships never appeared, and a book written about them didn't paint them in the light Applewhite and Nettles had hoped for, their recruiting didn't diminish. At one of their first recruiting efforts, Applewhite and Nettles told the crowd, "If our message speaks to you, then follow us. If you follow, then you must obey everything we say. That includes giving up your possessions, your family, and your entire identity."[6]

Even though their message may have sounded bizarre and outlandish to most people, nevertheless they began to recruit individuals few would expect them to, including a film editor, an accountant, college students, a former military officer, musicians, and even a wealthy real estate developer. This last recruit proved to be very beneficial to the group because of his ability to negotiate leases for the various pieces of property the cult would occupy over the years. In the 25 years the cult existed, hundreds of people would pass through the group, many staying for a while and then dropping out. Some would join, leave, and then rejoin. A small core, though, joined up and never left. Many of the cult members deserted families, homes, and jobs to join up. One woman, who had just given birth to twins, gave the babies and three other children to family members and then left to join the cult. Another couple gave their 10-year-old daughter to some friends before joining up.

As with most cults, once inside Heaven's Gate life became very controlled. Applewhite and Nettles structured the cult members' days so they had something to do every waking moment. In the early days of the cult, regulations required members to check with Applewhite or Nettles every 12 minutes for instructions, but they eventually dropped this requirement. Instead, the leaders developed and wrote a procedural manual as thick as a telephone book that covered everything from how long to take a shower to how to cut carrots to which way to pull the razor when shaving. In addition, no one in the cult ever did anything alone. Each member always had a partner (whom the leaders switched regularly to prevent romantic attractions) to watch over them and particularly to watch for backsliding and prohibited behaviors, such as trusting one's own judgment, showing too much curiosity, or wanting attention. Also, except Applewhite or Nettles, no one in the cult could make a definite statement about anything; instead, they had to couch their statements with phrases like "I'm probably not correct, but..." or "I may be wrong, but...."

Sex, despite the control maintained by the cult leaders, remained one of the biggest problems that the group faced. One of the most important tenets of the group was that all earthly passions had to be overcome. However, since the cult contained many young members, Applewhite and Nettles had to be on constant watch to prevent "slippages." Finally, to stifle sexual urges, one of the male cult members suggested that the men in the cult be castrated. Although at first Applewhite rejected the idea, eventually eight members of the cult, including Applewhite, had their testicles surgically removed in Mexico.

"They couldn't stop smiling and giggling," said one of the cult members about those who had been castrated. "They were excited about it."[7]

Even with all of the control and the stifling of sexual urges, membership in the Heaven's Gate cult was not without its amusements. The members watched "approved" television programs, such as *Star Trek* and *The X-Files*. However, during these viewings, members had assigned seating and leaders instructed them to turn away if they felt sexually aroused by any actor or actress. The cult also made trips to see "approved" movies, such as *Star Wars*, and even visited Las Vegas for gambling and shows.

Regardless of Applewhite and Nettles's success in managing the group, cult activities and the cult's existence itself nearly came to an end in 1985. After Nettles died of liver cancer that year, Applewhite appeared for a while to be at a loss for what to do, the two of them having been so close for so many years. Once, after her death, he reportedly asked other cult members, "Am I crazy? Should I tell everyone to go home?"[8] Eventually, however, Applewhite regained his sense of purpose and his belief that he had come from the Level Above Human.

After the 1993 incident involving the Branch Davidians in Waco, Texas, Applewhite became increasingly worried that his group was next on the FBI's hit list, and he began taking serious security precautions, including not meeting with new recruits until they had been in the cult for several months. Another security precaution involved the building of a "safe refuge" in the New Mexico desert. There the group had a building constructed of cement blocks and old tires. The cult even purchased several firearms. However, enthusiasm for a shoot-out with the authorities ran very low in the group, and finally Applewhite said he had received psychic instructions from Nettles (who had died almost a decade before) to abandon the fortress in New Mexico.

In May 1993, the Heaven's Gate cult began to seriously look for new recruits, which included placing advertisements in newspapers telling readers that they had one last chance to join them and advance to the Level Above Human. The cult also paid for a satellite broadcast of 12 homemade videos about their philosophy. However, the response to these advertisements turned out to be extremely meager, and Applewhite, though disheartened, wouldn't give up. He felt that it was his mission on Earth to spread the word and recruit people for the next level.

While this type of recruitment was very expensive, the group was able to afford it because one of the core cult members had come into a modest inheritance (reportedly $300,000 to $400,000) that gave the cult a small measure of financial security. However, eventually the cult spent the entire inheritance.

In October 1996, the cult moved into a 9,200-square-foot, seven-bedroom, nine-bath mansion in a gated community outside San Diego, California, called Rancho Santa Fe. They reportedly paid $7,000 a month to rent the mansion. To pay the rent, the group formed Higher Source, a computer business that designed Web site home pages. Because they reportedly did their work very well and, more importantly, only charged about one-fourth of what other Web design companies charged, they brought in considerable business.

Somehow, possibly through Internet reports or the radio show *Coast to Coast,* the cult became convinced that an alien spaceship, bound for Earth to take the Heaven's Gate cult members to the next level, lay hidden behind comet Hale-Bopp, which had been discovered in July 1995. An amateur astronomer had photographed what appeared to be an object trailing comet Hale-Bopp, and he talked about his discovery on the radio show. Courtney Brown, director of the Farsight Institute in Atlanta, also interviewed on the radio show, said that "three professional psychics had detected the comet-trailing object and found it to be a metallic object full of aliens."[9] Eventually though, professional astronomical photographers demonstrated that what the amateur astronomer had photographed was actually just a background star distorted by the telescope lens. Despite this, however, the cult members became convinced that comet Hale-Bopp was the "marker" they had been waiting for and that it signaled it was time to dispose of their bodily containers in anticipation of being picked up by the UFO. Applewhite also preached that Earth was about to be "spaded under" and that the comet was a sign it was time for him and other cult members to leave.

The cult members, excited about finally being picked up, purchased an expensive telescope in an attempt to see the alien spaceship. When they couldn't locate anything following the comet, they returned the telescope, complaining to the clerk at the store where they purchased it that they couldn't find the spaceship. "Well gosh," the clerk recalled them saying, "we found the comet, but we can't see anything following it."[10]

An article in *The New Yorker* said that the philosophy of Applewhite's cult was, "We think that an alien spaceship is trailing the comet; observation through a capable telescope shows no such spaceship; therefore, let's get rid of the telescope."[11] Even though the telescope didn't show the cult members a spaceship trailing the comet, they still believed the time had come for them to advance to the next level and to leave their human containers behind.

In anticipation of this, the cult members made videos in which all but one of the 39 members said goodbye. The cult members appeared in the videos to be very upbeat. "We couldn't be happier about what we're going to do," said one female cult member. "We are all happy to be doing what we are doing," said another woman.[12]

Applewhite also gave one last offer to prospective recruits. "You can follow us, but you cannot stay here," he said on the cult's Web site. "You may even find your 'boarding pass' to leave with us during this brief 'window.'"[13] Before committing suicide though, Applewhite instructed, individuals must first call out his or Nettles's name so that the UFO would be alerted to pick them up.

The Heaven's Gate cult then got busy. On March 23, 1997, Comet Hale-Bopp made its closest approach to Earth. Working in four shifts of 15, 15, 7, and 2 people and assisting each other, the 39 members of the Heaven's Gate cult who lived at the San Diego mansion—21 women and 18 men, ages 26 to 72—swallowed pudding laced with lethal amounts of phenobarbital and then washed it down with vodka (which increases the sedative effect of the phenobarbital). After this, each cult member fastened a plastic bag over his or her head, lay down on a bed with a packed bag on the floor next to it, and, covered with a purple shroud, quietly died. Authorities who first viewed the scene three days later said that all members of the cult wore identical dark jogging suits and new black Nikes, and all had short-cropped hair (leading the authorities to mistakenly believe at first that all 39 victims were men). All the cult members also had identification in their pockets. The house, witnesses later said, appeared immaculately clean and neat.

On March 26, 1997, after receiving a FedEx package from the cult, Richard Ford, a cult member who lived away from the San Diego mansion, became suspicious and went to Rancho Santa Fe to check on the other cult members. Going inside, he found the bodies of the 39 cult members and called the authorities. Soon afterward, Ford, who also goes by the name Rio D'Angelo, began negotiating a deal with ABC television for a movie about the cult.

However, the story doesn't end with just the 39 suicides in the mansion. On March 30, 1997, the police discovered a 58-year-old recluse dead in his home in northern California, draped in a purple shroud similar to those of the Heaven's Gate cult members. A suicide note found next to the body said, "I'm going to the spaceship with Hale-Bopp to be with those who have gone before me."[14]

In May 1997, at a Holiday Inn near San Diego, two former members of the Heaven's Gate cult, Wayne Cooke and Charles Humphrey, ingested applesauce and phenobarbital, then chased it with vodka. Cooke died, but Humphrey survived. For a while after being released from a mental hospital, Humphrey preached on college campuses about the cult's beliefs, but he became discouraged by the lack of response he received. In February 1998, authorities, acting on a tip from his daughter, found Humphrey's body in a tent near Ehrenberg, Arizona, his suicide attempt successful this time. Before joining the cult, Humphrey had been a computer programmer and the founder of a successful computer company.

While the coroner eventually ruled all the deaths to be suicide, not everyone agrees. "I don't consider it suicide," said Janja Lalich, a cult expert. "I consider it murder. [Applewhite] controlled it, he called the shots. These people were pawns in his personal fantasy."[15]

In March 2002, to mark the fifth anniversary of the Heaven's Gate cult suicides, Rio D'Angelo put the cult's 1992 Ford van on eBay, setting a minimum price of $39,000. Although at one time he was supposed to help write a TV movie about the Heaven's Gate cult, that project apparently fell through.

"I'm really the only one left," D'Angelo told a reporter for the Associated Press, lamenting that while five years ago he had turned down a tabloid's offer of $1 million for the exclusive rights to his story, today he'd take the money.[16]

The Heaven Gate belief system about a flying saucer appearing and rescuing cult members from the turmoil of a rapidly disintegrating Earth may sound like bizarre wishful thinking to many readers, but Heaven's Gate is in no way alone in their theology. There are a number of groups in existence today, most with many more members than the Heaven's Gate cult, whose theology also centers around extraterrestrials in UFOs rescuing Earth, though none of these groups fit my definition of a cult.

Because I sent away for some resource material while researching an earlier book, I somehow got on the mailing list of the Unarius Educational Foundation out of El Cajon, California. Unarius is an acronym for Universal Articulate Interdimensional Understanding of Science. In a very colorful brochure I received in 1999 from this group, they invited me to take part in the annual Interplanetary Concave of Light at the New World Teaching Center of the Unarius Academy of Science in El Cajon, which is about fifteen miles east of San Diego.

The brochure stated that this annual conference is in preparation for the landing of more than 30 spaceships on 67 acres of land owned by the Unarius Educational Foundation near El Cajon. These ships, according to the brochure, will contain representatives of the Interplanetary Confederation. After reportedly becoming concerned when they found that human beings had begun using atomic weapons, these representatives decided it was time to precondition earthlings for a spaceship landing and an awareness that we are part of a larger galactic civilization (this preconditioning, Unarius members claim, has been the Unarius Educational Foundation's mission for many years). According to the brochure, when this landing occurs, it will be a turning point for mankind because our "Space Brothers" will lead us on a path of peace and spiritual enlightenment.

In 2001, according to the Unarius Educational Foundation, a spaceship of Pleidians, residents of the Taurus star system, would land on a portion of Atlantis that would well up out of the Bermuda Triangle. Alta, the ambassador of the Interplanetary Confederation, would then, through a mental link with the residents of Earth, provide information about the changes Earth would undergo as a member of the Interplanetary Confederation. Alta, according to Unarius, is from the Pleidian planet Vixall. This failed 2001 date, however, was not the only date that has been predicted by Unarius for the earth landing of the Pleidians. The landing was originally supposed to be in 1974, then 1975, then 1976, and finally 2001. Undoubtedly, a new date is forthcoming.

The failure of Uranius's predictions for when an alien landing will take place doesn't seem to stem the group's belief that the alien landing will occur soon and perhaps have even been hurried by the events of September 11, 2001. "The recent terrorist attack was a great shock to all of us," the Unarius Web site said. "It is not happenstance that the Muons from planet Myton will soon land on Earth. Their arrival is part of a vast plan, a Grand Design for the spiritual advancement of humankind. The plan, masterminded by Advanced Intelligences, has not been set back by these acts of terrorism, for it has already set in motion the positive energies of the new cycle that are serving as a counterbalance to dissipate the negative energies."[17]

For anyone who might have qualms that the Unarius philosophy runs counter to the teachings of the Bible, a sidebar in the brochure I received states, "The Archangel Uriel is the overshadowing spiritual force guiding human kind into the 21st century. 'The future of mankind,' Uriel has stated, 'is positive and progressive, I promise you!'" The archangel Uriel, incidentally, used to be, before dying, one of the founders of the Unarius Educational Foundation, Ruth E. Norman, who died in 1993. She and her husband, Ernest Norman, now the archangel Gabriel, met at a psychics convention and founded Unarius in 1954. The Unarius Educational Foundation presently has learning centers in the United States, Canada, England, New Zealand, Nigeria, and Poland.

Another UFO group founder, George King, who stated that his full name was Sir George King, OSP, Ph.D., Th.D., D.D., Metropolitan Archbishop of the Aetherius Churches, Prince Grand Master of the Mystical Order of St. Peter, H.R.H. Prince De George King De Santori, and Founder President of the Aetherius Society, established a group called the Aetherius Society in 1954. According to newspaper articles, King claimed that between 1954 and just before his death in 1997, he had received more than 600 mental transmissions from the Cosmic Masters, who selected him to be the "Voice of the Interplanetary Parliament." Before receiving this calling, King drove a taxi in London.

According to the Aetherian belief system, flying saucers manned by
benevolent aliens constantly patrol Earth to protect its inhabitants from
the "Black Magicians," who are evil aliens that want to enslave Earth. The
benevolent flying saucers once even put an invisible shield around Earth
to ward off the Black Magicians. Aetherians also believe that the Cosmic
Masters have sent charges of positive spiritual energy to the tops of 19
selected mountains and that anyone climbing these mountains can partake of the energy. The mountains include Mt. Baldy in California, Mt.
Adams in New Hampshire, and Castle Peak in Colorado. A recent pilgrimage to the top of Mt. Baldy included Aetherians who are teachers,
accountants, and business owners.

"You'll find most of the members here are quite balanced in their lives,"
said an Aetherius Society member in California. "We're not kooks, we're
intelligent people."[18]

In late 2003, the Aetherius Web site listed their "cosmic activities" as follows: "One of the responsibilities of the Mission Team members is to monitor world events looking for areas where extra spiritual energy may be
required, for example, peace talks, hurricanes, floods, and outbreaks of
violence. When a situation is discovered that looks like it can be helped
through a concentrated flood of energy, the Mission Team organizes a
release of spiritual energy from either our Prayer Power batteries or other
energy held on our behalf."[19]

A group that has been in the news constantly because of its claims to have
cloned a human being is the Raelians. The Raelians believe that mankind
originated when a race of aliens called the Elohim visited Earth and created
mankind in a laboratory. The founder of this group, a former journalist
named Claude Vorilhon, who now goes by the name Rael, claims that aliens
transported him onto a flying saucer in 1973, where he found that he had
been selected to deliver the Elohimians' message about mankind's origins.
The Elohimians told him that they will openly come to Earth and give
mankind some very advanced technology, but only when there is world
peace, and only after an embassy has been built for them in Jerusalem. By
2002, the Raelian movement had raised more than $7 million to build this
embassy but as yet had not been able to acquire the Israeli government's
approval to proceed with the building. If Israel doesn't agree to allow them
to build the embassy by 2035, Rael warns, the Elohim will take away the
protection they have been giving Israel from its neighbors.[20]

The Raelian movement presently claims to have between 50,000 and
55,000 members in 84 countries.[21] In 1997, the Raelian movement raised a
worldwide furor when it announced the formation of Clonaid, a company
that planned to clone human beings for infertile couples and homosexu-
als. The company stated it also planned to offer a service whereby cells
from a loved one could be stored for future cloning. An ad on Clonaid's
Web site in late 2002 stated that the company is now offering cell preser-

vation for American soldiers serving in the Middle East, with the idea that a soldier killed there could be brought back through cloning. Also, according the company's Web site, the ultimate goal of Clonaid is eventually to be able to transplant the memory and personality of the cloned individual, thereby giving a person immortality.

In July 2002, Clonaid again raised a public furor when it announced to the worldwide news media that its scientists had already implanted a human clone into a South Korean woman (cloning was not illegal at the time in South Korea). A spokesperson for Clonaid said the woman, at the time of their announcement, was two months into the pregnancy. Independent confirmation of this claim, however, could not be made. In September 2002, Clonaid claimed that they had moved the woman out of South Korea in anticipation of a government ban there on cloning. In October 2002, Clonaid claimed that their scientists had recently implanted several more women with cloned embryos. On December 27, 2002, Clonaid announced that the first birth of a cloned human being had occurred but offered no proof of this.

"Our goal is to do a cloned baby and a very healthy one," said Dr. Brigitte Boisellier, a former biochemistry professor who now works for Clonaid. "We should disclose in December the results of the implantations to the scientific community."[22]

Cloning, however, is not cheap. Reportedly, a couple who lost a child has paid Clonaid several hundred thousand dollars so far to clone their dead child, which, according to the parents, has not yet been done.[23] Apparently, running the Raelian movement also isn't cheap as most members of the Raelian movement are required to tithe at between 3 and 10 percent of their net worth. Incidentally, Rael, the group's Web site says, is available for public speeches about cloning for a fee of $100,000.

Another UFO group has published *The Urantia Book*, which they claim is a collection of transmissions received by a patient of Dr. William S. Sadler from supermortals called the Revelators. This 2,000-page book, which has more than 600,000 copies in print and has been translated into seven languages, is a combination of the Bible and UFO lore. It contains 200 different sections dealing with such topics as supernatural beings, the local universe, the teachings of Jesus, and other matters dealing with Urantia (Earth).

Along with the groups talked about so far, there presently exist many other smaller groups whose belief systems center around aliens from other planets somehow affecting mankind, both for good and for evil. Sociologists claim that UFOs as the forces of good and evil are a product of our modern, technological society, that they are the modern day equivalent of elves, fairies, and angels.

"Space aliens, U.F.O.'s are playing the role that angels, God, Satan used to play," said Catherine Wessinger, a professor at Loyola University in

New Orleans. "They are unseen, superhuman powers who can hurt us or help us."[24]

Interestingly enough, in addition to all the groups I've talked about, a large segment of the United States population—nearly half according to a 1996 *Newsweek* poll—also believes in UFOs and that the earth has been visited by creatures from other planets.[25] Among the believers is Joe Firmage, a self-made millionaire and one-time CEO of USWeb, a company valued in the billions. He resigned his position as CEO, however, after claiming that an extraterrestrial had visited him. After leaving USWeb, Firmage decided to dedicate himself to spreading what he believes is the truth about UFOs and extraterrestrials: that they exist. Using his own money, he placed a full-page advertisement in *USA Today* and is paying to have his book, *The Truth,* published.

"Imagine one day we could plug our Internet into theirs," Joe told a reporter for the *Washington Post.* "That would be cool."[26]

Former astronaut Edgar Mitchell, a graduate of the Massachusetts Institute of Technology and the sixth man to walk on the moon, is another believer in UFOs. Mitchell has started a drive to persuade Congress to allow individuals with high security clearances to talk about UFOs. "Many of these folks are under high security clearances, they took oaths and they feel they cannot talk without some form of immunity," said Mitchell.[27]

One of the things Mitchell wants these people to talk about is the dispute concerning what happened in July 1947 at Roswell, New Mexico, where, according to some reports, a flying saucer crashed. Although in 1947 the federal government at first stated that it had recovered a "flying disc," it later retracted the story. Several times the federal government has stated it has no proof that UFOs or extraterrestrials exist. The problem with using this statement as proof, however, is that the federal government has lied so often, the cover-up at Waco and Agent Orange being two examples, that it is not possible to tell when the government is telling the truth. For example, my wife and I were watching a program recently on the History Channel about the health of the presidents of the United States, and about how the government has hidden the ill health of various presidents from the public. A White House spokesperson appearing on the program stated that he believed that if it is for the public good, the government should lie.

In early 2001, as part of my research for another book, I attended an international UFO conference. Hundreds of people attended this conference, and almost all, I found, believed totally in UFOs. However, the proof offered at this conference could only be described as thin to nonexistent. Although many people at the conference had anecdotes about UFO encounters, the only proof I saw offered were some videotapes of lights moving across the sky. No shapes could be distinguished in these videotapes, only lights that moved, which the audience accepted unquestion-ingly as UFOs but which I felt were more likely commercial aircraft or satellites.

At this conference, one of the individuals who claimed to be in contact with UFOs also claimed that he could have a UFO land by the hotel swim-ming pool after lunch. When, of course, nothing happened, the man tried to appease the obviously disappointed people by explaining that the UFO had sensed too much negative energy and decided not to land.

Also at the conference, several speakers claimed that 2001 was the year that the truth about UFOs would finally come out; one speaker even claimed to have inside information that the president would make an announcement about the reality of UFOs in May 2001. Of course, this didn't happen. Now a UFO group claims that 2003 will be the year.

"By the end of the year [2003], you'll see something," said George Faw-cett of the Mutual UFO Network (MUFON). "Most times we make a prophecy, it never happens. [But] I've never seen so much happen in one year."[28]

One of the interesting things I discovered at the UFO conference I attended was that many reported UFO spottings have been near a restricted area of Nevada, where conference attendees believe Area 51 is located (a supposedly top-secret base where the government keeps recov-ered alien spacecraft). True, the area is restricted, but that is because it is where the government conducts top-secret research. Stealth aircraft, for example, which certainly could be mistaken for UFOs, were reportedly developed and tested there.

The point of this chapter, however, is not to decide if the government is lying about Roswell and about extraterrestrial beings visiting us, or even whether UFOs are real or not. It is also not to evaluate the credibility or believability of any of the UFO groups. These groups simply hold to alter-native belief systems that they certainly have a right to believe in if they wish. The point of talking about them is to show that they are fertile ground for individuals like Applewhite, cult leaders who can use these belief systems for their own benefit and often to the detriment of cult members.

In the next chapter, I will discuss cults that have philosophies that are the opposite of most UFO groups. Rather than the belief that UFOs will bring the earth into a time of peace and prosperity, doomsday cults believe that the earth and all its inhabitants are heading for a future of doom, death, and destruction.

CHAPTER 9

Doomsday Cults

"The bombs are coming!" Elizabeth Clare Prophet, the leader of a cult known as the Church Universal and Triumphant, announced to her followers. "The bombs are coming!"

According to several news magazines and reports from ex-members, acting on Mrs. Prophet's warning that a nuclear holocaust was imminent in March or April 1990, several thousand members of the Church Universal and Triumphant sold their belongings, left family members who didn't belong to the church, and then streamed into the bomb shelters in Montana that they had gone deeply in debt to build. For days afterward, the members trembled as they prayed intensely, waiting underground for the Soviet attack that Elizabeth Clare Prophet had claimed would wipe out most of the United States. What brought about this belief by several thousand people that the end of the world as we know it would happen soon? Why would seemingly rational people pay huge sums of money to an organization for protection they didn't need?

In 1958, Mark L. Prophet, after making the claim that he had been contacted by the "Ascended Masters," whom he described as "immortal, God-free beings," established the Summit Lighthouse, whose declared purpose was to disseminate the teachings of the Ascended Masters. These beings, Prophet explained, were souls who have finished their cycle of reincarnation, have balanced all their karma, and now live with God, no longer having to be reborn. The method used by Mark Prophet to disseminate the teachings passed along to him by the Ascended Masters became a periodical called the *Pearls of Wisdom,* which eventually would be published weekly by his organization.

In 1961, Prophet met Elizabeth Clare Wulf, whom he later married. Mark Prophet immediately put his new wife through intense training to become another "messenger," or someone through whom the Ascended Masters could speak. She eventually became the messenger for Saint Germain and the Great White Brotherhood (*white* referring to the aura of the members, not their race). The Great White Brotherhood contains Western saints and Eastern masters. Elizabeth Clare Prophet, however, has further declared that, in addition to the Ascended Masters, "I am a messenger speaking on behalf of God."[1]

In 1966, the Prophets moved their organization from the East Coast to Colorado and then on to California. During this time, in order to spread the teachings of the Ascended Masters, they also established a Montessori school and Summit University. In 1973, however, Mark Prophet died and Elizabeth Clare Prophet assumed total control of what in 1974 would become known as the Church Universal and Triumphant. Eventually, the church would establish 230 study groups in 35 countries around the world. In 1978, the headquarters of the Church Universal and Triumphant moved to a 12,000-acre site just north of Yellowstone Park in Montana, which the group had purchased from magazine tycoon Malcolm Forbes. It was here that the church constructed the bomb shelters.

The teachings of the Church Universal and Triumphant are Judeo-Christian with a mix of Eastern mysticism. The following was posted on their Web site in late 2003: "Sponsored by the ascended masters Jesus Christ and Gautama Buddha, the church embodies principles, practices and rituals that are based on the essential truths found at the heart of all faiths. It is a church where Eastern and Western spirituality converge. The mystical paths of Hinduism, Buddhism, Judaism, Christianity, Zoroastrianism, Taoism and Confucianism are infused with new revelations from the ascended masters.... Experience the faith that brings together the oneness of the Great Tao, the Universal Christ, the Buddha, the Shekinah, the I AM THAT I AM, Brahman, and Allah."[2]

The primary theology of the Church Universal and Triumphant is that the soul must pass through many lifetimes until all its karma is balanced. Once this balance is achieved, the soul can then return, purified, to live forever with the Divine Source. To become a member of the Church Universal and Triumphant, individuals must officially accept all tenets of the church and tithe 10 percent of their income. Also, belonging to the church at one time meant strict diet restrictions, limits on the amount of sex a member could have with a spouse, rapid-fire chanting, the necessity for intense study of the works of Elizabeth Clare Prophet, and a vow of secrecy.

"Life inside the cult was chaotic," Cathleen Mann, a former member of the Church Universal and Triumphant told me in an interview. "Fear was the predominant motivator. Mrs. Prophet led with an iron fist, and her rule was law. There were extensive rituals to perform, including long hours of decreeing, which is fast-paced chanting. There were a multitude of tasks to take care of, lots of reading, and a strict environment."[3]

Recently, though, the church has loosened some of its requirements and has lessened its authoritarian structure. This has been done in an attempt to attract new members and to woo back those who left.

"I hated to be (considered) a cult," said Church Universal and Triumphant's president Gilbert Cleirbaut, whose church is on a list of disapproved religions in his home country of Belgium. "I really could understand why people were afraid of us. But at the same time they also misunderstood why we were different."[4]

As with many cults, Church Universal and Triumphant members were expected to live under the strict rules of the cult, which included a frugal lifestyle, but these rules didn't apply to Elizabeth Clare Prophet. Elizabeth reportedly likes to indulge herself in the finer things of life, including expensive clothing, costly jewelry, an elegant house, and first-class travel.

"She was the head of the organization, she deserved nice things," said former church member Peter Arnone. "The church has an explanation for everything. They said, 'She meets dignitaries from all over the world and needs to make an elegant presentation.' But she lived an ostentatious lifestyle compared to the way her staff was living."[5] Reportedly, at one time, Elizabeth Clare Prophet had ten members of her staff assigned to a one-bedroom apartment.

Arnone further stated that he left the church at Christmas in 1992, disgusted with the control that he says dictated what colors to wear, who to marry, and even when husbands and wives could have sex. "This is a very destructive organization," he adds. "It has hurt many, many people."[6]

"The group taught you to view Mrs. Prophet as 'the mother of the universe,'" Cathleen Mann told me. "In fact, she was called Mother by all her followers. She demanded (and got) instant and complete obedience. She was worshipped as a god walking the Earth."[7]

In the late 1980s, Elizabeth Clare Prophet claimed that she had begun receiving messages from the Ascended Masters warning her that a nuclear holocaust was imminent. At Prophet's direction, church members borrowed money and mortgaged their homes to pay for bomb shelters at the Montana headquarters (most cult members didn't worry about going into debt because they believed the nuclear devastation would wipe out their debts anyway). Prices for the bomb shelters ranged from $5,000 to $200,000. Church members additionally purchased stockpiles of food, water, batteries, clothing, and other necessities. Many cult members thought that weapons would be needed because looters were likely to appear after the holocaust. To this end, Prophet's fourth husband, Edward Francis, purchased $100,000 worth of semiautomatic weapons and 120,000 rounds of ammunition under a false name, for which the police arrested him and he served a jail sentence in 1989. After getting out of jail, he left Mrs. Prophet and ran off with the children's nanny.

When Elizabeth Clare Prophet finally announced to her congregation that the Ascended Masters had told her the nuclear holocaust would come in March or April 1990, several thousand cult members headed for the bomb shelters. When the nuclear attack didn't come, however, the church lost many members who felt they had been defrauded, but many also remained, believing that it was only their intense prayer that had averted the attack.

Not discouraged by the failure of her 1990 prediction of a nuclear doomsday, in late 1996, Prophet reportedly told her congregation, "We need your sacrifice. The world is about to fail. I don't know where the bombs are coming from. But we must be ready."[8]

In January 1998, however, doctors diagnosed Elizabeth Clare Prophet with epilepsy and Alzheimer's disease; consequently, she has retired from an active role in the church. Because of Prophet's poor health, the failed prophecies about a nuclear disaster, and the resulting loss of a large percentage of the church membership, the Church Universal and Triumphant has lately fallen onto hard financial times. In addition, the cult leaders are having a difficult time explaining the apparent incongruity of how the messenger specially selected by the Ascended Masters could be struck down with a disease such as Alzheimer's.

"Elizabeth Clare Prophet has been the magnet for this movement and she's running out of gas," said Arnone, who belonged to the cult for 22 years. "America is not as naive as it used to be. People are more distrustful of cults with charismatic leaders."[9]

Recently, breakaway members of the Church Universal and Triumphant have formed their own group in Vermont called the Temple of the Presence. Several members of this congregation claim that because illness prevents Elizabeth Clare Prophet from serving as a messenger for the Ascended Masters, they have been chosen as the new messengers. The Church Universal and Triumphant, of course, disputes this claim, even though the church is yet to name a successor messenger for Mrs. Prophet.

In an attempt to relieve its money problems, the Church Universal and Triumphant has, in the last five years, laid off several hundred of its workers and is selling off some of its property in Montana. The new leadership of the Church Universal and Triumphant is also attempting to remove the stigma of being a doomsday cult, and is instead trying to move the organization more toward the mainstream.

"To speak about those things is to go constantly backwards to that bad reputation that we had," said Church Universal and Triumphant president Gilbert Cleirbaut, speaking about the church's "shelter phase" in the 1980s and 1990s. "That's why I don't want to go back to the shelters…[We need to] position our church in a way that there is less focus on the guns, but more on what are the good things [we] do, where we are a benefit to society rather than we create problems to society."[10]

However, not everyone agrees with this new stance. "The idea of cataclysm has been a part of the church's thinking since the beginning," said Erin Prophet, Elizabeth's daughter and a former church official. "They really can't just turn around and say that's not what we're about anymore."[11]

Practically everyone has seen the cartoon with a character wearing the sandwich sign that proclaims, "The End Is Near!" While this is meant as a joke, throughout history a large number of people have proclaimed with all seriousness that they have unique knowledge that the end of the world is coming. Through this proclamation, many prophets of doom have attracted large groups of followers who believe that these doom forecasters have some type of special insight, special vision, or special relationship with God that gives them inside knowledge about the impending end of the world. Once this belief system is established, the doomsday forecasters then have tremendous control over the lives of the people who believe in them.

In June 1523, for example, a group of astrologers in London predicted that on February 1, 1524, the end of the world would begin with a huge flood that would inundate London. Their prediction caused a widespread panic, and because of the prediction, more than 20,000 people left their homes and headed for high ground.

In 1831, a farmer named William Miller announced that his in-depth study of the Bible had determined that Jesus would be returning to Earth on April 3, 1843, and on that day, God would take the faithful to heaven and then destroy the world and all its sinners. When this date passed with no Second Coming, Miller recalculated and stated that the actual date was July 7, 1843, then March 21, 1844, and finally October 22, 1844. On each date, thousands of Miller's followers gathered on hilltops all across the country, devoutly and intensely praying as they waited for the end to come. Even after "The Great Disappointment," as October 22, 1844, became known, many of Miller's estimated 100,000 followers, who eventually became known as Seventh Day Adventists, remained faithful to him.

More recently, in 1963, Richard Kieninger wrote a book titled *The Ultimate Frontier*, in which he tells how at age 12 he met Mr. White, who represented the Brotherhoods, a group of galactic leaders and earthly religious leaders (Jesus, Buddha, Mohammed, etc.). White told Kieninger that, even though Kieninger was only a reincarnated Egyptian pharaoh, the Brotherhoods had chosen him as the person who was to prepare the world for its ultimate destruction, first predicted by Kieninger to occur before 1976. Kieninger often claimed that America would never see its 200th birthday. In 1970, Kieninger and a group of his followers purchased

240 acres of farmland in Illinois and founded the town of Stelle, building it to withstand the coming earthquakes and other calamities.

The town of Stelle, constructed around the idea of survival, and so consequently allowing only those who subscribed to the group's beliefs to live there, eventually threw Kieninger out when his womanizing came to light. Kieninger moved to Texas, where he founded a new doomsday group, the Adelphi Organization, and also designated a new date for the end of the world, May 5, 2000, when a planetary alignment would reportedly tear the earth apart. The town of Stelle, in the years following the ouster of Kieninger, eventually moved away from many of its former doomsday beliefs and now allows nonbelievers to live there.

More recently, in June 2002, Australian news media reported that the Catholic Church outlawed a cult within the church called the Order of St. Charbel. The leader of the Order of St. Charbel is William Kamm, a lay worker also known as Little Pebble. His followers believe he will likely be the next pope. Over the years, Kamm has predicted many doomsday-type catastrophes. Living in New South Wales, Australia, Kamm claims that the Virgin Mary speaks to him on the 13th of each month at 3:00 P.M. At these encounters, Mary passes on the prophecies he publishes. Some of the doomsday prophecies Kamm has made include America would be annihilated by nuclear weapons in 1986, the Antichrist would take over the world in 1990, Halley's comet would destroy the earth, Pope John Paul II would announce that Little Pebble would be the next Pope, and a tidal wave would engulf the island of Guam in 1993.

Although Kamm has prophesied hundreds of unfulfilled calamities, the failure of all these predictions has not discouraged him. In a June 27, 2002, press release, Kamm stated, "Over the years I have announced to the world many prophecies relative to serious events.... [I]t is a fact that not all of them have eventuated at the time suggested, but you should keep in mind that none of them have been canceled. Rest assured, those yet to come are now much closer than before."[12]

In a July 10, 2002, press release, Kamm made more dire predictions: the Pope will turn up missing, the stock market will collapse, a comet will strike the earth and kill one-fourth of the population, a white cross will be seen in the sky for seven days as a harbinger of the "end times," and other calamities.[13] In an earlier press release, Kamm claimed that the Virgin Mary had revealed to him that Comet 76P Kohoutek had struck the moons of Mars and that one of the moons, Phobos, had been sent on a collision course with Earth. Because of this approaching catastrophe, he advised his followers to stock up on drinking water, canned and dried food, warm clothing, and medical supplies.

While this sounds like a person suffering from serious delusions, the Order of St. Charbel reportedly has 500,000 members in 160 countries. The Catholic Church, in issuing its decree outlawing the cult, said that

Kamm's teachings are false, harmful, and contrary to the teachings of the Catholic Church. Reportedly, most members of this cult take Kamm's predictions very seriously; consequently, their beliefs have broken up families because of conflicts between believers and nonbelievers, and have financially strapped cult members trying to prepare for the end of the world.

Catholic Bishop Peter Ingham said in the decree outlawing the Order of St. Charbel that the cult has sparked many family breakdowns. "[T]hose apparition messages are clearly not of supernatural origin," said Bishop Ingham, "but they affect people's lives, if people take him seriously, they follow him."[14]

On August 9, 2002, the police in New South Wales, Australia, arrested William Kamm and charged him with four counts of Aggravated Sexual Assault, one count of Aggravated Indecent Assault, and one count of Aggravated Act of Indecency. These crimes reportedly involve sexual acts with the children of cult members.

Naturally, the first question that will come to the minds of most readers is, Why do cult members stay in cults once the predictions of the cult leaders have proven to be false, and even more so, as in the case of Kamm, proven to be false numerous times? Interestingly, social scientists have found that, while a false prediction, doomsday or otherwise, will cause some cult members to leave, it actually strengthens the belief and commitment of many cult members. I will discuss this phenomenon much more thoroughly in chapter 14, but suffice it to say here that the doomsday predictors themselves are also seldom discouraged when their predictions fail. They usually just set a new date for the doomsday or predict a new type of approaching catastrophe.

Another question many readers might ask is, Why do some cult leaders make predictions of doom over and over? The reason is that to keep members in the cult, cult leaders need to ingrain followers with a sense of uniqueness and importance, with a sense they are the only group on Earth with their purpose. What better way to do this than by proclaiming a future doomsday that only the cult members will survive or that only the cult members can prevent? Also, to justify making cult members work extremely hard for extremely long hours, cult leaders need a reason for this sense of urgency. What better method than to forecast a fast-approaching doom that only the cult members can prevent or survive through their hard work?

According to social scientists, doomsday groups tend to form in times of rapid social and cultural change as a way for people confounded by these changes to deal with them. But occasionally, regardless of the prevailing social atmosphere and conditions, doomsday cults form simply as a means for the leaders to steal money or possessions from their followers. For example, in July 2000, newspapers reported that a court in South

Korea sentenced two doomsday cult leaders to 10 years in prison for swindling cult members out of an estimated $35 million. The cult, called Chunjunhoe, or Heaven's Gathering, reportedly had 150,000 members and a theology built around Confucianism. The cult leaders had encouraged members to sell all their worldly belongings and give the proceeds to the cult before the world ended on February 19, 2000, when the earth would lose its spiritual energy. Prosecutors said the authorities had discovered that the cult leaders were preparing to leave the country with their members' money several days before the announced doomsday.

Of course, occasionally doomsday cult predictions that don't come true can backfire in other ways on the cult leaders. In September 1999, the authorities in Indonesia reported that three cult leaders had been beaten to death by cult members who had been told that the world would end when the calendar turned to 9/9/99. The cult members had reportedly sold all their possessions and given the proceeds to the leaders in preparation for the end of the world.

"The members were really mad," said a village chief in East Java.[15]

As has been shown throughout history, the threat of an approaching doomsday is the perfect vehicle around which to form a cult. Not only does the leader offer cult members a way to escape the certain death and destruction of the doomsday, but preparing for the impending global disaster gives cult members a sense of urgency and importance, which the leader can use to justify exhorting them to work harder and harder and longer and longer for the cult. Also, when cult members truly and completely accept the belief in an impending doom, it is much easier for the leader of the cult to persuade them to give up all their worldly goods, or, as in the case of the Church Universal and Triumphant, to borrow money and mortgage property for the cult. After all, none of it will matter anyway because the world is about to end.

Doomsday cults are not the only type of cults that forecast a dark future for their members. In the next chapter, I will discuss a type of cult that also does this and which is, without a doubt, the most dangerous type of cult to its members and occasionally even to nonmembers: the suicide cult. As I will show, suicide cult leaders, though obviously psychologically troubled since they usually take part themselves in the group suicide, must have tremendous charisma and persuasive powers. They must be able to convince cult members that group suicide is not only the necessary and proper thing for the group to do but also that it will be a personally rewarding act.

CHAPTER 10

Suicide Cults

On October 5, 1994, as reported by hundreds of news outlets, authorities in Switzerland discovered 23 bodies in the burned ruins of a farmhouse in Cheiry. The same day, 50 miles away, other Swiss authorities uncovered 25 bodies in three burned chalets in Granges-sur-Salvan in the Alps. Across the ocean on that day, Canadian authorities discovered 5 burned bodies in a villa in Morin Heights, about 50 miles northwest of Montreal. In December 1995, authorities searching a burned house near Grenoble in the French Alps found 16 bodies. In March 1997, the Canadian authorities uncovered 5 burned bodies in St. Casmir, about 50 miles southwest of Quebec City. What did all these tragedies have in common? Most of the adult victims belonged to a cult known as the Solar Temple.

Formally known as the International Chivalric Order Solar Tradition, the Solar Temple cult was believed to have had nearly 600 members at its height. One of the leaders of the cult, Luc Jouret, a homeopath physician, had convinced his followers that he was the reincarnation of a fourteenth-century member of the Order of the Knights Templar. He also claimed that his daughter, Emmanuelle, was a "cosmic child" who had been conceived without sex. Preaching a mixture of Christianity, New Age philosophy, ecological doomsday predictions, and Eastern mysticism, Jouret convinced his followers that death was only an illusion and that by committing ritual suicide and leaving their bodies behind on Earth, they would be reborn on a world that orbited the star Sirius.

In this case, unlike the Heaven's Gate cult, it wouldn't be alien spaceships that would transport the cult members to their new home, but rather the spirits of Ascended Masters who would help convey the souls of cult

members across the vastness of space to their new home on another
world. However, Jouret also preached that before the group could leave
for Sirius, their sins committed while on Earth must and could only be
expiated by fire and that, most importantly, the fiery suicide ceremony
had to take place during a solar equinox. In compliance with these ceremonial requirements, some of the cult members rigged up propane tanks
and gasoline so that they would explode and burn down the houses in
which they lay waiting.

Unlike most cults, however, the members of the Solar Temple didn't live
together in a commune, but rather lived in their own homes. Many of the
cult members had been wealthy, educated, and influential people. Members included politicians, businessmen, a journalist, police officers, a psychotherapist, an architect, and civil servants. Also unlike most cults, the
members often hid their membership from friends and family members.

However, very much like most cults, the Solar Temple offered its members something they craved: a feeling of being involved in a unique and
monumental undertaking. Jouret offered cult members the promise of an
opportunity to escape from a dying planet and, more important, the
promise of eternal life. He preached to the cult members that they were
part of a specially selected, elite group.

"We went about our daily lives, but we didn't belong to this world,"
said a former Solar Temple member. "Jouret made us feel we were a chosen and privileged congregation."[1]

As with most cults, however, belonging to the Solar Temple cost the
members dearly. Some members reportedly gave the cult more than
$1 million, which cult leaders Jouret and Joseph Di Mambro, who had ear-
lier led a cult known as the Foundation Golden Way, spent lavishly on
themselves. Some reports claim that the cult leaders amassed more than
$92 million.

In October 1994, when authorities started discovering the bodies of
Solar Temple members at the various suicide locations around the world,
they found that some of the victims lay in a starburst pattern on the floor,
their feet pointing toward each other, while in other locations the bodies
formed crosses. They also found many of the Solar Temple members
wearing long flowing gowns of different colors, which apparently designated rank within the cult. But the police also discovered something more.
A number of the dead hadn't committed suicide but had been murdered.
Authorities described the burned-out scenes as mass murders followed by
mass suicides. At one of the scenes, for example, police discovered a 3-
month-old boy, who Solar Temple leaders had labeled as the Antichrist,
with a wooden stake driven through his heart. His parents were found
nearby, stabbed to death. At another scene, two girls, age 2 and 4, the
daughters of Solar Temple members, had been shot through the forehead.
Several of the adult victims had as many as eight bullet wounds, while

others had been poisoned. Apparently true to their beliefs, Jouret and Di Mambro lay among the corpses authorities discovered on October 5, 1994.

During the mass suicide/murder that occurred near Grenoble in December 1995, reportedly 14 individuals, including three children of the cult members, ages 6 years, 4 years, and 19 months, were given the sedatives myolastan and digoxine. After the medications took effect, two other cult members, one a police officer and the other an architect, shot the 14 individuals with rifles and then arranged their bodies in a ceremonial pattern. The two men then killed themselves, and afterward, all 16 individuals burned in a preset fire that consumed the building in which they lay. This group had reportedly felt "left out" when the original three groups of Solar Temple members died in ceremonies on October 5, 1994, and wanted to catch up with them.

As the only partially bright moment of these incidents, in the Canadian suicide in 1997, three teenage children of Solar Temple members talked their parents into sparing them. The parents drugged the teenagers and placed them in a shed near the suicide scene. The parents then died in a fiery explosion of propane tanks and gasoline.

"Physically speaking, the kids are doing fine," said an agent of the Quebec Youth Protection Agency. "But psychologically speaking, they are traumatized and under a state of shock."[2]

Naturally, police in Europe and Canada conducted investigations into the deaths, but most of those responsible, they found, had died in the explosions. One of the alleged leaders of the Solar Temple cult, though, did stand trial. However, on June 25, 2001, a French court cleared Swiss orchestra conductor Michel Tabachnik of any crimes involving the deaths of Solar Temple members. Prosecutors had charged him with allegedly inciting cult members to take part in suicide pacts. During his trial, Tabachnik admitted he'd had links to the Solar Temple, but he denied any role in the deaths. Witnesses at the trial claimed that Tabachnik had written much of the cult's literature and was third in command of the group. However, French authorities appealed the acquittal, and a new trial was set for june 2004.

Unfortunately, the story of the Solar Temple may not be over. There still exists a sizable number of Solar Temple members worldwide. "Yes, there are Solar Temple members remaining in Quebec," said Pierre Robichaud of the Quebec Provincial Police. "They say they are inactive but, unfortunately, we cannot say without doubt that, yes, they are inactive."[3]

While the incidents just described would certainly strike most readers as bizarre, they are by no means unique. In January 1998, according to newspaper reports, Spanish police on the island of Tenerife in the Canary Islands raided a group of apartments and arrested a German psychotherapist, Heide Fittkau-Garthe, who police said was going to lead her cult in a group suicide. Reportedly, Fittkau-Garthe had convinced cult members that the earth was about to be destroyed by an "Earth-axis leap," and that the only way to escape the coming doom was to climb to the top of a dormant volcano on Tenerife, where they would be rescued by an alien spaceship. If the ship didn't appear, she told cult members, they were then to commit a mass suicide.

Thirty-two Germans and one Spaniard, most well educated and financially comfortable, had just days before boarded planes for the Canary Islands when Fittkau-Garthe contacted and told them that the time for the end of the world had come. Fortunately, a relative of one of the cult members alerted the police, and they stepped in and averted a possible tragedy. In the leader's apartment, the police found poisonous chemicals they believed were going to be used in the mass suicide.

On May 22, 1999, a court charged Fittkau-Garthe with attempted murder in the mass suicide plan. The court ordered her to be held without bond.

Just the thought that a loved one might belong to a suicide cult should send icicles through the veins of any normal person. But how could a cult leader hold such power over seemingly intelligent people? The individuals in the incident just described and those who died in the Solar Temple cult tragedy, for example, were mostly well-off financially and highly educated. How can a cult leader convince apparently rational, intelligent people that committing suicide will lead them to a better life in another world or dimension?

I will answer this question in more detail in a later chapter; here it is sufficient to say that the dynamics of cult life make such decisions seem rational and reasonable at the time to cult members. The members have come to hold the cult leader in such awe and esteem that they believe that every word he or she tells them comes directly from God or some other indisputable source, so it must be true.

"The seducing aspects of the leader's teaching can lull members into a very distorted emotional space where they can lose their ability to determine what is appropriate or not appropriate," says Rosemarie White, clinical director of the Institute for Suicide Prevention in Los Angeles. "So death becomes something to be welcomed for reasons that the leader explains."[4]

Often, as I will show and as some of the incidents talked about so far have already shown, it can also be deteriorating events either inside or outside the cult that can push cult leaders into deciding that mass suicide is the answer. For example, preceding the Solar Temple suicides, there had apparently been a considerable amount of squabbling and dissension within the cult. Reportedly, a number of Solar Temple members and ex-members had been complaining about the extravagant spending of Jouret and Di Mambro. That, and a government investigation allegedly under way into the Solar Temple, could have been what led Jouret and Di Mambro to conduct the mass suicides on two continents. In the case of Jim Jones and the Peoples Temple, described in chapter 3, it was also dissension within the group and pressures coming from outside the group, specifically Congressman Leo Ryan's investigation, that pushed Jim Jones into the final White Night mass suicide.

"History shows that a suicide event in a cult is often tied to some force outside the cult—one that is pushing it ever deeper into a psychological position of defense," says an article in the *Christian Science Monitor*. "The cult leader may begin to lose power, or the calculations of the leader on the basis of reality begin to lessen."[5]

In addition, suicide cult leaders often possess an apocalyptic view of the world, and as a consequence many times forecast an imminent doomsday. Because the world is going to end anyway, and usually in a violent way, suicide, the leader preaches, is a viable option to escape this, particularly since the group, because of its special mission, will be taken directly into heaven, to some other dimension, or to another planet.

Regardless of the cause or the reasons, mass suicides within cults seem to keep occurring and likely will continue to occur as long as cult members continue to follow charismatic, but unstable, leaders. This thought alone should be enough to galvanize opposition to cult membership by family members and friends of anyone considering joining a cult. It was this fear that caused family members to go to a judge to have the police retrieve a 16-year-old girl from the God's Salvation Church cult in Garland, Texas, talked about in chapter 3. The family feared that when the cult leader's predictions failed to come true and God didn't appear worldwide on television or come to Earth in a spaceship, then the cult leader might feel backed into a corner and do something drastic, such as order a mass suicide. Considering the many past tragedies in such cults, the actions of the family were certainly prudent.

For any reader who believes that suicide cults were just a problem of the twentieth century, or for anyone who believes that since the new millennium has arrived without a Second Coming or the end of the world that this type of thinking has stopped, I can say unequivocally that this is not true. The following recent incidents demonstrate that suicidal thinking within cults is still alive and well.

In April 2000, the police in Peru rescued 86 members of a cult who, believing that the world was about to end, had been convinced by cult leaders that a ritual, collective suicide by starvation was the only way to salvation. The cult leaders, arrested by the Peruvian police, had also convinced cult members to sell all their property and give them the proceeds.

On October 31, 2001, according to European news reports, prosecutors in the Netherlands announced that they had opened a criminal investigation into a cult called the Efraim Society, which has its headquarters in the small Dutch town of Puttershoek, though the meetings of the cult are held in secret, undisclosed locations. The leader of the cult, Heinrich vanGeene, claims that he is the reincarnation of the prophet Elijah. The task of the cult, which authorities believe numbers around 100 people, is to gather the "Bride of Christ" so that this group can be raptured. The Bride of Christ are selected people who believe in and ascribe to the cult's theology and, according to the cult's leader, will be the only ones raptured.

Although on its Web site, which is translated into 11 languages, the Efraim Society claims not to be a cult, most of the message sounds very much like a cult. For example, the Web site states, "Read, if possible quietly, as much of this Web site as possible and ask God the Holy Spirit if he will help you understand it. If you are touched by Him, don't let go then and, particularly, do not listen to others."[6]

As this statement shows, cult leaders never want prospective or current cult members to talk over what they are being told by the cult with someone not attached to the cult. They want no outside, unbiased opinions concerning what the leaders are telling cult members and prospective recruits. In furtherance of this cutoff from outside sources of information, vanGeene has ordered Efraim Society members to get rid of all televisions, radios, magazines, and newspapers. He has also ordered them to resign from any church they belong to.

Like most cult leaders, vanGeene claims to have access to knowledge unknown to others. For example, the Efraim Society Web site states, "We are allowed to understand God's will and the mysteries that God has hidden in the Bible more than anyone."

The Web site goes on to say, "Leave everything behind you. Truly everything!.. Putting it very bluntly, you will have to hate everyone who doesn't agree with you, and especially everyone who is against you choosing the Lord. Don't let opponents of God confuse you by saying 'But isn't God love?' or such false arguments. No one can ever match the love of God or even comprehend the scope of it. But He hates anyone who wants to take you, who are His Bride, away from Him, and He expects you to hate them too. Beware also of close family. When the devil has the opportunity he will certainly use this family to take you away from your heavenly Bridegroom."[7]

Cult leaders like vanGeene usually try to shut cult members off from any outside relationships, family or otherwise, and from any voices of reason that could counter what the cult leaders are saying. Cult leaders also usually try to instill an "us against them" mentality within the cult. As can be seen from the message on the Efraim Society Web site, this is exactly what this cult is trying to do.

On his Web site, vanGeene has proclaimed several dates for the end of the world and the consequent rapture for the members of his cult: late September 2001; November 7, 2001; November 11, 2001; November 21, 2001; and December 21, 2001. When the rapture didn't occur on any of these dates, vanGeene explained it by saying that God had postponed the rapture because the Efraim Society had not met two necessary preconditions.

"The bride must be good enough, and must be full in number," vanGeene says. "After all, God says, 'My house must be filled.' Supposedly we do not yet meet one or possibly both conditions."[8]

While these proclamations sound like those of any fervent religious sect, what started the authorities investigating the Efraim Society was that parents who belonged to the cult had taken their children out of school in anticipation of the end of the world. In addition, in expectation of the pending rapture, the children's parents had quit their jobs. But what really concerned the authorities was a statement attributed to vanGeene: "If He (God) doesn't come for us, we will go ourselves."[9] Given the number of vanGeene's failed prophecies for the end of the world, the authorities fear that vanGeene might soon begin to worry that the members of his cult will start to have doubts about his legitimacy, and, as implied in his statement, in his desperation to keep control he might engineer a mass suicide.

In another cult incident reported in European newspapers in September 2002, the French police went on alert because of the possibility of a mass suicide by a cult called the New Lighthouse Movement, which reportedly believed that the world would end on October 24, 2002. The group also believed that before the end of the world, they would be transported by flying saucers to a new life on the planet Venus. This cult includes a doctor, a civil servant, and a teacher. The leader of the group, who had previously been a hitchhiker in the area, had earlier forecast that the world would end in February 2002 and then on July 11, 2002. When the July date passed without the prophesied apocalypse and consequent rescue by flying saucers, one member of the cult killed himself and two others attempted suicide. Authorities ordered the alert because they worried that the cult leader, fearing dissension in his group, might lead the cult in a mass suicide when his third prediction fails.

Also in September 2002, three members of a Buddhist-based cult in Cambodia committed suicide by self-immolation. Three other cult members attempted suicide by stabbing themselves with knives, but all three survived.

"They poured 60 liters of gasoline into bathtubs, sat in them and then set fire to them," said Chhim Sakhon, a police official in Cambodia. "We could not save their lives."[10]

Apparently, the leader of the cult had convinced members that ritual suicide was the only way that cult members could get into heaven. However, while preaching the necessity of ritual suicide, the leader of the cult backed out of killing himself at the last moment. He later told the police that he didn't have to take part in the ritual suicide because he was already holy enough.

"The ringleader was smart," said Sakhon, "he didn't do it."[11]

As the events described in this chapter clearly show, certain cults can be extraordinarily dangerous. In these cults, members don't have to worry as much about losing their life's savings, their identity, and their relationship with family members as they do losing their very lives. But what really makes suicide cults dangerous is that cult leaders bent on group suicide are seldom willing to allow reluctant members to escape, but, as I have shown with Jim Jones and the Solar Temple, are instead often ready to force the individuals to take part in the cult's death.

While I have listed cults so far in categories that describe their main characteristics, it has been obvious that some cults share traits with several types. However, as I will show in the next chapter, some cults are so different or so unusual they simply can't be placed into a specific category.

CHAPTER 11

Other Cults

"It's all very stimulating stuff in the beginning...," said a former member of the Fellowship of Friends in a 1996 *Los Angeles Times* article. "But there's no doubt it's a cult. Our lives were totally controlled."[1]

Is this man talking about a cult formed around a wild-eyed guru who preaches that all members should embrace poverty and the simple life? Is he talking about a cult that rejects all worldly pleasures, and whose members spend their days praying, chanting, or meditating?

Hardly. According to reports in several California newspapers, the Fellowship of Friends is a pleasure- and consumer-oriented cult. Founded in 1971 by former schoolteacher Robert Burton, the Fellowship of Friends believes that true spiritual awakening can only come through experiencing the finest things life has to offer: fine food, fine wine, great art, great writers, great music. In his book *Self Remembering*, Burton stresses "the education and discipline of the emotions, the importance of living in the present, a love of beauty, and an understanding of its capacity to create higher awareness."[2]

True to his beliefs, Burton, who lived out of his car before founding the Fellowship of Friends, has built a lavish mansion, which he named Apollo, in the style of a French chateau on a 1,300-acre estate in the northern California Sierra foothills. There, among terraced hills supporting a vineyard that produces award-winning wines, the members of the Fellowship of Friends can come and study under a man whom they believe to be both spiritually advanced and a prophet.

Burton, who claims he is guided by 44 angels, including Benjamin Franklin, Jesus, and Plato, is believed by members of the Fellowship of Friends to be near godlike and also privy to information from "higher sources." As a result of his claimed direct contact with these angels and higher sources, Burton predicted that an earthquake in 1998 would swallow up all of California, except for Apollo. He has also predicted that a nuclear holocaust will destroy most of world in 2006, but again spare Apollo, which will then become the center of the movement to reestablish civilization in the post-holocaust world.

While his prediction of a California-swallowing earthquake, of course, didn't come true, this didn't humble Burton. He carries on as though he'd never made a mistake. Like most cult leaders, Burton either ignores or attempts to rationalize his mistakes, while also attempting to control every aspect of his followers' lives. Within the Fellowship of Friends, this control includes regulating the members' sex lives and diets, ordering them to abstain from any form of negativity, and even directing them to abstain from the use of certain common words, such as *I* or *thing*. Burton has also forbidden members to dye their hair, have mixed-breed pets, ride bicycles, or smoke. Smoking, incidentally, is so strenuously outlawed that Burton has instructed cult members to sniff when greeting each other to catch renegades. Burton fined one couple $1,500 each for violating the no-smoking rule. One former member of the Fellowship of Friends claimed that the cult leaders, besides barring him from having sex with his girlfriend, also ordered him to urinate only on the side of the toilet so as to make less noise. While most Fellowship of Friends members have jobs and homes, Burton discourages members from mingling or socializing with people outside the Fellowship, including family, whom Burton sees as "spiritually dead."

The leadership of the Fellowship of Friends doesn't see these constraints as brainwashing, however. "The Fellowship does not engage in brainwashing," said Girard Haven, a member of the group's board of directors. "We may have a charismatic leader and strong feelings about higher forces and our own spirituality, but we know what we are doing. We are not doing it blindly."[3]

Unlike many cults, though, the Fellowship of Friends doesn't recruit from the masses, but instead recruits mainly from groups of well-educated and well-heeled individuals. New recruits are often located after Fellowship of Friends members go to bookstores and plant Fellowship of Friends' bookmarks in selected metaphysical books that reflect the beliefs of the cult. Prospective members who respond to the telephone number on the bookmark are invited to attend lavish dinners at expensive homes. Only after being appraised by Fellowship of Friends members can prospective recruits be invited to join the cult, whose membership includes many doctors, lawyers, artists, and musicians.

Recruiting well-heeled members certainly paid off. In the late 1990s, the Fellowship of Friends had 65 centers around the world (in late 2003, their Web site, which is translated into 10 languages, states that they now have only 30 centers) and employed approximately 500 people. The group's overall worth in the late 1990s was estimated at $26 million, while Burton's annual salary was at least $250,000. Many of the Fellowship of

Friends' employees work at the cult's winery, which is located on their property in northern California. According to recent news articles, the Fellowship of Friends produces 25,000 cases of wine a year, which is reported to be of high quality.

Along with the winery, the Fellowship of Friends has its own collections of fine art and rare literature, as well as its own opera company, orchestra, theater troupe, and museum. In addition, Burton has decorated the mansion at Apollo with expensive antiques and paintings. One of Burton's favorite sayings is, "Beauty creates its likeness in those who pursue it."[4]

Because of all these expensive possessions, belonging to the Fellowship of Friends is naturally very costly. The cult requires members to tithe 10 percent of their incomes, while wealthy members pay much more, in special assessments, to enable the Fellowship of Friends to purchase sculpture, paintings, rare books, antiques, and other items that will "lift the spirituality" of the cult members. The annual income of the Fellowship of Friends in the mid-1990s exceeded $5 million.

However, all is not rosy for the Fellowship of Friends. In recent years, large numbers of its members have been leaving, causing a serious cash flow problem. The trouble began for the Fellowship of Friends in 1995 when a cult member sent an open letter to the membership accusing Burton of sexually seducing him. He said Burton brainwashes members into a state of "absolute submission," allowing him to feed a "voracious appetite for sexual perversion."[5] Following this disclosure, other male members came forward with similar accusations, including the cult's former financial officer, who said he felt pressured to join Burton's male harem.

"They don't see it coming, and when it comes, they don't know what's happened," said Charles Randall about Burton's aggressive homosexual advances toward Fellowship of Friends members.[6]

Another male member of the cult who also claimed Burton aggressively pressured him into having sex said, "I had never had a homosexual encounter before this. But he [Burton] told me it was the wish of C-influence (the group's term for higher forces, or gods) that I have sex with him."[7] At all-male dinners hosted by Burton, members say he has been known to boast that "one hundred boys would not be enough [for his sexual appetite]."[8]

To these charges, Burton's attorney has responded, "We don't think a [sexual] relationship between a leader and a member of the congregation is abusive in and of itself."[9] However, two lawsuits filed by former Fellowship of Friends members claiming sexual abuse have been settled out of court.

Former Fellowship of Friends officials who have left the cult also aren't kind in their evaluation of Burton and his organization. "The Fellowship is a dictatorship, a predatory dictatorship," said Thomas Easley, an artist and former leader who left the cult after a homosexual relationship with Burton. "I should know. I was a leader."[10]

Former Fellowship of Friends financial officer Charles Randall said, "I thought it was the one true way, but as it turns out, it was just a cult."[11]

The point to the preceding anecdote is that a cult can be formed around almost any belief or philosophy. Also, this anecdote shows that, to succeed, a cult doesn't have to be aimed at the uneducated, the emotionally challenged, or the poor. As shown by both the Fellowship of Friends and the Solar Temple (discussed in the previous chapter), cults can also attract well-educated, wealthy, and seemingly mentally competent people. All that's needed is a charismatic leader who followers believe has some type of special insight, some type of special knowledge unknown to the rest of the world, or some type of special direct pipeline to God or ascended beings. To attract followers, the cult leader then offers to share this information or knowledge with cult members. This belief in the leader's gift quickly becomes a strong magnet that pulls people in because gaining this insight or knowledge from the cult leader, members believe, will make them part of an elite group who are a step above regular human beings.

This special insight of the cult leader, incidentally, doesn't have to be only knowledge gained through conversations with spirits, ghosts, or God. Some cults can be formed because followers believe that their leader has a special insight into how to make the world a better place. For example, according to a 1996 article in the *New York Times* and other news accounts, Eugenio Perente-Ramos believed that a revolution of the working class against the ruling-class bureaucracy could occur at any moment, and that he would figure prominently in both the revolution and the world afterward. The world following the revolution, he preached, would be a working-class paradise. With this belief system, Perente-Ramos founded a cult that recruited many idealistic, politically left-leaning college students. His cult went by several names, including the National Labor Federation, the Provisional Communist Party, the Eastern Farm Workers' Association, and the Women's Press Collective. Perente-Ramos convinced his followers that they were part of a great underground movement that would right society's wrongs and bring social justice to the world.

As with most cults, however, once in Perente-Ramos's group, members found themselves expected to give total and complete obedience to both the leaders and the rules of the organization, which included communal living with other cult members in a group of Brooklyn buildings called "the cave." Although most members thought they would be helping the poor escape their plight, they instead spent most of their time in fundraising and in doing hour after hour of meaningless paperwork. Additionally, in the evenings, leaders required the members to attend political lectures that often continued until the early morning hours.

"Time was precious," said a former National Labor Federation member. "Every minute was pre-scheduled. They kept you so busy that you didn't have time to think about leaving."[12]

Like most cults, every detail of daily life for individuals in the National Labor Federation became strictly regimented. Every task had to be accomplished according to detailed written instructions. Even things as simple as how and where to lay a pencil on the desk had been spelled out in a manual for cult members.

"And once you start working for them you are so busy with the minutiae that you don't realize that they aren't living up to their promises," said a former cult member. "They would talk all this revolution then take in all of this money, and then they wouldn't do a thing."[13]

In 1996, following up on a routine complaint of a crying baby, the police in New York City arrested 35 members of the National Labor Federation at their Brooklyn headquarters and seized 26 rifles, 5 shotguns, 16 pistols, and 2 machine guns. They also confiscated five canisters of black powder, which can be used in making explosive devices. The police, though, found no indication of what the cult had planned to do with all these firearms and explosives.

Cult leaders like Perente-Ramos like to tell or write boastful autobiographies of themselves, but reality is almost always much less exciting. A former wife of Perente-Ramos stated that he was actually born Gerald William Doeden in Idaho, had changed his name several times, and was unstable. Additionally, she said that he had greatly exaggerated his involvement with Cesar Chavez's labor movement and his relationship with Chavez. Nonetheless, though Perente-Ramos died in 1995, his organization still exists today.

"It was a totalitarian cult which trained its cadres to believe they were the only true revolutionaries in the United States," said Chip Berlet of Political Research Associates. "The guns were proof of their seriousness."[14]

Other cults can be formed around such innocuous causes as self-improvement. After taking many courses and spending huge sums of money, often attracted by fraudulent claims of what they will accomplish, individuals are drawn deeper into the group and persuaded to begin recruiting new members so the group can bring in even more money. An article in the May 1994 issue of *Redbook*, "I Lost My Husband to a Cult," tells of a married couple's experience in a self-improvement group called Lifespring. Immediately after joining, the couple found their lives being controlled by this group as they were pressured into taking more and more courses, consequently giving the group more and more money. Eventually, the husband left his wife and children to become a recruiter for Lifespring.

"Cults like Lifespring are like a psychological prison: What they do is narrow your world," says Marcia Rudin, director of the International Cult Education Program. "You leave friends and destroy relationships for a false high."[15]

Some cults have also formed around psychotherapists and other types of mental health therapists with a belief that these individuals have the only cure for people with certain problems. These cult leaders then make their patients near slaves to them through the therapy, and often set up communal living arrangements so they can control every aspect of the cult members' lives. The article "After Synanon," in the March 29, 1998, issue of the *Los Angeles Times Magazine,* details life inside a group called Synanon, a drug and alcohol recovery program that had its start in the 1960s in Santa Monica, California.[16] Its leader, Charles E. Dederich, may have started with lofty goals and ideals but eventually turned Synanon into a cult through which he controlled every aspect of the lives of his followers. In 1980, a court convicted Dederich of encouraging an attack on a lawyer representing individuals who were suing Synanon.

Far too often, though, cults form simply and only for the purpose of benefiting the leader. For example, several Florida newspapers in 2000 reported that Richell Denise Bradshaw claimed she was the "Daughter of God and the sister of Jesus." As such, she claimed, she deserved to live in luxury. "I'm the queen," she stated. "I am here to reign."[17] Bradshaw called herself Queen Shahmia.

As Queen Shahmia, Bradshaw lived in posh, luxury hotels and traveled first-class. Her followers would peel her fruit, soothe her feet, comb her hair, and bathe her. Wherever she walked, her followers would spread flower petals in her path. Eventually, however, Queen Shahmia found that the donations gathered by her followers were not enough to meet her expenses. She told her followers that God was angry because of the paltry donations they were getting. She ordered them not to ask politely for money anymore but just to take it.

In January 2000, Florida police arrested three of Queen Shahmia's "manservants" for a string of robberies. The police also eventually arrested the Queen who, in July 2000, a court of five counts of robbery, one count of conspiracy to commit robbery, and one count of grand larceny. The court sentenced her to 25 years in prison.

The Queen's three manservants, however, told the court that they should all be set free because God had given them permission to do what they were doing. "I know that we plundered the earth," one of them said, "but we plundered the earth with permission."[18]

From the anecdotes in this and the preceding chapters, certain questions naturally arise: Why do some people find cults appealing? How do cults locate and recruit these people? How do cults indoctrinate their members into the total acceptance of a belief system that to outsiders appears absurd? In the next three chapters, I will examine these questions, which have no simple answers. As I will show, the involved processes are intricate and complex, requiring cult leaders to have an in-depth understanding of the psychology of human needs and wants, which they then prey upon to establish and maintain their cults.

CHAPTER 12

The Appeal of Cults

In 1993, Gail Maeder broke up with her longtime boyfriend, and soon afterward a boutique that Gail and her boyfriend had opened went out of business. Following these events, Gail suddenly left town and disappeared without a word to anyone. Frantic family members finally heard from her several months later when she sent them a note through the mail. In it she wrote, "You are probably wondering what I have decided to do with my life. Until recently, nothing has ever been able to offer me any real motivation."[1] The message was written on a recruiting flyer for a group called Total Overcomers Anonymous. This group would later become better known as the Heaven's Gate cult.

In March 1997, sheriff deputies went to the Heaven's Gate headquarters in San Diego. One of the 39 suicide victims they found inside was Gail.

Readers will naturally wonder why any reasonable, rational person would be attracted to a group that believes UFOs are in route to Earth to pick them up and transport them to a better existence. Even if the person believed that the UFO story were true, why would he or she believe that the aliens would choose the members of a nomadic group who often begged for food and lived in campgrounds as the ones to transport to a new world? Wouldn't there be many more valuable people the aliens would choose instead?

The more important, less rhetorical, question is, What attracts a person to a group that for most people, with just a little rational thought, ought send up red flags? What is the draw to these groups?

In her book *Cults in Our Midst,* Professor Margaret Thaler Singer states that many people, like Gail Maeder, who are attracted to cults are in emotional turmoil or in a highly transitional phase of their lives. They are going through a period during which the stability in their lives has collapsed. These people, Dr. Singer finds, are often willing to suspend rational thinking if they believe that doing something such as joining a new group of people will end the turmoil and bring solidarity back into their lives.

Dr. Philip Zimbardo, in his article "What Messages Are Behind Today's Cults?" states this about the appeal of cults: "Imagine being part of a group in which you will find instant friendship, a caring family, respect for your contributions, an identity, safety, security, simplicity, and an organized duty agenda. You will learn new skills, have a respected position, gain personal insight, improve your personality and intelligence.... Your leader may promise not only to heal any sickness and foretell the future, but give you the gift of immortality, if you are a true believer."[2]

With this kind of almost magical promise, readers can likely understand why Gail Maeder, in her low emotional state, would be attracted to the Heaven's Gate cult. Often when a person is at an emotional low, the appearance of a cult recruiter seems almost as if fate has destined the person to belong to the group. "Anytime you have people who feel hopeless and helpless," says Stanley Pollack, founder and director of Teen Empowerment in Boston, "they are prone to go where they think they belong."[3]

Many times, when a person has had emotional and business setbacks like those Gail experienced, they seem no longer to have an identity; they seem to have no direction or purpose in life. A cult will promise to remedy that. As an article in the *Detroit News* states, "Cults appeal to those who have no identity: 'I used to be no one, but now I'm part of a group. I didn't have any direction, but now I know the real truth!'"[4]

"There's nothing freaky at first," said a woman identified in a 1994 issue of *Cosmopolitan* only as Beth, who became involved in what she thought was simply an ordinary religious group. "You can't know what's in store for you."[5]

Beth had just moved to North Carolina, where she didn't know anyone, and her mother had just started treatment for cancer. Feeling lonely and frightened, Beth desperately needed the comfort of friends; as a result, she joined a church that at first, she reports, seemed like a fun place to be. There were lots of activities and lots of people who paid attention to her. But then the true nature of the group surfaced. Soon after Beth joined, the leaders began restricting her choice of clothing, attempting to stifle her activities with anyone outside the group, and even trying to decide whom she dated within the group. The group also demanded that Beth tithe 10 percent of her income to them and then demanded that she quit her job and take one they had selected for her.

Individuals like Beth who are in an emotionally vulnerable state, as Dr. Singer pointed out earlier, become very susceptible to the lure of security and fellowship that groups such as Beth's church seem to offer. Times of vulnerability tend to neutralize critical thinking.

Dr. Michael D. Langone explains it this way on the American Family Foundation Web site: "Conversion to cults is not truly a matter of choice. Vulnerabilities do not merely 'lead' individuals to a particular group. The group manipulates these vulnerabilities and deceives prospects in order to persuade them to join and, ultimately, renounce their old lives."[6]

In an article in the *Cultic Studies Journal*, Dr. Margaret Long explains why her brother became particularly vulnerable to cult recruitment: "In my brother's case risk factors included being new to the community, being separated from his family, having a new job, the recent death of his mother, and the recent breakup of an engagement to be married."[7]

Erika Van Meir, a mental health therapist who does approximately one-third of her work with former cult members and their families, told me, "It seems many [cult members] I have met, and those I have worked with, got involved at some transitional time in their life. Often they were vulnerable and made contact with a cult recruiter who happened to present a belief system, program, or ideology that made sense to the person. Nice-sounding beliefs combined with the intense attention (called 'love bombing' in the literature) and flattery that recruiters bestow upon their recruits make the groups very appealing."[8]

In an interview, cult exit counselor Mitchell Mack, Jr., told me about the factors he has found that seem to make cults attractive to some people: "People attracted to cults are usually looking for structure in their life; they're looking for independence," he said. "People are looking for purpose and meaning. Cults give people the answers to all of life's questions."[9]

Anyone can be drawn to a cult environment in times of emotional vulnerability, as the preceding anecdotes have illustrated. But Madeleine Landau Tobias and Janja Lalich, in their book *Captive Hearts, Captive Minds*, state that experts have also found there are certain predisposing factors that can make a person more vulnerable and the appeal of cults more powerful. These factors are the following:

1. Dependency—the desire to belong, lack of self-confidence.
2. Unassertiveness—inability to say no or express criticism or doubt.
3. Gullibility—impaired capability to question critically what one is told, observes, thinks, etc.
4. Low tolerance for ambiguity—need for absolute answers, being impatient to obtain answers.
5. Cultural disillusionment—alienation, dissatisfaction with the status quo.
6. Naïve idealism.
7. Desire for spiritual meaning.
8. Susceptibility to trance-like states—in some cases, perhaps, because of prior hallucinogenic drug experiences.
9. Ignorance of how groups can manipulate individuals.[10]

Steven Hassan, in his book *Combatting Cult Mind Control*, tells how, as a college student, he had broken up with his girlfriend and thought he would never find true love. He also felt other pressures.

"At that time I felt extreme pressure to make a big contribution to humankind," he said. "I had been told all my life how intelligent I was and how much I would accomplish when I grew up. I was going to graduate in another year, and time was running out."[11]

Steven also felt that he wasn't doing enough to right the injustices of the world, even though he had earlier become a foster parent to a child in Chile. "I looked out at the world and saw so much in the way of social injustice, political corruption, and ecological problems that it seemed I could offer little."[12]

Consequently, Steven became an easy target when four youths approached him in the campus cafeteria and engaged him in a conversation about an organization they belonged to that was doing something dramatic about everything he saw wrong in the world. They convinced him to go to several lectures and meetings, and eventually he became one of the top American recruiters for the Unification Church, or the cult that is better known as the Moonies.

While many people believe that cults only appeal to fringe people in our society, those with mental or emotional problems, or only to those with a limited capacity to make rational, sound decisions, this is just a stereotype, and like most stereotypes, it doesn't show the real picture. Cults can also appeal to the best in our society if the person is approached at the right time in his or her life.

The results of a study of 12,415 people who took part in the National Survey of Families and Households had some interesting findings in relation to who is attracted to cults. For example, the study found that the lower a person's stake was in conformity, the greater that person's chances were of joining a cult. But, interestingly enough, the survey also found that each year of education actually increased the odds that a person would be attracted to a cult.[13]

A young man identified in a 1997 article in *Good Housekeeping* only as Josh had just transferred from an art school in San Francisco to a school of design in New York City. According to his mother, Josh "was the kind of kid who worried about everything from racism to oil spills to world peace."[14] Along with relocating to a new school 3,000 miles across the country, Josh had also just taken on a new job in New York City and was planning to share an apartment there with an old friend. In addition to all these stresses, Josh's father, with whom Josh had had little contact most of his life, had suddenly called him and then, just as suddenly, wanted nothing to do with him again.

Josh's mother, after discovering that Josh hadn't moved into the apartment, hadn't shown up for the new job, and hadn't reported for classes at the new school, naturally became alarmed. She became even more alarmed when he unexpectedly called her one day.

"Hi, Mom!" he blurted. "I'm in the Moonies!"[15]

Josh apparently felt that the burden of all the new responsibilities he suddenly found himself under was more than he wanted to bear. For anyone who had always had a parent around to provide guidance in making tough decisions, being away from home for the first time and suddenly propelled into adulthood can cause intense psychological stress and often confusion about what to do. Consequently, for a young man like Josh, a group such as the Moonies, with its structured life and no decision making, can look very attractive.

According to an article published in the journal *Adolescence*, "Cults attract youths experiencing psychological stress, rootlessness, feelings of emptiness and being disenfranchised, and identity diffusion and confusion. Such youths come from all walks of life and all classes of society. Cults seem to offer confused and isolated adolescents a moratorium—a period of dropping out, or a 'time-out'—as well as a highly structured sense of belonging and a means of escape from being 'normless.'"[16]

An obvious question is, What do all the people in the incidents talked about so far in this chapter have in common? It is apparent that they were all going through emotionally difficult times in their lives. Major changes or disruptions had just occurred that drastically shook up their lives. Their feelings and emotions, because of these changes or disruptions, were strung out taut. Consequently, these individuals often felt stressed out and depressed and were looking for something that would give them solutions to their problems.

According to the book *Combatting Cult Mind Control,* "Surveys of present and former cult members indicate that the majority of people recruited into destructive cults were approached at a *vulnerable time of stress in their lives.* The stress is often due to some kind of major transition: moving to a new town, starting a new job, breaking off a relationship, experiencing financial instability, or losing a loved one."[17]

Individuals suffering emotional pains because of these stresses, therefore, occasionally either seek out cults or are attracted to the idea of a cult when a cult recruiter approaches them. In particular, people who are at an emotional crossroads in their lives, have just been divorced, have just had a significant person in their life die, or have just had some other sort of large, distressing life change, feel attracted to the closeness and protectiveness of cults. Once in a cult, members seem to have close friends in the other cult members, they seem to be totally accepted as a person who is a valuable asset, they have what they believe to be a supernaturally wise person guiding them, a person who seems to have answers for all of life's difficult problems, and they are freed from having to make any more tough decisions. All decisions, often even very minor ones, are made by the cult leaders. For a while, this type of life can feel very comforting to individuals who have been under a large amount of emotional stress, but after the stress passes, this life can become imprisoning and suffocating.

Occasionally, cults also appeal to people who find that traditional religion doesn't seem to offer them the answers they are seeking or the fellowship they desire. "What you find in every religion, it seems to me, is a promise of a miracle and a promise of mystery and a promise of meaning," says Lonnie Kliever, a religious studies professor at Southern Methodist University. "These are the things that lots of people hunger for."[18]

Jim Martin, associate editor of *Ex-Cultworld* magazine told me in an interview what attracted him to a group called The Way International: "I didn't have much of a spiritual upbringing. I never went to church much. The Way seemed to have all the answers about what religion should be. There seemed to be lots of love in the group."[19]

Bill Honsberger, an expert in cults, adds, "Most people who end up joining a cult think they are joining one of the most sincere, profound groups. They might be lonely, discouraged. . . . In some ways they might be disillusioned about God. Along comes people who really seem to care for you—that's pretty seductive right there."[20]

At other times, though, people are attracted to cults simply because they are lonely and looking for companionship. Lorna Goldberg, in the book *Recovery from Cults*, says, "For some time afterward in therapy there is a discovery that part of the cult's appeal was to escape from a sense of loneliness that developed in early childhood and adolescence."[21] Adding to this, a 2001 *London Times* article about the Solar Temple cult, talked about in chapter 10, said this about how a woman became one of its members and eventually one of its victims when she died in a mass murder/suicide: "Her children had left home and her husband was monopolized by his business interests. It was then that she met a Swiss homeopath called Luc Jouret (one of the cult leaders)."[22]

While it's true that cults can appear very attractive to individuals undergoing emotional turmoil, a very common belief among many members of the public is that cult recruiters, in addition to looking for the type of people talked about so far, also look for individuals who have moderate to sometimes severe psychological problems, because these individuals are usually easy to deceive. However, former cult recruiters say that, rather than the mentally troubled, they tried to target bright, idealistic people who, with the proper indoctrination, could become valuable cult members. They add that those with mental problems, on the other hand, aren't nearly as valuable because they are likely to be disruptive to the cult. One researcher, who reviewed several studies of the psychological health of present and former cult members, states, "The studies in this area could be summed up by concluding that cult members tended to have strong needs for authority and certainty in their lives, but no evidence of pathological mental states."[23]

Steven Hassan adds, "[W]hen I was a leader in the Moonies we selectively recruited 'valuable' people—those who were strong, caring, and motivated. People with emotional problems, on the other hand, always had trouble handling the rigorous schedule and enormous psychological pressures we imposed on them. It took lots of time, energy, and money to recruit and indoctrinate a member, so we tried not to waste our resources on someone who seemed liable to break down in less than a year."[24]

Given that most new cult members are not psychologically troubled but are bright and idealistic, cults must, to keep members from leaving once the initial effect of cult membership has worn off, somehow make their members feel that they have to stay in the cult because their presence is vital to the success of the cult's mission. What this mission is, of course, depends on the cult. To create and maintain their appeal, some cults have been formed around the claim that they will right social injustices of the poor and disadvantaged, while other cults have made much larger claims as to the value of the work they are doing. Some cults claim that they are part of an elite group involved in work that will be not only beneficial but no less than world shattering in its effect on mankind. As the foundation to such a claim, cults must make their members believe that Earth is on the verge of collapse, and that the only thing that will save the Earth and mankind is the work that the cult is doing. Although most of this world-saving work turns out to be imaginary, cult leaders continue to assure members that what they are doing, no matter how it looks, is going to save the world.

"[M]any former members confess that at first they felt a kind of wonder, as if they had drawn near something awesome," says cult counselor Janja Lalich. "They experienced a sense of exhilaration, excitement, passion, or expectation that was almost overwhelming."[25]

For some cult members, though, even saving the world is not enough. Therefore, some cults have to offer an even greater incentive to be appealing, especially to the recruits who are highly educated, financially well-off, and seemingly sophisticated. To do this, cults offer these prospective members an opportunity to take part in events and experiences that are outside the realm of ordinary human experience. As I demonstrated in chapter 10 with the Solar Temple cult, many of its members were sophisticated, well educated, and even very wealthy. To attract these types of individuals, the cult leaders offered them the opportunity to be magically transported to a world circling another star.

"These modern-day pied pipers offer, among other things," says Professor Margaret Thaler Singer, "pathways to God, salvation, revolution, personal development, enlightenment, perfect heath, psychological growth, egalitarianism, channels to speak with 35,000-year-old 'entities,' life in ecospheres, and contact with extra-terrestrial beings."[26]

While claims such as these may sound outlandish to many readers, a powerful part of human nature is the desire to be a unique and special individual, to be totally unlike the common man. This trait was clearly seen in the case of the cult called the Fellowship of Friends, talked about in chapter 11, in which members saw themselves, rather than spiritually dead like the common man, as an elite group who alone understood and appreciated the beauty of fine things. This desire to be a unique and special individual can often override a person's ability to properly judge cult claims.

"People lead mediocre lives," says Hank Hanegraaff, president of the Christian Research Institute, talking about the Heaven's Gate cult, "and so these leaders exploited expectations of joining an elite."[27]

Staff writer for the *Washington Post* Joel Achenbach sums up the appeal of cults this way: "Three things, all three of them as old as mankind, draw men to these groups: A shot at life after death. A special role in the universe. Someone to believe in."[28]

Former Church Universal and Triumphant member Cathleen Mann told me in an interview what attracted her to what she eventually discovered to be a cult: "I was attracted by many things: the complex doctrine, the fact that the group had a charismatic female leader, the mystery of the multilayered practices, the drama and chaos created by the leader, the uniqueness of the teaching, and the beautiful physical location of the group's headquarters in Paradise Valley, Montana."[29]

In addition to all the reasons mentioned so far, though, cults often appeal to young people simply because the groups are seen as a way to rebel against established authority, a desire that often runs high during adolescence. Rob Tucker, in his article "Teen Satanism," says this about joining a satanic cult: "It advocates a kind of fierce independence that includes anarchy, rebellion, and radical self-sufficiency at a time in teens' lives when attitudes toward authority are being shaped. It advocates the rejection of any form of authority, whether religious, societal, or parental."[30]

Adolescents, of course, can be attracted to satanic or occult cults not just because of their philosophy of giving free reign to one's impulses, to say nothing of the excitement of belonging to a group that is so far outside the norms of accepted society, but also because of the claims that members of these cults will have access to supernatural powers. Those drawn to these types of cults believe that they will have access to powerful mechanisms that they can use to satisfy whatever cravings or desires they have, no matter how outlandish they seem. Satanism in particular promises its adherents immediate gratification. However, unlike many adolescents attracted to cults, those attracted to satanic or occult cults have often previously drawn the attention of school administrators and the authorities. According to Rob Tucker, "They are often described as 'loners,' are underachievers, and generally present as 'problem' kids."[31]

Yet even for adolescents who join what appear to be peaceful religious cults, making such a decision can still be seen as an act of rebellion against their parents. Steven Hassan, a former recruiter for the Unification Church, says, "I have also noticed that many idealistic young people recruited into cults are struggling to assert their individuality, and some are going through a period of rebellion."[32]

However, for some young people who join cults, this act can also occasionally be an attempt to live up to the parents' and their own expectations. Therapist Lorna Goldberg says in the book *Recovery from Cults,* "William Goldberg and I noted that adolescents who seem particularly vulnerable to cults are those who have high expectations for themselves and are ready to see the best in others."[33]

Researchers such as the Goldbergs additionally find that some young people are attracted to cults because once they are free of their parents they become bewildered by the multitude of choices and decisions they must make. Life turns out to be much more complicated than they had suspected. Joining a cult simplifies life because all choices and decisions are made for cult members. Also, often young people see the adult-controlled society at large as stagnant and closed to young people. Society to them doesn't seem to address the issues they see as important.

Dr. Philip Zimbardo states, "Cults represent each society's 'default values,' filling in its missing functions. The cult epidemic is diagnostic of where and how society is failing its citizens."[34]

Interestingly, studies have also found that cults are more appealing to certain groups of people. For example, research has shown that the percentage of Jews in cults is far higher than the number of Jews in the general population. Estimates of the proportion of Jews in cults range from 20 percent to 50 percent. And while there are some exceptions, such as Jim Jones's Peoples Temple cult, the majority of cult members are white. In addition, a large number of Catholics find cults appealing. According to an article in the *Cultic Studies Journal,* some experts say this is because Catholics are used to absolute authority in their belief system.[35]

Finally, sometimes the appeal of a cult can come just from people wanting very badly to believe in someone or something. This would explain why, according to newspaper accounts, an estimated 4,000 people have flocked to an extremely remote and inhospitable area of Siberia to visit a commune called the City of the Sun. Sergei Torop, a 41-year-old former traffic officer from Minusink, Siberia, who claims he is the reincarnation of Jesus Christ, founded this commune as a part of his ministry.

"It's all very complicated," said Torop, who now goes by the name Vissarion. "But to keep things simple, yes, I am Jesus Christ. That which was promised must come to pass. And it was promised in Israel 2,000 years ago that I would return, that I would come back to finish what was started."[36]

While Vissarion has not performed any miracles that would verify he is who he says he is, many people still devoutly believe, or want to believe, that he is Jesus Christ. The thousands of people who have left their homes to hear Vissarion speak include many professional people, such as doctors, former Red Army senior officers, performers, teachers, former government ministers, and others.

However, as with many cults, people wanting to live in Vissarion's commune or belong to his group, called the Church of the Last Testament, must first give up all ties with the past and all their worldly belongings. "To accept me, people must give up everything they own," Vissarion preaches. "The rich will find it very difficult to enter the kingdom of heaven, very difficult."[37]

Also as in many cults, dissent within the Church of the Last Testament is not tolerated. "If someone says to me that he knows better than me, how can they?" said Vissarion. "How can they know anything at all if it is I who make the rules? The rules need to be made by me before they can exist."[38]

Following in the footsteps of many other cult leaders, Vissarion has attempted to instill a feeling of urgency and uniqueness for his group. In 2002, he prophesied that a comet will strike the earth in 2003. While destroying much of the earth, the comet will spare the City of the Sun and its inhabitants.

Although the many people who have given up their previous lives to reside in a deserted area of Siberia under extremely harsh conditions believe that Vissarion is truly Jesus Christ, including a former colonel of Russia's strategic missile forces who is Vissarion's high priest, others insist that Vissarion is just a con man who fraudulently deceives followers into giving him their possessions. Many of Vissarion's detractors point out that not only does he live very well off of his followers, but he also had his revelation about being Jesus Christ only after being laid off as a traffic cop.

For all of the reasons discussed in this chapter, the promises that cults make can have a strong attraction to certain segments of our society. Of course, while all these promises sound very appealing, the members usually discover that the cult falls far short of its promises. However, by that time, along with physical and sexual abuse, the cult has usually also inflicted serious damage to the person's psychological and emotional well-being, to the person's finances, and to the person's relationships with family members and friends outside the cult. Often it can take years after leaving a cult to undo the damage it has done.

Yet, while there obviously exists a pool of people seemingly ready for cult recruitment, there also exists a larger segment of society that finds cults' promises silly and cult membership completely unattractive. Therefore, to avoid wasting time and resources when they want to attract new members, cults must know whom to approach when recruiting. As I will show in the next chapter, cult recruiting can be very sophisticated and extremely deceptive.

CHAPTER 13

Cult Recruitment

When Corey Slavin's grandmother, whom she loved dearly, died, the loss left her feeling depressed and despondent. Even though Corey had a good life and an excellent job, she told writer Paula Dranov, whose article "The Frightening Lure of the Cult" appeared in a 1994 issue of *Cosmopolitan*, "I felt I was in over my head. My self-esteem was very low."[1] To overcome this, Corey turned to a coworker who seemed to be very sympathetic to her plight, and eventually Corey poured out her story to her. After they got to know each other, Corey found that she and the coworker seemed to share many common interests, and soon what Corey believed was an intense friendship developed between them. Actually, however, Corey was unknowingly being recruited into the Church Universal and Triumphant, one of the doomsday cults I talked about in chapter 9.

Not until long after their "friendship" began did Corey find out that the woman, whom she admired intensely for seeming to have all the answers and a life completely in order, was actually a member of a cult and was in the process of recruiting Corey into the group. Before Corey managed to escape the cult's grasp, she spent eight months living and working at its headquarters in Montana, and the group got away with more than $65,000 she had inherited from her grandmother.

"The Bible-based cult focuses on such universal human vulnerabilities in their recruitment strategies," states an article that appeared in the *Cultic Studies Journal.* "In their dealings with newcomers church members try to give the impression of having achieved spiritual transcendence...They strain to radiate a 'Christ-like' sense of joy and timelessness, and to be unaffected by the usual disappointments of daily life. Visitors might conclude that cult members are not burdened by normal emotional baggage, the kind which magnifies daily upsets and triggers irrational reactions to significant others."[2]

Typically, a cult wants to bring in new members because, like Corey, they bring with them money to increase the cult's income. Consequently, both new and long-time cult members often find themselves pressured by cult leaders to bring in more and more new recruits. To do this, they must naturally make more and more contacts. How new members are found, though, depends on the inventiveness of the recruiter.

After graduating from college and spending a year in menial jobs, Janet Joyce, according to the book *Captive Hearts, Captive Minds*, finally landed a position as an activity therapist in the psychiatric ward of a hospital in New Jersey. Among her new responsibilities were hiring and supervising several people. Unsure of herself in her new position as boss, Janet sought help in making herself a better supervisor. A friend she spoke with about her concerns recommended a therapist in New York City that she said would be of great help to Janet, and after attending several sessions with the therapist, Janet agreed.

The therapist soon invited Janet to parties and introduced her to many people Janet found interesting. As a result, Janet started going out on dates and to other social events. Eventually, the therapist suggested that Janet move to New York City to be closer to her new friends and her therapy. Considering this a good idea at the time, Janet moved into a house where, unbeknownst to her, all the residents were patients of her therapist or other therapists who belonged to the same organization that Janet's therapist belonged to: an intensely controlling psychoanalytical cult called the Sullivanians. The leaders of the Sullivanians believed that they had to control every aspect of their patients–cult members' lives, no matter how minor, and that this could only be accomplished through a communal living system. This control even extended to the belief that children should be separated from their parents, which led to accusations of child abuse against the group.

"Soon I had moved into a household connected to the group, although I was not fully aware of this or what it meant," Janet said. "I knew that it was a social scene—people to hang out with, people with similar political views...people who wanted to make changes in the world."[3]

Once Janet had moved into her new home, her therapist suggested that she break off all contact with her family and outside friends, and before long, Janet found herself isolated and only taking part in activities with others in the house. In addition, Janet's therapist began making all of her decisions for her, and if Janet resisted any of the therapist's decisions, the other members of the household would pressure her to comply and tell her that she really didn't know what was best for her, that she should trust her therapist. For the next 17 years, Janet's life became totally controlled by the Sullivanians until finally she could muster the strength to break free.

Janet's experience shows that some groups have advanced beyond the "approach cold on the street" method of cult recruitment. Some cults now also attempt to recruit people sent to them under false pretenses. For example, in addition to Janet's experience, some cults prey on unsuspecting people who sign up for what appear to be innocent self-improvement courses but are really just a subterfuge for cult recruitment. This has even been known to happen when businesses send their employees to what are supposed to be business-related courses. Cult leader Frederick Lenz, also known as Rama, whom I discussed in chapter 7, often used this method of recruitment for his cult.

Erika Van Meir, a family therapist in Atlanta, Georgia, who works with former cult members and their families, told me about her own attempted recruitment into a cult: "I had a personal experience myself as a trainee, finding out that the so-called 'legitimate therapy practice' I was interning with was connected to a 30-year-old Marxist-Leninist cult. It was unbelievable to realize what was going on and then try to alert other mental health professionals."[4]

Steven Hassan, the former cult member mentioned in the previous chapter, tells about agreeing, after meeting and speaking with several people in a university cafeteria, to go to a meeting of a group that seemed to focus on the same social problems he was concerned about. However, when he asked about the nature of the group, he received deceptive answers.

"I asked if they were a religious group," Hassan tells in his book *Combatting Cult Mind Control*. "Oh, no, not at all," they laughed, telling him they were part of something called the One World Crusade, a group that, like Steven, wanted to correct certain social problems.[5]

Steven attended several of the group's lectures, which he said he found interesting but a bit shallow. However, when he tried to ask questions about the lecture information, he found himself constantly put off. Finally, he told the group he was leaving, but almost immediately he found himself surrounded by people begging him to come back to another lecture, which he reluctantly agreed to do. At the next meeting Steven attended, he found himself constantly corralled by people who said one flattering thing after another to him. It wasn't until he found himself at a weekend workshop far out of town, and with no way back, that someone finally told him that the group he was involved with was actually the Unification Church, or the Moonies.

"Cult recruiting is a form of confidence game," says Professor Margaret Thaler Singer. "They'll get the lonely kids, the new kids in town, the kids who just transferred. Some of the cults actually train people to go to school grounds and see who's at the edge of the crowd that no one is paying any attention to."[6]

Steven Hassan adds, "They lied a lot, which is the major thing readers should know. No one joins a cult—they get recruited. The major difference between legitimate organizations and cults are the legitimate ones are upfront, they don't have to lie and deceive to get new members."[7]

As I talked about in the last chapter, cults like to recruit people during vulnerable periods in their lives, people who are looking for supportive friends and are therefore less likely to see the deceit of the recruiters or to question their motives deeply. Most of these individuals just feel happy to have found a person or a group of people who appear willing to accept, understand, and support them, not realizing that they are actually being recruited into a cult.

An immediate question some readers might have is, Why should we be concerned about cult recruitment? What difference is there between a cult recruiting someone and the Masons, the American Legion, or the local Baptist church recruiting new members? We don't oppose or try to stop these groups from recruiting. Why should we oppose or stop cults? The difference is that cults recruit people into groups that, according to my definition, are involved in criminal activity. As I show throughout the book, cults have recruited members and then defrauded them out of their life's savings, have physically and sexually abused them, have held them at locations against their will, encouraged them to commit crimes such as arson and robbery, and have even murdered them or encouraged them to murder others. This is why the public should be concerned about cult recruitment.

"In working with several thousand individuals who have been in cults," says Professor Margaret Thaler Singer, "I have not been told by one of them that he or she went out looking for a guru to set her or him up in prostitution, flower selling, cocaine dealing, gun smuggling, child abuse, or living off garbage, which were the ways these various individuals had ended up while in the cult."[8]

But just how does a typical on-the-street recruitment into a cult take place? How are potential cult members initially spotted and contacted? First, a recruiter looks for a likely prospect, often someone who appears to be lonely or troubled. Cult recruiters are told to look for individuals who appear to be left out of the crowd and lost. The recruiter, who in many cases is an attractive male or female, then approaches the person with a smile and says hello, afterward engaging the person in a conversation and attempting to gauge the person's personality and discover the person's feelings and attitudes about certain issues. After a short conversation, the recruiter can tell whether the person should be a target or whether he or she should just move on to another possible recruit. Does the person seem to crave company? Is he or she idealistic and concerned about social problems? Does the person seem to be searching for meaning? These are all signs of good cult recruitment material. Often it is a person's good qualities, such as being trusting and wanting to help others, that make him or her vulnerable to cult recruitment.

"From my experience," says Herbert Rosedale, a cult expert, "people who get involved in destructive cults had a weak moment at which they were susceptible to recruitment....They are not dysfunctional people. They may be among the most idealistic, brightest people in the world."[9]

As for the idea that cults like to use attractive individuals as recruiters, I found this to be very common among the former cult members I spoke with. "I was at a book sale at a mall," former cult member Jim Martin told me, "and I was approached by these three model-type females."[10] The three women, who were cult members, eventually recruited Jim into the cult.

"I picked up a pretty hitchhiker," said former cult member Karl Kahler. "It turned out she was a member of a cult called The Way International."[11]

"I joined the Hare Krishnas during my senior year at the University of California," Nori Muster told me about her cult recruitment. "The way the group recruits is to send single men out to talk to women."[12]

If the cult recruiter finds that the person approached seems to be a likely prospect, the recruiter then begins agreeing with and reinforcing the person's beliefs. Cult recruiters try to make themselves sound very much like the possible recruit. People naturally tend to be attracted to other people who agree with them and who like and support the same things they do. Cult recruiters also use certain buzzwords they know will bring about a positive response from the type of recruit they are looking for, words and phrases such as *world peace, salvation,* and *love,* among others. Former cult members usually say that their recruiter seemed like the nicest, most sincere, most caring person they had ever met. Interestingly, as a police officer, this is the same description I hear from victims when they describe the perpetrators of con games.

However, once the initial contact is made, the person looks to the recruiter like a likely prospect, and the hook is set, the next thing the recruiter must do is persuade the person to go to some location where the cult will be able to exert control. As in Steve Hassan's case, a number of people who have been recruited into cults tell about agreeing to go to a meeting at some isolated location only to find out too late that it is actually a three- or four-day event and that they have no transportation back to where they came from. Any potential recruit who shows resistance and says he or she wants to call family or friends for a ride back is usually told that the telephones at the lecture location just happen to be out of order. The cult recruiter, of course, assures the person that he or she will be given a ride back after the event is over. However, after three or four days, many of these individuals have already been converted.

Another cult recruitment technique is to persuade the prospective cult member to attend a meeting or event where he or she will be cut off not only from the outside world but also from any conflicting information, so the recruit cannot compare what is being presented against any other viewpoint. While at this meeting, the cult constantly bombards prospective members with information and allows them very little time for rest and reflection. After enough of this intense and prolonged bombardment of information, the new recruit is often so exhausted that his or her reasoning capacity and ability to resist have been severely reduced.

However, one of the most important things a cult does when recruiting new members is to isolate them from other new recruits so there is no one to compare notes with about what the organization is, what it is doing, or what they've been told. Usually, the only people surrounding the potential recruit are long-time cult members. Reportedly, the Unification Church has a rule that states no first-week people are allowed to talk to other first-week people. This is to keep new recruits from comparing notes and realizing too soon what they are getting into.

The potential recruit, after being isolated from outside sources, is then "love bombed" with hugs, flattery, attention, and sometimes with good food and other amenities. Love bombing naturally tends to make a lonesome person feel that he or she has at last found a group of people who really care, and it consequently makes the recruit who is craving affection want to be part of the group. It is only later that the abuse—physical, financial, mental, emotional, and sexual—begins.

In an interview, cult exit counselor and former cult member Steven Hassan told me about how the use of both guilt and love bombing kept him from walking away from the group when he knew he should have: "The first inkling I had that this group wasn't what they said they were was one snowy night when we were driving into the Tarrytown estate. They said, 'By the way, this weekend we're going to have a joint workshop with the Unification Church.' I said, What workshop? What church? I thought this wasn't religious. They immediately said, 'What's the matter, Steve, are you closed minded? What's wrong with you, Steve?' They had turned it around on me."

Steven then went on to tell me, "I felt like running. I could have, and should have, just walked away from the estate in the snow and hitchhiked or tried to get to a phone somewhere and called my family. But they just seemed like such nice people. They just seemed so friendly. And so I didn't. That started my journey."[13]

During this love-bombing period, cult recruits are given only very edited information about the group that is recruiting them, with any specific questions by the potential recruit either ignored or many times put off with the promise that they will be answered at a later time. Often potential recruits are kept so busy, and are many times so sleep deprived, that they don't have the time or a clear enough head to do any serious contemplation about what they are being told. This continues until the person's resistance is so broken down that he or she is now pliable and ready for indoctrination into the group.

The anecdotes given so far in this chapter all share one common feature: the people recruited into these cults were never told until far into the recruiting process that they were being approached by a group involved in illegal activities. Very, very seldom will a cult ever let prospective recruits know ahead of time what they are really getting into. Most cults realize from experience that prospective members must first be conditioned and made ready before being told the truth about the group they're being invited to join. Most cults will only tell a new member about their true nature once they believe the recruit is ready to actually become part of the cult.

As the anecdotes so far in this chapter clearly show, very few of the people who join cults ever immediately realize the true nature of the group they are being recruited into. Yet recruiting attempts made by cults are unsuccessful simply because the attempts are seen for what they really are. People know it's a cult and say no thank you. In a study of 1,000 randomly selected high school students in the San Francisco area, 54 percent reported having been approached by a cult recruiter, while 40 percent reported three to five such encounters.[14] Like the individuals in this study, most people contacted by cults decline any offers by recruiters.

Yet, even with so many failures, many cults still manage to steadily increase their numbers. How? Attorney Lawrence Levy, who has successfully sued cults many times, told me in an interview, "Cults give a lecture and 500 people attend. Four hundred and fifty get up and walk away by the end. Fifty go look at the cult's published material and buy something. Five come back for more information, and out of this five, the cult captures three or four people for their group. If you give enough lectures during the year, you can entrap a lot of people."[15]

Readers may wonder how the members of groups who profess to be religious or who claim to be on a crusade to correct social wrongs can knowingly lie and deceive in order to recruit new members. Doesn't this cause a conflict with the recruiters' consciences? According to Dr. Gregory S. Blimling, author of an article published in the *Cultic Studies Journal,* "One must remember that cult recruiters, both those specifically trained for the purpose and those who are simply zealous new members, are motivated by a commitment to the worthiness of the cult. When they deceive, manipulate, or coerce another person into the steps leading to a conversion, they do so with the unshakable belief that they are helping that person to become closer to 'God' or whatever other principle, deity, or experience they are professing."[16]

Another article from the *Cultic Studies Journal* proposes a further reason that cult members can deceptively recruit without it causing a conflict with their consciences: "Cult members generally disdain outside society because they feel their special mission places them above laws and accepted social norms. They therefore believe they are justified in lying and deceiving others. (The Unification Church speaks of 'Heavenly Deception,' Hare Krishna members speak of 'Transcendental Trickery.')"[17]

The individuals who recruited Steven Hassan, for instance, emphatically denied that they were part of any religious organization, even though the group they belonged to, the Unification Church, is very much a religious group. Recruits simply don't get any real information about the cult they are being recruited into until much later in the recruiting process.

As another example of deceptive recruiting, former cult member Janja Lalich tells of her experience: "I was told we would be unlike all other groups on the Left because we were led by women and because our leader was brilliant and from the working class. I was told we would not follow the political line of any other country, but that we would create our own brand of Marxism, our own proletarian feminist revolution; we would not be rigid, dogmatic, sexist, racist. We were new and different—an elite force. We were going to make the world a better place for all people."[18] What eventually happened, however, was that Lalich found herself trapped for years in a closed, totalitarian cult that allowed no dissent or independent thought.

I have talked so far about how cult recruiters look for lonely, troubled individuals, but these recruiters also report receiving training concerning what else to look for when recruiting. Because cults want to recruit bright, idealistic people, recruiting often takes place on college campuses. A poll by a major news service found that 40 percent of all respondents said that there were cults active on their campuses.[19] Should colleges be concerned about cults recruiting on their campuses? My answer to this question would be that the Heaven's Gate cult, which ended in a 39-person suicide, recruited on college campuses.

According to the article "Residence Halls and Cults: Fact or Fiction?" which appeared in the *Cultic Studies Journal*, "It is also known that first-year students are targets for cults. First-year students face the challenges of adapting to their new surroundings, taking on new academic responsibilities, and developing new relationships. In addition, residence halls are prime recruiting grounds. Cult members have been known to walk the hallways of residence halls on the weekends to find lonely students."[20]

Why are cults so interested in college students? Professor Margaret Thaler Singer observes, "What the cults want to recruit are average, normal, bright people and especially, in recent years, people with technical skills, like computer skills. And often, they haven't become street smart."[21]

Interestingly, cults also often target foreign college students for recruitment. Jane R. Lindley, in the book *Cults on Campus: Continuing Challenge*, gives what she sees as the main reasons for this recruitment of foreign students:

1. They are often alone and homesick, particularly when they first arrive in the United States.
2. They are usually governed by cultural norms which dictate politeness.
3. They are out of their own cultural milieu and have a difficult time discerning genuine overtures of friendship.
4. They are eager to learn about the host country's customs and therefore welcome the opportunity to meet Americans.[22]

Along with recruiting college students, however, cults now also have their eyes set on another group for recruitment. Cults have discovered that elderly people are not only easy to recruit but also often have tucked away considerable sums of money, typically savings from a lifetime of work—money the cult wants. Therefore, cult recruiters now often cruise malls, parks, and other areas where the elderly congregate, again looking for the lonely, lost person.

"Older adults are appealing to cult recruiters not only because they often have weak ties with immediate family members," says an article in the *Journal of Humanistic Education & Development*, "but also because they have the financial resources to contribute to the cult."[23]

Herbert Rosedale, an attorney who has handled many cult cases states, "I know of a number of cases in which people have impoverished themselves. It runs the gamut from people who were solicited to make six-figure donations to those who have nothing but their Social Security checks to give. It's devastating—both to individuals and to their families."[24]

In an article that appeared in *Modern Maturity* magazine, the authors note, "No longer satisfied with recruiting wide-eyed and penniless youths, the cults have shifted their focus to older people—even those who have little more to offer than their Social Security checks and small pensions." In the article, a cult recruiter describes how she cruised the hallways of nursing homes looking for possible recruits. "No one ever stopped me," the former cult recruiter said. "The authorities probably thought I was someone's granddaughter; they were happy to have someone visit."[25]

Interestingly, no matter who the likely prospect, cult recruitment has grown and advanced with the times, and quite often today the first contact with a cult recruiter doesn't come face-to-face, but rather on the Internet. Yet still, as with face-to-face recruiting, Web sites set up for cult recruiting usually don't reveal the true nature of the group doing the recruiting. For many cults, the Internet has proven very lucrative for their recruiting efforts.

"The Internet puts them in touch," says Larry Trachte, a professor at Wartburg College in Iowa. "Instead of standing in airports, all of a sudden they have contact with millions of people."[26]

William M. Alnor, in his book *UFO Cults and the New Millennium*, adds this about Internet cult recruiting: "Prior to the Internet there were more built-in curbs on ideas. Editors of newspapers and magazines served as gatekeepers, individuals with the power to ignore or discredit wacky ideas instead of publishing them. The Internet has allowed anyone with know-how and a standard modern computer equipped with a modem to go on-line to receive and disseminate ideas worldwide, without being curbed or censored by an editor."[27]

Rick Ross, a cult exit counselor who maintains a cult information Web site, says, "[T]he Internet has proven a powerful recruitment tool for cults. It allows them to disseminate information cheaply and to reach upper middle-class loners who may be more likely to own computers. More sophisticated cults are looking for people who are in a high socioeconomic bracket."[28]

This cult Internet recruitment, besides possibly enticing a person into a cult that can wreck havoc with the person financially and emotionally, can have an even darker, more ominous edge to it. Unfortunately, since a large majority of cult members, both young and old, say that they were recruited during a time when they were at a low emotional point in their life, often brought on by high stress, a number of cults have used this fact to assist in their recruiting. The Heaven's Gate cult, for example, reportedly recruited on Web sites designated for those concerned about depression, which often accompanies emotional turmoil and high stress.

"It's really ruthless to exploit people on the basis of their illnesses," says psychiatrist Louis J. West about Heaven's Gate's recruiting techniques. "To go after people with medical problems because you know they're more vulnerable...and pull them into something that could cost them their lives is as bad as you can get."[29]

But it can actually get even worse than this. According to Japanese newspaper reports, when the Tokyo police examined a number of CD-ROMs confiscated from buildings owned by the Aum Shinrikyo cult (responsible for releasing poison gas in the Tokyo subway system, killing 12 people and injuring thousands, as discussed in chapter 2), they found huge e-mail address lists of Japanese college students. The authorities believe that the cult may have sent out more than 40,000 e-mails in an attempt to recruit college students.

Although a large number of cults now use the Internet for recruiting because setting up and maintaining a Web site is relatively inexpensive, other cults, particularly those with considerable financial resources, still like using the more conventional, though more costly, methods of advertising as a means of recruitment. The Unification Church, for example, ran a two-page advertisement containing a message from their leader, Reverend Moon, in dozens of newspapers around the world. The ad cost $25,000 to run in just one Minneapolis newspaper.

As has been shown, many people have been susceptible to cult recruitment at a vulnerable point in their lives. On the other hand, many similarly vulnerable people have rejected the overtures of cult recruiters. What are the factors that make cult recruitment successful with some vulnerable people but not with others?

Social psychologist Dr. Robert Cialdini has found through his research that there are six principles that are used to influence others. These principles are the rule of reciprocity, commitment and consistency, social proof, liking, authority, and scarcity.[30] As described in the following list, how much these factors affect a person and guide that person's decision-making process will often decide who succumbs to the lure of the cult and who doesn't.

1. Reciprocity: This rule states that individuals usually attempt to give back, in kind, what another person has given them. Some individuals, to rid themselves of the uncomfortable feeling of owing someone, will often agree to a request for something far larger than what they have gotten. For example, in cult recruiting, long-time members of a cult will often tell some very personal things about themselves, which then commits the recruits to tell something just as personal, or even more so, about themselves. The cult leaders can then use this information to pull the individuals in even deeper or as blackmail to keep them in line later on.

2. Commitment and consistency: People generally like to appear consistent in what they say, believe, and do. Once a potential member agrees and gives in on something that the cult requests, that person will often, in an attempt to appear to be consistent, continue agreeing and giving in until a commitment to the group seems the logical course of action.

3. Social proof: People usually will accept ideas or follow leaders if it appears to them that everyone else is, and particularly if it appears that famous people are. This is the reason cults often attempt to recruit famous people as spokespersons. Cults also purposely cut recruits off from any outside sources of information, from any unbiased input, so the consensus on the cult belief system the recruit witnesses comes only from other cult members.

4. Liking: People naturally prefer to be around individuals they like and who like them. As previously mentioned, recruiters will "love-bomb" prospective members with flattery, hugs, and statements of approval, giving the potential cult members the overall feeling that they have found a group of people who truly love, admire, and care about them. Few individuals can resist the impulse to like these people and consequently want to be around them.

5. Authority: Most people are raised to recognize that it is proper and necessary to obey legitimate authority in our society. Consequently, once a potential cult recruit accepts and believes that a cult leader is godlike and all knowing, the less likely it is that this person will question whatever the leader says. The new cult member soon believes that if the leader says it, it must be true, it must be right.

6. Scarcity: People give more value to opportunities if they believe they are rare and difficult to come by. Cults therefore make potential members believe that they are offering them the chance to be part of a unique group that is an integral part of some world-shattering event or that they are offering them the chance to have access to information known only to a select few in the world. This makes belonging to the cult look that much more attractive to recruits.

Based on the socialization processes they have undergone during their lives, some individuals can be extremely susceptible to these six factors, while others can be much less susceptible. In addition, the degree of stress or emotional turmoil a person is under at the time of cult recruitment can cloud a person's judgment and also make him or her more or less susceptible. But experts such as Professor Margaret Thaler Singer find a person's willingness to be recruited into a cult can also stem from who the recruiter is. In her book *Cults in Our Midst*, Professor Singer states, "In a recent survey of 381 former members of 101 different cultic groups, 66 percent stated that their initial contact with their group came through a friend or relative."[31]

Actually, while I have talked about the most common methods of cult recruitment, there is really no method cult members won't use if they believe it will be successful. For example, as I talked about in chapter 11, the cult called the Fellowship of Friends recruited new members by leaving their bookmarks in books that promoted the cult's view of the world. Monte Kim Miller, leader of the Concerned Christians cult, talked about in chapter 6, used radio broadcasts and audiotapes to attract recruits. The Heaven's Gate cult, talked about in chapter 8, purchased a full-page ad in *USA Today*.

Often, as previously mentioned, it is a family member or a trusted friend who introduces a person to a cult. "I was introduced to the cult (the Church Universal and Triumphant) by a professor in my psychology master's program," former cult member Cathleen Mann told me.[32] Former cult member Robi Klee told me that her mother worked with people who she thought were very nice but who she later found out, after Robi and her mother had been recruited, were actually members of The Way International cult.[33]

Cult recruiting, no matter what the method, can best be described by a quote from a former member of the Peoples Temple cult: "When you meet the friendliest people you've ever known, who introduce you to the most loving group of people you've ever encountered, and you find the leader to be the most inspired, caring, compassionate and understanding person you've ever met, and then you learn that the cause of the group is something you never dared hope could be accomplished, and all of this sounds too good to be true, it probably is too good to be true!"[34]

Regardless of whatever recruiting methods cults decide to use, the key to success is always to get prospective members interested enough to attend group meetings. Once this is accomplished, indoctrination into the cult's belief system can begin. As I will show in the next chapter, this indoctrination, which can be more intense and thorough than the worst kind of prisoner-of-war brainwashing, often brings about a psychological metamorphosis, after which a once bright, inquisitive person becomes an unthinking robot who will follow the orders of cult leaders without question.

CHAPTER 14

Cult Indoctrination

Like many other young people, Adam Berkowitz wasn't sure what to do with his life after graduation from college. Thinking it would be an adventurous and fun thing to do before settling down to a serious job, he decided to join two friends in a cross-country trek in a van. According to an article in the May 1997 issue of *Current Health,* the vehicle broke down in Boulder, Colorado, and Adam found his way to a coffeehouse frequented by college students and area teenagers. It was there that he met the man who would promise him a major part in a profound undertaking, but who in the end would instead enslave him.

Adam noticed the man, who called himself Ron, sitting in the corner of the coffeehouse giving tarot card readings to patrons. Adam watched the readings for a long time and found himself drawn to the man's charisma.

"I was mesmerized by his presence," Adam said. "I spent 10 hours listening to him. At the end of the day, several of us held hands in a circle, and Ron told us we should come and live with him."[1]

Like many people at a crossroads in their lives, at a time when nothing is certain, Adam found himself vulnerable, and consequently allowed himself to be unknowingly recruited into a cult. Adam and several others accompanied Ron to the motel where he was staying and listened to him speak all night. Then Ron did a tarot card reading on Adam. The cards, Ron interpreted as he slowly turned each one over, said that he was destined to become Adam's teacher. At that point, drawn by Ron's charisma and persuasiveness, Adam agreed to become part of Ron's group.

For the next month, Adam and the other recruits stayed at the motel, where for hour after hour they studied New Age writing and listened to Ron lecture, getting only a few hours of sleep and quickly grabbing a low protein meal between study and lecture times. Like most cult leaders, Ron wanted to give the cult members a feeling of eliteness and earthshaking importance. He told them that the world was about to end and that it was the cult's job to prepare for it.

"It was amazing how quickly we believed what Ron said," Adam later recalled. "A kernel of truth was at the bottom, but the rest was fabrication. Once you accept the first lie, the rest is easy."[2]

Shortly after Adam joined the cult, Ron had him cut off contact with everyone outside the cult, including family members. He convinced Adam that his family didn't respect him or what he was doing and that to properly carry out the cult's task, which at first consisted mainly of long hours of study, he must have nothing to do with anyone outside the group.

Along with the nonstop study and lectures, cult members also had to take part in a regular confession/criticism ceremony, in which they stood up in front of the group and confessed their sins and wrongdoings, followed by the other members sternly criticizing them. The criticized cult members, after being told they were worse than nothing, naturally wanted more than ever for Ron to help them become the kind of person they should be. But as soon as the cult members began to feel that they were becoming much better people, the confessionals and group criticisms would start all over again. Adam quickly learned that the best way to avoid this ceremony of criticism was never to say anything critical of Ron or the cult, never to show any independent thought, and to talk only positively about whatever Ron preached. He found that the cult members who criticized Ron or showed any independent thought were most often the targets of the group criticism.

Naturally, maintaining a cult such as this is expensive, and to help with the cost of running the cult, Ron had Adam get a job in a video store. Adam, of course, had to turn his paycheck over to Ron, who also persuaded Adam to take out and give to him $8,000 in cash advances against a credit card that belonged to his parents.

When Adam's parents got the bill for $8,000, they knew Adam had to be in trouble. After a little investigation, they found that he was involved in a cult, but to their surprise, they also found that he refused to talk to them about it or even discuss the idea that he should leave. Adam's parents wouldn't give up though, and to avoid a threatened visit to the cult headquarters by Adam's parents, Ron allowed Adam to visit his parents at their home. Fortunately for Adam, his parents, on discovering that he was part of a cult, sought professional help. When Adam visited his parents' home, exit counselors contacted by Adam's mother and father were there and were eventually able to convince Adam that Ron had duped him. Adam decided not to return to the cult.

"It's a 'cult' if it's designed to disable the ability of the individual to think for himself so as to make him psychologically dependent on the commands of the cult leadership," states an article in the Internet magazine *Rewired*.[3] This is exactly what happens to many cult members, and it is exactly what happened to Adam.

But why should we be concerned about how a group indoctrinates its new members? Some readers might argue that many religious and other types of groups also attempt to persuade new members that their purpose is good and that their group is unique. While this is true, the difference between that and the indoctrination by cults is that the desired result of cult indoctrination is not just to have a member who is enthused and excited about belonging to a group. The desired result of cult indoctrination is to create mindless robots who will never question the cult leadership and who will carry out the cult leader's orders, no matter what they are. And as I have shown in the many incidents reported so far in this book, these orders can often include criminal acts such as financial fraud, assault, kidnapping, and even murder. This is why the public should be concerned about cult indoctrination.

Another question many readers will have after reading the anecdote at the beginning of this chapter is what kind of power could Ron have had that would make Adam convert so totally to the cult's belief system? Adam, after all, was not some gullible teenager. He was an adult who had graduated from college. What kind of power did Ron have that would allow him to bend Adam's mind to his will?

First, Adam is by no means an isolated case. As I have shown in the incidents discussed in this book, many thousands of people have been converted to near mindless robots who are willing to do a cult leader's bidding without question. In Adam's case, he not only became a servant of the cult, but also turned his back on his family and even misappropriated $8,000 of his parent's money to give to the cult. But again, Adam's case was not that unusual.

"I worshipped Wierwille (the leader of The Way International) without question," a former member of the cult told a reporter for the *Chicago Sun-Times*. "So do many others. If he had told me to kill myself, I would have done it. If he had told me to kill somebody else, I would have done that, too."[4]

Commitment of this magnitude is hard for many people to understand. Yet it occurs regularly in the thousands of cults in our country. Indoctrination or thought reform of this magnitude, however, cannot be done in an afternoon. It takes time and considerable effort. It also happens a little at a time, in hardly noticeable steps, so that the victims don't discern a radical change in themselves as it is occurring. Only after leaving a cult do the victims usually see how much they have changed and how subtly the changes occurred. But how does this come about? How can ordinary, rational people be willing to take the first step in accepting the cult's belief system? Shouldn't they realize the cult members are trying to change them and be on guard against it?

In the book *Recovery from Cults*, Dr. Geri-Ann Galanti, in a chapter titled "Reflections on 'Brainwashing,'" tells of her experience going undercover to investigate what people had claimed was brainwashing, or thought reform, by the Unification Church (Moonies). Even though she knew that these people were attempting to influence her and to change her behavior and belief systems, she said she nevertheless still found herself doing many of things they wanted her to do. "I was beginning to act like them," she reports, "cheering wildly at mediocre performances, reporting attitudes that I felt would meet with their approval, actively participating in games and songs from childhood."[5] And this was a person who knew all the subtleties of thought reform and what the group was trying to do to her. To Dr. Galanti, however, the people were just so nice and so friendly, it was difficult for her to ascribe evil motives to them, even though she was well aware of the many reported abuses within the Unification Church.

"Cults are just extended con games," Professor Margaret Thaler Singer told me.[6] Indeed, the police do find that in con games, as in cult indoctrination, the people conducting the con seem so honest, so nice, and so caring that the victims say it's impossible to ascribe evil motives to them. Consequently, victims of con games, and cult indoctrination, believe that whatever the person tells them must be true and that anything they agree to do for the person could never be harmful to them. The person is just too nice for that.

Dr. Robert J. Lifton, in his seminal book on mind control, *Thought Reform and the Psychology of Totalism*, states that mind control, such as the type used by cults, is achieved through the manipulation of eight things:

1. Milieu control
2. Mystic manipulation
3. Demand for purity
4. Confession
5. Sacred science
6. Loading the language
7. Doctrine over person
8. Dispensing of existence.[7]

MILIEU CONTROL

With milieu control a cult leader attempts to control the total environment of the potential cult members. Cult leaders do this by isolating the cult recruits from outside influences, so that the only influence recruits experience is that of the cult leader and longtime dedicated cult members. This can involve actually physically segregating cult recruits in some isolated location where they see no one but other cult members, or it can involve psychologically isolating recruits, in that cult leaders convince the recruits that only the cult and its members know the true path and that all outsiders, who are misinformed and doomed, must be avoided.

As a part of this milieu control, cult leaders also regulate what media sources, if any, recruits get to see, hear, and read, and they particularly forbid recruits access to any media sources that might promote critical thinking. Another method of milieu control involves assigning each new cult recruit an older cult member who is then expected to watch over him or her to be certain the new recruit is not influenced by outside sources. These watchers make certain the recruit can never have a "reality check" by talking to someone not totally committed to the cult. Some cult recruits report their watchers even going to the bathroom with them.

In addition, cult leaders want to keep new members from knowing exactly what is going on with their indoctrination, or to even know that it is occurring, so they won't realize the final goal of the cult, which is total control of its members. Cult leaders do this by performing the indoctrination in small steps, often so small and subtle that new cult members cannot see what is happening or how they are slowly changing. And since cult recruits see or talk to no one outside the cult, there is no one to tell the cult recruits that they are changing. Also, isolating new cult members strip them of any support group outside the cult; consequently, new members must depend on other cult members for emotional and other types of support. Soon new members become totally dependent on the leader and other cult members, and, after this, total control can be established and maintained.

MYSTICAL MANIPULATION

"Cult leaders center veneration on themselves," says Professor Margaret Thaler Singer. "Priests, rabbis, ministers, democratic leaders, and leaders of genuinely altruistic movements keep the veneration of adherents focused on God, abstract principles, or the group's purpose. Cult leaders, in contrast, keep the focus of love, devotion, and allegiance on themselves."[8]

This veneration of cult members for the leader is one of the main purposes of cult indoctrination. However, for a cult leader to convince followers to give him or her this veneration and devotion, the leader must be seen as larger than life. Cult leaders must demonstrate and prove to cult members that they do indeed have the special relationship with God or the supernatural powers they claim to have. This is often accomplished through simple ruses. Jim Jones of the Peoples Temple cult, for example, hired people to claim they were ill or crippled and then be miraculously healed by him. Also, Jones would have confederates circulating through the congregation who would surreptitiously report to Jones what members of the congregation were saying. Jones would then repeat these comments from the pulpit, making the members believe he had supernatural powers. In addition, Jones would have longtime members of his congregation visit the homes of new members, and while there, ask to use the bathroom. While in the bathroom, the longtime members would look through the medicine cabinet to see what medications family members were taking. Jones would then use this information to make new members think he had received word from God about their illnesses.

At an American Family Foundation conference I attended, I went to a seminar titled "Anyone Can Be Fooled." The seminar leader, besides teaching, also works as a stage magician. Of course, most of the seminar attendees, including me, didn't know about the instructor's ability as a stage magician and so he astounded us with his ability to perform what appeared to be supernatural acts—until he explained to us how he did them. Then, like Sherlock Holmes explaining to Watson how he made his deductions, it all seemed so simple and not supernatural at all.

A *London Times* article about the Solar Temple cult, talked about in chapter 10, tells about how one of its leaders, Joseph Di Mambro, convinced members he had supernatural powers. "Jo brandished a sword and cried, 'By the powers invested in me, I trace a protective circle around this holy assembly.' It was mumbo-jumbo with light tricks and the occasional hologram thrown in. But it fooled members, who tended to be well-heeled, well-educated, and well-connected."[9]

The extent to which cult members are indoctrinated into the belief that their leader is larger than life, however, never becomes more apparent than when outsiders who have not been indoctrinated meet or interview the cult's leader. While the people inside a cult may see their leader as God or godlike, outsiders, and particularly mental health professionals, often see a much different image. They often see individuals with serious psychological problems. Dr. Saul Levine, a Canadian psychiatrist, offers this assessment: "Their leaders are paranoid, sometimes very disturbed, but they fully believe that they are absolutely right."[10]

Despite many times demonstrating these psychological problems, cult leaders still often truly believe they are personal representatives of God and try to prove it by making prophecies through information they claim God has given them about approaching disasters or miracles, prophecies which, of course, ultimately fail. Many people might believe that after these prophecies have failed, the cult would break up since members would not want to stay in the cult once they see that their leader apparently doesn't have access to divine information after all.

Although failed prophecies by cult leaders can cause some members to leave, many don't because of a psychological phenomenon called "cognitive dissonance." This phenomenon makes some cult members become even more dedicated to the cult after a prophecy fails. The cult member ties up a great deal of his or her existence in the beliefs of the cult, and then something happens, or rather doesn't happen, that threatens that existence. Because individuals have a psychological need to maintain order and balance in their lives, in these instances, the only way they can do that is by rationalizing why the predicted event didn't occur, but to do it within the framework of the cult belief system.

Cognitive dissonance theory, developed by Leon Festinger, states, "If you change a person's behavior, his thoughts and feelings will change to minimize the dissonance."[11] What he is saying is that a person's thoughts, feelings, and behavior tend to be in unison, and if one of them changes or is altered for some reason, the other two will change to minimize the discrepancy. In his book *When Prophecy Fails,* Festinger tells about a UFO group whose leader convinced the members that a UFO was en route to rescue them from the impending end of the world. The members sold all their belongings or gave them away and then went to a mountaintop to await the end of the world and their rescue by the UFO. Although one might expect the group members to become disillusioned and ready to quit the group when the end of the world didn't come and the UFO didn't appear, most group members became even more committed because their earlier behaviors had also caused changes in certain mindsets and attitudes about the group. If they radically changed their behavior by leaving the group, they would also have to radically change their belief systems and attitudes, something most people find extremely difficult to do. They would have to admit to themselves that they had been completely and totally wrong in everything they had believed and done, which is an incredibly difficult thing for most people to do. Instead, it was much easier for the group members to accept the leader's explanation for the failure of the prophecy (in this case, the explanation the leader gave was that when the aliens in the UFO saw the holiness of the group members they decided to spare the earth) than to change their belief system.

A quote from a former cult member explains why people stay in cults even though leaders abuse them, even though nothing promised is ever accomplished, and even though prophecies fail: "After you've made a commitment of this magnitude, it's hard to admit you've made a mistake, and you'll go to great lengths to rationalize what you've done."[12]

DEMAND FOR PURITY

A major part of most cult belief systems is that the cult ideology is right, and everything else is wrong. The cult, during its indoctrination of new members, sets up a sharp dividing line. There are no shades of gray, only black and white. The cult ideology is right, and anything that disagrees with it is wrong. Period. There is no middle ground. Members who accept this line of narrow thinking tend to lose the objectivity that is needed when dealing with matters of human behavior and morality, which are not black or white, but mostly gray.

CONFESSION

As Adam found out in the incident at the beginning of this chapter, confession and criticism are a large part of the methodology of cult conversion. Cult members are made to confess over and over the sinfulness of their lives before joining the cult, and they therefore begin to see everything and everyone they dealt with before coming to the cult as sinful. After enough confession, a cult member feels completely unworthy, and consequently is much less likely to believe that he or she has the right to question or criticize cult leaders or the cult ideology. In addition, a large part of this ceremony also involves being criticized, often brutally, by other cult members, usually for having questions or some type of independent thought. New members soon learn that the best way to avoid confession and criticism is to accept the cult ideology without question, and to never say anything critical of the cult ideology or the cult leaders.

In cases where this doesn't work and cult members continue to question ideology or cult practices, cult leaders often throw it back onto the members, insisting that if members have any questions about the leaders or the cult's ideology, then the members must be the ones with problems, not the cult or its ideology. This assertion is usually reinforced by strong peer pressure not to question the cult's actions or its leaders, because they are always right. In a cult, the person questioning or complaining is *always* wrong.

"Questions are deflected," says Dr. Michael D. Langone in the book *Recovery from Cults*. "Critical comments are met with smiling pleas of 'no negativity,' or some other 'thought terminating cliché.' If prospects or new members persist in 'negativity,' they may be reminded of personal problems or guilty memories they have revealed to leaders, or they may be subjected to subtle ad hominem attacks that short-circuit their questions. Examples of such personal attacks might be 'you're intellectualizing' or 'you're being divisive.' Doubt and dissent are thus interpreted as symptoms of personal deficiency."[13]

Because of all of this, cult members often experience difficult times mentally and emotionally when they begin to have doubts about their leader or the cult's objectives. The cult members know that any criticisms voiced will be turned back on them, and so consequently the members don't know what to do. Recognizing this, and to keep the members productive rather than troubled, cult leaders often teach their members methods to use that will stop any of these "negative" thoughts. These thought-stopping processes, such as chanting, praying, repeating a mantra, and talking in tongues, are then used by the cult members to stop questions about the cult ideology and other negative thoughts. They are used to stop cult members from ever testing reality. The only reality is the cult and the cult philosophy.

"Cults teach you to stop thinking," said Steven Hassan. "Reality is completely redefined."[14]

Another way cult leaders stifle questions and criticism is by devising exhausting work schedules for all cult members so they will have little free time for such negative reflections. In many cults, every single minute of a person's day is accounted for with some type of task. There is absolutely no free time to reflect on what they're doing. In addition, the cult has preached and convinced its members that everything outside the cult is Satan's domain and all the people his servants. Therefore, the cult members feel intense dread at the thought of leaving the cult and naturally want to stop these types of negative thoughts. Soon, because of all this, as far as the cult members are concerned, the cult is always right no matter what.

In addition, cults lessen the likelihood of members questioning or complaining by attempting to establish a feeling of personal powerlessness and dependency on the cult. They do this by keeping the members off balance. A member may be praised one day and harshly criticized the next. A member may also be given information one day that is contradicted the next.

"They were masters of saying one thing on Monday, something else on Tuesday, and by Friday yet another," Maureen Dilley, a former member of The Way International, told me. "At the same time, on Friday they would maintain that Monday and Tuesday never occurred."[15]

To be kept off balance, members might also suddenly find themselves switched to different duties or to a different, unknown location. In addition, members might be given impossible tasks and then forced to confess their sinfulness for failing. The members often feel so worthless they believe they don't have the right to question or complain.

SACRED SCIENCE

The belief system of the cult must be seen by cult members who want to avoid the harsh confession and criticism ceremonies as sacred and holy. After enough time, the belief system is finally viewed as so holy that any questioning or criticism of it becomes the worst kind of blasphemy. Accepting the belief system as holy writ is actually comforting to many cult members because it not only makes them believe they are part of an elite group, one of the few in the world who know the real truth, but it also simplifies the world by seeming to answer all life's difficult questions.

To do this, the doctrine of a cult must be one that, as in religious doctrines, cannot be disproved. It must appear global and awe-inspiring. Yet it must also appear consistent and symmetrical enough to be believable. Like members of most major religions, a committed member of a cult doesn't demand proof of the group's beliefs, but accepts them on faith because they seem to answer major questions about life.

LOADING THE LANGUAGE

Cult leaders often like to change the meanings of certain common words so that only the cult members know what they mean when they use them. The use of this jargon then gives the cult members a feeling of exclusiveness and eliteness. In addition, cults teach members to use "thought-stopping" clichés. When faced with a possible viable argument against the cult's ideology or the cult leadership, members can use these statements or expressions to shut off all further discourse or interaction. They are flat statements that deny the existence of any reality other than that of the cult.

Yet to really bind people to a group, along with a private language, cults also often change the way their members look or dress. A distinctive hairstyle or mode of dress or uniform binds a person tightly to an organization by giving him or her a sense of belonging to an exclusive group.

DOCTRINE OVER PERSON

Members of cults eventually come to believe that the ideology of the cult is the only true answer to all questions of life. Therefore, if a cult member has a concern or question about the cult ideology, the problem is not with the ideology but with the cult member. The overall effect is that the cult's ideology becomes more important than any of its members.

DISPENSING OF EXISTENCE

Once a cult member has totally accepted the ideology of the cult, everyone outside the cult is seen as misguided, misinformed, and often evil. There is only one right way—the cult's way. Following this logic, members are told, and many believe, that if they leave the cult, they are evil and terrible things will happen to them. To keep members loyal and tied to the cult, leaders often spread fabricated stories about the terrible things that have happened to those who have left the group, how evil the people outside the cult are, and how particularly evil the people are who would steal them away from the cult.

Steve Hassan, telling his story about life inside the Unification Church (Moonies), says, "I had been repeatedly told horror stories about deprogramming. I had come to believe that group members were brutally kidnapped, beaten, and tortured by deprogrammers—Satan's elite soldiers committed to breaking people down and destroying their faith in God.... Fear of the outside world, particularly of parents, was drilled into our minds."[16]

"The indoctrination is so complete, and the peer pressure so great," says Joel Friedlander, a former member of the Fellowship of Friends, talked about in chapter 11, "that gradually the old you is replaced by the new you who believes all the propaganda, including the line that eternal damnation is the price of getting out."[17]

An article in the *New York Times* gives a vivid example of the power of thought reform used by cults: "The effectiveness of such manipulations was chillingly revealed in Diane Sawyer's interview on ABC last week with Rio D'Angelo, the 40th Heaven's Gate member who left a month before the suicides. Like a brainwashing victim in *The Manchurian Candidate,* he easily rattled off answers to questions about his beliefs but couldn't respond to the simplest queries requiring him to recall the house he inhabited with Ro (one of the two leaders of the Heaven's Gate cult)."[18] To totally bind members to this group, however, reportedly all members of the Heaven's Gate cult wore identical wedding rings to symbolize being wed to the cult.

The effect of thought reform in cults is often so pervasive that months, and sometimes years, after people have actually managed to get out of a cult, they will look back on their time in the group and say they can't believe what they were convinced of or what they did while they were in the cult. The thought reform came in such small, subtle segments that the people seldom saw it for what it was or saw the transformation that the cult indoctrination had made in them.

Confirming and adding to Dr. Lifton's eight conditions of thought reform above, Professors Margaret Thaler Singer and Louis Jolyon West have developed a list of 10 elements they have found are likely to be used in any successful cult indoctrination:

1. Isolation of the recruit and manipulation of his environment.
2. Control over channels of communication and information.
3. Debilitation through inadequate diet and fatigue.
4. Degradation or diminution of self.
5. Introduction of uncertainty, fear, and confusion, with joy and certainty through surrender to the group as a goal.
6. Alternation of harshness and leniency in a context of discipline.
7. Peer pressure, often applied through ritualized struggle sessions, generating guilt and requiring open confessions.
8. Insistence by seemingly all-powerful hosts that the recruit's surrender—physical and spiritual—depends on identifying with the group.
9. Assignment of monotonous tasks or repetitive activities, such as chanting or copying written material.
10. Acts of symbolic betrayal and renunciation of self, family, and previously held values, designed to increase the psychological distance between the recruit and his previous way of life.[19]

While cults have seemingly only been using thought reform since the 1960s, its history is longer than that. An article in *Psychiatric Annals* describes how the Chinese Communist Party began using thought reform as early as 1929. "Neither mysterious methods nor arcane new techniques were involved; the effectiveness of thought reform programs did not depend on prison settings, physical abuse, or death threats. Programs used the organization and application of intense guilt/shame/anxiety manipulation, combined with the production of strong emotional arousal in settings where people did not leave because of social and psychological pressure or because of enforced confinement. The pressures could be reduced only by participants accepting the belief system or adopting behaviors promulgated by the purveyors of the thought reform pro- grams."[20] Although cults have fine-tuned a few of these processes, today they use much the same system as the Communist Chinese did to force cult members to accept what often seems to outsiders to be a total com- mitment to some outlandish philosophy or theology.

The same article in *Psychiatric Annals* lists six conditions present in a thought reform program:

1. Obtaining substantial control over an individual's time and thought content, typically by gaining control over major elements of the person's social and physical environment.
2. Systematically creating a sense of powerlessness in the person.
3. Manipulating a system of rewards, punishment, and experiences in such a way as to promote new learning of an ideology or belief system advocated by management.
4. Manipulating a system of rewards, punishment, and experiences in such a way as to inhibit observable behavior that reflects the values and routines of life organization the individual displayed prior to contact with the group.
5. Maintaining a closed system of logic and an authoritarian structure in the organization.
6. Maintaining a noninformed state existing in the subject.[21]

Further, psychologist Edgar Schein has outlined three stages— unfreezing, changing, and refreezing—that people go through when their thought processes and attitudes are changed by cult thought reform:[22]

1. Unfreezing: In this stage, a person's old and long-held views of the world are challenged as being wrong. The cult then bombards recruits with information on what the correct worldview is. This information flow often comes so fast or lasts for so long that the recruit eventually begins to have serious doubts about his or her personal beliefs, and isn't sure what to believe. Many cults also use group criticism or self-confession to enhance the unfreezing.
2. Changing: Once the person begins seriously doubting the accuracy of his or her old worldview, acceptance of the cult's view becomes easier and more possible. During times of anxiety and confusion, people often look to what

others are doing or to what decisions others have made as a guide for their own behavior. Since cults control a person's environment during indoctrination and conversion, the only other people the recruit usually sees are long-time cult members, so all actions and decisions reflect the cult belief system. And once a person makes a commitment to even part of the cult's philosophy, he or she is likely to make more commitments. Before long, the recruit has fully accepted the cult's philosophy.

3. Refreezing: After a recruit appears to have accepted the cult's philosophy or worldview, cult members reward positive behavior with hugs, expressions of approval, and so on, and conversely punish any questioning or backsliding with criticism and shunning. A recruit soon learns that the path of least resistance, and the best way to avoid criticism, is to toe the cult line. After enough time, the life of devotion and unquestioning obedience to the cult leader seems proper and normal.

To guard against members becoming unfrozen and consequently questioning or criticizing the cult, most groups have the members carefully watch each other for any signs of independent thought, and often establish strict rules meant to stifle any chances of backsliding. For example, the Heaven's Gate cult, talked about in chapter 8, had a long list of offenses for its members, including the following:

1. Taking any action without checking with my partner first.
2. Trusting my own judgment or using my own mind.
3. Having private thoughts.
4. Having inappropriate curiosity.
5. Inappropriately offering suggestions, second guessing, or jumping ahead of my teachers.[23]

It doesn't take much study of these rules to know what kind of dependent, mindless servants the Heaven's Gate cult wanted its members to be. That 38 members of this cult meekly and obediently followed their leader, Marshall Herff Applewhite, into death shows how pervasive thought reform can be.

Of course, cults can also have their own additional processes that they use when indoctrinating new members. These include feeding cult recruits high-starch, low-protein diets that, when combined with sleep deprivation, break down a new member's ability to resist psychological pressure.

"Lack of sleep augments suggestibility," says Dr. Jean-Louis Valatx in discussing his research on sleep deprivation, "that is, if actions are suggested, the person will follow through, even though he wouldn't have if he hadn't been sleep-deprived."[24]

During the indoctrination of new recruits, cults will also often use, along with the above, other physiological processes that will either make the recruits more malleable or make them believe the cult has shown them a true spiritual experience. For example, cults will many times have recruits undergo some type of repeated chanting or exercises that will cause them to hyperventilate. One of the effects of hyperventilation is a lightheadedness or dizziness, along with a loss of the ability to perform critical thought. Intense hyperventilation can also bring on the feeling of unreality, which the cult claims is actually a divine state or message.

Other cults will attempt to get new recruits into these states by the use of hypnosis or through inducing trance states. These are called altered states of consciousness, and during these times, individuals are much more susceptible to suggestion. In addition, while in these states, a person's analytical and reasoning abilities become seriously hampered. Naturally, cults never tell recruits they are going to be put into trance states or hypnotized; rather, they lead recruits through seemingly innocuous activities that result in these states. For example, a phrase repeated over and over in a cadenced, singsong tone can bring a trancelike state. Other cults will use guided imagery, in which listeners are told to try to picture themselves in some type of scene the speaker is describing. Guided imagery can often induce a hypnotic state, making the individual more malleable and ready for indoctrination.

Although the procedures and methods cults use in indoctrination can vary, Dr. Langone, an expert on cults, says that almost all cult indoctrinations have three stages: deception, dependency, and dread.[25]

1. Deception: Cults deceive new members as to what the group really is, what it can do for them, what the group is actually proposing to accomplish, and the size of the commitment expected of cult members.

2. Dependency: Through various methods, including isolation, stripping away of the old identity, severing of old relationships, inducing guilt for the sins of their lives before the cult, and punishing critical or negative thinking, cults make new members totally dependent on the cult for support, emotional and otherwise. Once individuals have found that their sense of self has been destroyed and consequently they are confused about what to believe in "the easiest way to reconstruct the self and obtain a new equilibrium is to 'identify with the aggressor' and accept the ideology of the authority figure who has reduced the person to a state of profound confusion."[26]

3. Dread: Once the new member has become thoroughly indoctrinated, cults then infuse him or her with a feeling of dread over losing the psychological and emotional support of the group. In addition, cults make members believe that if they do ever leave the group, terrible things will happen to them.

Despite their thorough indoctrination of new members, most cults still have to continuously reinforce the indoctrination to be certain members don't start slipping backward into precult behaviors or even slip away from the cult altogether. As I have pointed out, cults can reinforce indoctrination in various ways. However, one of the most unique ways this was accomplished was a method used by The Way International, an organization founded in the 1950s by Victor Paul Wierwille, who, like most cult leaders, made his "official" history much more interesting than it really was.

According to news reports and several books about the organization, Victor Paul Wierwille, a defrocked minister of St. Peter's Evangelical and Reformed Church, established The Way International at his family farm in New Knoxville, Ohio, in 1955. At its height in the mid-1980s, The Way International had offices or centers in all 50 states and in 40 foreign countries. By Wierwille's death in 1985, more than 100,000 people had attended his "Power for Abundant Living" seminar (at $200 each), and in 1985, The Way International reported revenues exceeding $30 million.

In September 1942, when Wierwille was 25 years old, he claimed that God spoke to him and told him that He would teach him The Word as it had been taught in the first century, that Wierwille would know The Word better than anyone in history, and that afterward Wierwille was to spread The Word to others. As a part of this miracle, apparently so that Wierwille would know it was really God speaking to him, Wierwille claimed that God caused a near blizzard to strike the small Ohio town where He spoke to him.

"The sky was so white and thick with snow," Wierwille told others, "I couldn't see the tanks at the filling station on the corner not 75 feet away."[27]

The only problem with this "miracle" claimed by Wierwille is that, according to official weather records, no measurable snow fell in Ohio during September 1942. But like most cult leaders, Wierwille never felt terribly concerned about facts that disagreed with his story.

However, what may have started out in 1942 as an evangelical crusade eventually degenerated into a personality cult built around Wierwille. Members of The Way International saw him as being next to God, and because of this, most members could apparently overlook the fact that he lived in luxury while most of his followers toiled just above the poverty level.

"I believed that Wierwille walked more closely with God than any other human," said former The Way International member Karl Kahler, who wrote *The Cult That Snapped* to tell of his experiences as a member.[28]

"I believed he was a man who spoke directly with God," said Jim Martin about Victor Wierwille. Martin, associate editor of *Ex-Cultworld* magazine, also added this comment about Wierwille: "He could talk you out of your last dime and make you feel good about it."[29]

However, being a female member of The Way International, and particularly an attractive female, reportedly often brought with it pressure to have sex with Wierwille. Kahler discusses in his book how prevalent sexual coercion was in The Way International. He quotes a longtime member and leader of The Way International: "He [Wierwille] subtly taught that it was a woman's duty to meet the needs of a man of God.... [T]here was a 'big sex trip' going on, with Wierwille leading the charge. It was rampant among the leadership, well-concealed but promoted in a subtle way."[30] Kahler also quotes a former leader of The Way International who left to form his own ministry: "The guy [Wierwille] screwed thousands of women. He was a sex addict. He was an egomaniac, he was an alcoholic, he was a sex addict."[31]

Wierwille was able to get away with this sexual coercion because, like most cult leaders, he maintained strict discipline among his members. He warned his sexual victims not to talk to others about it, and most didn't. Supporting Wierwille in the sexual coercion and consequent cover-up was the practice in The Way International, as in most cults, for all decisions, even very minor ones, to be made by the leaders and never left to members. Therefore, when the leader said he wanted sex, most female members of the group didn't know how to disagree or disobey. No one ever questioned a decision, action, or order of Wierwille.

"While I was a member and under the mental control of TWI leaders," Pat Roberge, editor of *Ex-Cultworld* magazine told me, "if Victor Wierwille had ordered me to do something, I don't think that I would have hesitated to do anything ordered, including criminal acts."[32]

Recently, and as I will talk about in the next chapter, former members of The Way International have sued the group for this sexual coercion and other crimes they claim the cult committed. The cult has settled several of these cases out of court.

Interestingly, while Wierwille had always preached that cancer was an illness caused by devil spirits and that it showed negative belief, he contracted ocular melanoma, which eventually spread to metastatic melanoma of the liver, killing him in May 1985. Although The Way International remains active today, it isn't the organization it was under Wierwille. Since Wierwille's death, the group has suffered through a period of internal fighting. This internal fighting eventually led to the ouster of The Way International president L. Craig Martindale, who had been selected by Wierwille to replace him. Rosalie Rivenbark, a longtime member of The Way International, became its president in 2000.

For the purposes of this chapter, I want to examine The Way International's continuing indoctrination methods. What did this group do to reinvigorate its followers and make them want to continue working long hours for the group?

Although The Way International used conventional indoctrination techniques with its new members, the group also had a reindoctrination technique that was not only very successful but also extremely cost-effective because members paid to be reindoctrinated. Every August between 1971 and 1995, The Way International held what it called the Rock of Ages Festival. This musical festival (later to also include dance, drew an estimated 20,000 attendees every year.

"The Rock of Ages was a gathering of the flock to reinforce the belief of the members of The Way," former The Way International member Jim Martin told me. "The best way I could describe it was that it was like an old-fashioned revival/camp meeting/circus. There was lots of singing, lots of teaching, and lots of seminars. It lasted a week, and there was always something going on. We all had to pay $50 apiece to attend, and there was a lot of interaction at the Rock among The Way members. This was also where you'd get your new assignment."[33] Like the people leaving an old-time revival, after a week at the Rock of Ages Festival, most members of The Way International said they felt a renewed drive and commitment.

After reading what I've written so far in this chapter, many readers are likely to think, "Okay, maybe a cult can make a person believe in some outlandish ideology. But what kind of power can make members go along with a cult leader's decision to harm or kill others?"

To answer this question, Stanley Milgram, a researcher, conducted a series of experiments in the 1960s that demonstrated how even normal, law-abiding people can be coerced into harming others. In his experiment, Milgram led test subjects to believe that they were administering electric shocks to unseen individuals in the next room whenever the individuals didn't perform a task properly. Milgram found that his test subjects would deliver even what they thought were dangerously high levels of electric shock if they were ordered to do so by the experiment leaders. The test subjects would do this even though the individuals in the next room, who were not actually being shocked, would scream as though they were in intense pain.

In his book *Obedience to Authority,* Milgram states, "The essence of obedience consists in the fact a person comes to view himself as the instrument for carrying out another person's wishes, and therefore no longer regards himself as responsible for his own actions."[34]

Along with harming others though, cult leaders can often convince individuals to take actions totally out of character for them. This usually comes to the public's notice whenever a highly educated individual with a position of authority in society does something at the direction of a cult leader that he or she should have known would be disastrous.

An excellent example of this is Catholic Archbishop Emmanuel Milingo, who, according to new reports, shocked the Catholic Church in 2001 by marrying Maria Sung, a 43-year-old Korean woman chosen for him by Reverend Sun Myung Moon, head of the Unification Church. Milingo, who by Catholic Church rules and doctrine could not marry, left his new wife several months later.

"Maybe I was the object of a type of brainwashing," said Archbishop Milingo, trying to explain his actions. "I didn't realize what I was getting myself into. I only understood later that it (the wedding) was a way of them getting total control over me."

Milingo claims that Moon had planned to establish a new Catholic Church, with Milingo as its head. "It was all so strange," said Milingo. "It was like a strange dream."[35] In November 2002, after Milingo had spent a year in spiritual retreat in Argentina, the Vatican announced that he had been forgiven and would resume his duties in the church.

Actually, however, this type of thought reform is not just a phenomenon associated with cults. Throughout history, government leaders have often convinced others to take actions that most people believe they should have known would be disastrous. Scientists use the term *groupthink* to refer to this obedience to a decision that has the likely potential to be harmful and disastrous. Researcher Irving L. Janis coined the word *groupthink* for a type of decision making that causes highly cohesive groups to emphasize consensus rather than a careful and thorough analysis of a problem and its possible solutions. Janis defines the term this way: "Groupthink is a mode of thinking that people engage in when they are deeply involved in a cohesive group, when the members' striving for unanimity overrides their motivation to realistically appraise alternative courses of action...Groupthink refers to a deterioration of mental efficiencies, reality testing, and moral judgment that results from in-group pressures."[36]

In his book *Groupthink*, Janis defines eight attributes of a group that cause groupthink:

1. An illusion of invulnerability.
2. A faulty grasp of its own moral principles.
3. The skills for intellectualization and rationalization.
4. Advanced capabilities in stereotyping others.
5. A willingness to self-censor.
6. A desire to act with unanimity.
7. The ability to put direct pressure on dissidents.
8. A reliance on self-appointed mind guards to maintain the belief system of the group.[37]

Although Janis developed the groupthink theory to explain extraordinarily bad decisions by government leaders, such as the Bay of Pigs invasion and the escalation of the Vietnam War, it can also explain decisions made by groups such as Heaven's Gate and the vampire cults described in chapter 1. In his article "Expanding the Groupthink Explanation to the Study of Contemporary Cults," which appeared in the *Cultic Studies Journal*, Professor Mark N. Wexler states that "the chances of groupthink dramatically increase when cohesive groups with structural faults find themselves under stress from external sources in a crisis situation."[38] As examples of this, Jim Jones (talked about in chapter 3) found himself under tremendous stress when longtime group members decided to leave with Congressman Leo Ryan, and the cult known as the Movement for the

Restoration of the Ten Commandments (talked about in chapter 6) faced a revolt among its members when the world didn't end on December 31, 1999, which the cult leaders knew would eventually lead to a government investigation.

Interestingly though, while all the thought reform processes discussed so far work fairly well, research has shown that thought reform processes work better when they use positive reinforcement rather than negative pressures such as the threat of physical violence. Actually, the use of positive reinforcement to convert cult members comes as no surprise to any police officer who has ever worked as part of a SWAT team or a hostage negotiations team. These officers see the power of this type of thought reform all the time, and they have a special term to describe it: the Stockholm syndrome.

The name of this thought reform process came from a hostage incident that took place in 1973 at the Sveriges Kreditbank in Stockholm, Sweden. During this incident, the police found that as the time wore on, the hostages became very emotionally attached to the hostage takers. The police also discovered that, as the time passed, the hostages began voicing more fear of the police than they did of the hostage takers. One of the hostages, while talking on the telephone to the Swedish prime minister, even claimed that their abductors were not really holding them hostage but rather were protecting them from the police.

This syndrome, which appears to be an unconscious, long-term reaction, is caused by a combination of factors and has been seen many times in subsequent hostage situations. The case of Patty Hearst is probably the most celebrated example of the Stockholm syndrome. A group of terrorists kidnapped Hearst and held her hostage. Because of the effects of the Stockholm syndrome, she eventually joined the terrorist group and even took part in a bank robbery with them.

Studies have shown, however, that certain factors must be present before the Stockholm syndrome will develop. There must be positive contact between the hostages and hostage takers (any negative contact can block the development of the syndrome), and both the hostages and hostage takers must be under intense stress together. In addition, the hostages and hostage takers must see each other as human beings with feelings, needs, and problems.

This syndrome, incidentally, is a long-term condition that doesn't just fade away after a hostage incident is resolved. Hostages have been known to visit their abductors in prison and set up defense funds for them. In the Stockholm incident, one of the hostages even became engaged to one of her abductors. Many people who have been held hostage for long periods later say that they found themselves liking their captors and doing things for them that they never would have thought possible.

A study of former hostages posed the following question: "If rescuing police shouted for you to get down on the floor, but one of the hostage takers ordered you to stand, what would you do?" The overwhelming answer was that they would obey the hostage taker.[39] Because of the Stockholm syndrome, police officers must carefully judge whether to rely on intelligence given them by released hostages, as the released hostages will often lie to help the hostage takers, even though they are no longer in any danger from them. In addition, a SWAT team must carefully check all hostages when an incident is resolved because often a hostage taker will masquerade as a hostage and the hostages won't tell the police. It doesn't take much analysis to see how this condition can apply to cult members. During cult indoctrination, recruits are often held almost captive and are under intense stress with individuals who seem extremely friendly and loving to them. (For more information on the Stockholm syndrome, see my book *SWAT Teams*.)

I had a recent experience that showed me how a condition very much like the Stockholm syndrome can also have long-term, and seemingly unconscious, effects on its victims. I was having dinner at the 2002 American Family Foundation conference and was talking to a young lady sitting next to me. She told me how she had been recruited into a cult through a referral by a therapist she had been seeing for personal problems. She had been told the cult would help her with her personal problems, but instead the cult had been very abusive, and had worsened her personal problems. She then told me that she had retained a lawyer and was suing the therapist for referring her to the cult. When I asked her if she intended to also sue the cult and its leader, she actually pulled back in her chair at the suggestion. After a few moments, apparently seeing the contradiction in her behavior, she began trying to explain to me why it likely wouldn't do any good for her to sue the cult or its leader.

"We are far too cavalier about the impact of mind control and the impact of charismatic people, who, if they tell you often enough and intensely enough, can cause you to think that black is white and white is black," says Jackie Spier, a California state senator and a survivor of the mass murder/suicide at Jonestown, where she was wounded by the same gunfire that killed Congressman Leo Ryan. "Self-determination is eroded."[40]

One of the most important things about cults that I hope I've shown in this book is that these groups are inherently dangerous organizations. Few people who come in contact with cults for any length of time escape without some harm. Fortunately, as I will show in the next chapter, there are ways for family members and friends to keep other family members and friends from being attracted to cults to begin with, ways to rescue family members and friends who have been drawn into a cult, and ways for former cult members to legally strike back at cults that have abused them.

CHAPTER 15

Combating Cults

In February 1998, according to a *San Francisco Chronicle* article, a San Mateo County (California) jury awarded former cult member Anne-Marie Bertolucci $625,000 as compensation for the fraud and emotional distress she suffered while a member of the Ananda Church of Self-Realization. The leaders of the Ananda Church appeared stunned by the verdict.

"To be their target is an experience I would not wish on anyone," said Asha Praver, a minister with the Ananda Church of Self-Realization.[1]

The "their" Praver referred to are attorneys Michael Flynn and Ford Greene, who specialize in suing abusive groups and their leaders. Greene, in particular, has a special reason for wanting to pursue cult leaders in court. As a young man, he traveled to the Unification Church camp in Boonville, California, to retrieve his sister, who had joined the group. Instead, however, he found himself also recruited into the Moonies. He only stayed with the group for eight months, though, before leaving, totally disillusioned about his original commitment and convinced that organizations such as the Unification Church can be extremely dangerous. In the following years, he attended law school with the intention of using his education to fight such groups in the courtroom. And while he has been very successful, he doesn't want people to think that he is against religion. He says he is very careful "not to throw the baby of legitimate religious beliefs and practice out with the bathwater of deception and coercion."

Greene continues to explain, "I look to see whether a group is authoritarian or open. There are red flags. Secrecy is certainly one of them. Punishing or disregarding dissent is another. Uncritical and unconditional adulation of the leader is another. Exploitation, financial or sexual or labor, is another."[2]

While many cults like to hide behind the First Amendment in the belief that it puts them beyond the scrutiny of any investigative group, Flynn and Greene regularly use a 1988 California Supreme Court ruling, given in one of Greene's cases, that allows attorneys to investigate the actions of any religious group to prove illegal conduct. The ruling basically says that the First Amendment doesn't protect religious groups from claims of manipulation and exploitation.

Naturally, many cults don't look upon these two lawyers favorably. Their offices have been burglarized and ransacked several times. The attorneys even caught a private investigator, hired by the Ananda Church of Self-Realization, going through documents in Flynn's trash, and as a consequence the court reprimanded the defendants from the Ananda Church.

However, while opposed to abusive cults, which they vigorously pursue in the courtroom, these two attorneys are not opposed to unorthodox beliefs. Flynn, for example, once represented New Age guru Deepak Chopra in a lawsuit claiming defamation.

While the work of Flynn and Green should give hope to abused cult members or to the families of abused cult members, these two men are not the only attorneys vigorously opposing abusive cults. For example, the Church Universal and Triumphant, a group discussed in chapter 9, sued former member Gregory Mull, claiming he owed them $30,000 in notes he had signed in their favor. However, an article in the *Cultic Studies Journal* tells how Mull contacted attorney Lawrence Levy and how Levy, after hearing horror stories of Mull's treatment while in the group, countersued the Church Universal and Triumphant for fraud, extortion, intentional infliction of emotional distress, common-law involuntary servitude, unjust enrichment, and assault. Levy found that during Mull's 10 years in the Church Universal and Triumphant, he had lost his wife, his career as an architect, and his health.[3]

Levy says that the key to winning legal cases against groups like the Church Universal and Triumphant is to focus on actions, not beliefs. "I always let the jury know I don't care what they [the cult] believe," Levy told me in an interview. "That's none of my business. The First Amendment gives people the right to believe anything they want. But it doesn't give them the right to *do* anything they want."[4] Levy also believes that an attorney, before taking such a case, must learn about abusive cults and how they operate. Then, during the trial, the attorney can educate the judge and jury, who are usually unaware of the dynamics and destructiveness of many cults.

In Mull's case, the court found in his favor, awarding him $1,563,000. Although the Church Universal and Triumphant appealed the case all the way to the U.S. Supreme Court, it lost. The California Appellate Court, in its ruling supporting the verdict, described the Church Universal and Triumphant's treatment of Mull as "shameful, despicable, and reprehensi-ble."[5]

Although Mull became attorney Lawrence Levy's first case against a cult, Levy has since successfully sued cults more than a dozen times. "I've sued The Way International, the Church Universal and Triumphant, and I've sued Hare Krishna," Levy told me. "When you scratch the surface," he said, "and you don't worry about their religious interests, then you just find basic torts. They extort from you, they use undue influence. You get in somebody's pocketbook, though, they usually get upset."[6]

In *George v. International Society for Krishna Consciousness*, another case reported in the *Cultic Studies Journal*, the trial court ordered the Hare Krishnas, after losing an appeal to the U.S. Supreme Court, to pay damages of $5 million. The jury awarded this amount to the family of a member of the cult as compensation for the emotional suffering it caused them. The family's suffering began when their underage daughter joined the Hare Krishna movement and was continually shipped around the country to hide her from her parents, who were searching for her. In addition to the emotional distress, the father of the underage girl suffered a fatal heart attack that doctors said had been brought on by the strain of trying to find his daughter.[7]

In another case, according to news reports, Paul and Frances Allen reached an out-of-court settlement in November 2000 with The Way International. While the details of the settlement could not be disclosed, the Allens had originally sued The Way International for $50 million, alleging in their suit that the group engaged in a "pattern of corrupt activity," as defined by the Ohio Revised Code, "including, but not limited to acts of theft, fraud, coercion, assault, and rape." Although the judge in the case threw out two counts of the lawsuit, he upheld the claims that Mrs. Allen had been sexually victimized and that The Way International had engaged in a pattern of corrupt activity that included acts of assault and rape, and breach of contract.[8]

In May 2002, a suit filed by a Mr. and Mrs. Parker against The Way International, and handled by attorney Lawrence Levy, was also settled out of court. Although the terms of the settlement could not be disclosed, reportedly the Parkers were very satisfied by it.

In June 2002, another couple, the Peelers, filed a lawsuit against The Way International, seeking $75 million. The couple alleges that The Way International engaged in fraudulent misrepresentation and the sexual exploitation of some of its members.

Along with attorneys that sue abusive cults because of the mistreatment members suffer while belonging to them, there are also a number of legal firms that handle child custody cases involving a parent or parents who belong to a destructive cult. Articles in the February 1995 and January 1996 issues of the *Cult Observer* deal with how these cases are handled and litigated. In one article, New York City attorney Randy Frances Kandel goes into great detail about how law firms can successfully litigate child custody cases in which one parent is a member of a destructive cult.[9] As I have shown numerous times in this book, getting underage children out of destructive cults can be of extreme importance to their physical, mental, and emotional health—and occasionally it can even save their lives. However, what the article in the *Cult Observer* really says is that a parent wanting to obtain custody of a child whose other parent is in a destructive cult must be certain to retain a law firm that has experience and expertise in litigation against destructive cults. This is excellent advice because if these parents don't, their attorney is likely to see this as just a case in which a person doesn't agree with an ex-spouse's religious beliefs.

To effectively help a noncult parent gain custody of a child who has a parent in a destructive cult, the attorney will need to show, through expert testimony, how remaining in the cult will be highly detrimental to the child's health and well-being. However, this is not an easy task because many judges, juries, child social workers, and others are totally unaware of what goes on within a destructive cult. All too often they believe that the legal system shouldn't get involved in religious issues, which is what they mistakenly believe membership in a cult is. The attorney handling the noncult parent's case therefore must have experience with litigation against cults, because he or she must be able to show the judge and jury that the case is not a religious issue, and then educate them about what living in a cult can do to a child.

Many other legal issues can arise from cult membership, such as dissolving a marriage arranged by the cult or voiding contracts and monetary promises made to the cult. Often these contracts and promises are not legally binding, but to void them takes the services of an attorney with experience in dealing with destructive cults. Also, some contributions made while a member of a cult may be recoverable if it can be shown that they were obtained under duress or by fraud. Successful litigation in these cases takes careful planning and often requires, as in child custody cases, the introduction of expert testimony that can educate the court about both thought reform and life within a cult.

Naturally, litigation against abusive and destructive cults would be much easier if the members of the legal system were more aware of the dynamics of a cult. A number of the cult experts I spoke with suggested that law schools should be encouraged, when developing their curriculum, to include a course that would educate future attorneys about thought reform, undue influence by abusive groups, and what really happens to people in groups such as destructive cults.

Along with the civil remedies I've described in this chapter, former cult members can also bring criminal charges against cult leaders and members who have mistreated them. On February 9, 2000, according to newspaper reports, a California court sentenced cult leader Robert Martin

Lloyd, who in 1998 legally changed his name to Master David, to nine years in prison for the assault and rape of one of his female cult members. Master David, who claims to be the reincarnation of Jesus, at first insisted on representing himself because, as Jesus, he knows all, but eventually he decided to accept the services of a public defender. The government ordered Master David deported back to England at the conclusion of his sentence.

On September 24, 2002, an article in the *Great Falls Tribune* reported that during opening arguments at the trial of cult leader Arthur Sandrock, his attorney did not deny that Sandrock sexually molested two girls when they were ages 8 and 10 but said that his client shouldn't be held responsible because he was severely mentally ill. Sandrock was "in another dimension when he was committing these acts," his attorney said.[10] Sandrock was charged with 12 counts of sexual assault and three counts of the rape of a minor. The prosecutor also charged Sandrock with two counts of tampering with witnesses after Sandrock reportedly sent threatening letters in an attempt to convince witnesses not to testify at his trial.

Sandrock claimed to be "the high lord of Yawe" and "the Fourth Son of God." He allegedly told his victims that they were satisfying God's sexual desires by having sex with him, and that God would send them to hell if they refused.

In February 2002, the *Los Angeles Times* reported that the L.A. police arrested alleged cult leader Mogens Amdi Petersen and accused him of swindling his victims out of at least $10 million through TVIND, an organization Petersen founded that many people have called a cult. A college student, Martin Lewis, joined TVIND, thinking it to be a charitable group set up to help poor people. Lewis instead found himself in a cult, and rather than charity work, he claimed the group forced him to sell newspapers and flowers on the street.

"When I got home," Lewis said, "it was like I had escaped from prison. I want to warn others of this organization."[11]

On October 23, 2000, four members of the Honohana Sanpogyo cult pleaded guilty to swindling 15 people out of more than $6 million. Cult leaders reportedly told members that the problems for which members had sought the cult's help would only become worse if they didn't sign up for cult-run seminars, which cost up to $20,000 each.

Of course, some people don't want to have to wait for the legal system to act. Some people want to take more immediate and direct action against cults. In the Japanese village of Kitamimaki, for example, residents discovered that a vacant house in their village belonged to the Aum Shinrikyo cult, the group responsible for the poison gas attack in the Tokyo subway system, talked about in chapter 2. According to the *Washington Post*, the alarmed villagers, in order to keep any cult members from occupying the building, dug an eight-foot-wide ditch around the house, strung barbed wire, installed video surveillance cameras, and stretched helicopter-thwarting rope netting around the open areas near the house.

When five vans carrying Aum Shinrikyo members showed up and began unloading equipment at 4:00 A.M. one morning, the villagers on watch began ringing iron bells that serve as the village's fire alarm system. Within minutes, 500 villagers surrounded the cult members, loaded their equipment back into the vans, and escorted them out of the village.

"They are not a religious group, they are terrorists," said Masayoshi Mizushina, a village councilman. "We will never let them in here, and we will fight them by any means."[12]

Other people, angry at being victimized by alleged cults, also want to take direct action. For example, on September 3, 2002, according to Australian news reports, a former devotee of Mahariji, an Indian guru, attempted to ram his truck into a convention hall in Ipswich, Australia, where the guru was speaking. "I am one of hundreds of ex-premie of the Mahariji who came to realize he is nothing more than a fraud and fat cat who is living in the lap of luxury at the expense of his followers," said Neville Ackland, who claims to have given Mahariji nearly $500,000.[13]

Although not as forceful and direct as Ackland and the Japanese villagers, many colleges and universities, which are often fertile grounds for cult recruitment, have also taken steps to combat cults. The most important thing these colleges and universities are doing is trying to make new and impressionable students more aware of the possibility of cult recruitment on campus. To do this, many colleges and universities are giving talks about cults and cult recruitment during student orientation, and many others supply new students with handouts that give them the warning signs of cult recruitment. A number of colleges and universities have even banned groups from their campuses that have been found to use deceptive recruitment techniques.

"There are a significantly greater number of colleges and universities today that are aware of cult activity on their campuses," said Ronald Loomis, education director for the American Family Foundation. "And they are initiating programs to educate their students and faculty and staff about them."[14]

However, not all colleges and universities give these warnings, and those unaware students who are consequently recruited into cults are often, it has been found, recruited after they attend meetings, seminars, or retreats given by cults. At these functions, the students are never told the real nature of the group sponsoring the event. In addition, these events often take place at isolated locations away from the campus, to which recruiters offer the students a ride. On arriving at the site, the students often find themselves trapped there with no way back until the event is over. The book *Cults on Campus: Continuing Challenge* suggests that any students approached about attending a meeting or seminar by a group the students have never heard of should ask the person inviting them the following questions:

1. Is your organization known by any other name?
2. Who is the leader of your organization?
3. Can you give me the names of other students who have been to one of your retreats?
4. Does your organization operate on other college campuses? Which ones?
5. If someone decides he/she wants to leave before the seminar is over, how can he/she get back here?
6. Why have you chosen to recruit members by speaking to them on street corners rather than the more traditional ways of recruiting?
7. Exactly where is the retreat and how else (other than your bus) can people get there and leave?
8. How does your group get its money?[15]

Naturally, any evasive answers or refusals to answer questions should be a clear sign that the students need to tell the person they aren't interested. If the recruiter agrees to provide the names of other students who have attended the retreat, they should be contacted to learn more about the group and its purpose. Another good question college students should ask of any group trying to recruit them is, Does the group encourage its members to stay in school and succeed academically, or does it want students to drop out and work or study in the group? If the recruiter claims that the group wants its members to stay in school, students should ask for the names of members of the group who are still in college and contact them.

While this advice is tailored for college students, it can be used by anyone approached by what appears to be a cult recruiter. However, one of the things I have been told by practically every cult expert I've spoken with is that although the efforts some colleges and universities are making to educate new students about cults is certainly commendable, it is not enough. This type of warning and education must be given much sooner. As I stated in a previous chapter, in a study of high school students, 54 percent report having been approached by a cult recruiter, and 40 percent report three to five such contacts. Classes about the dangers of cults and the signs of cult recruitment should start not at the college level but in junior high and then be reinforced in succeeding grades. Studies show that people knowledgeable about cults are much better prepared to resist them.

In addition to the individuals and groups mentioned so far, even some national governments have gotten themselves involved in fighting abusive cults. Because of the illegal practices of certain cults, a number of nations have gone so far as to ban these groups from operating within their national boundaries. Other nations have formed agencies that investigate and report on possible abusive groups. Argentina, for example, has established the SPES Foundation, which monitors cult activity in the country. In 1984, the European Parliament passed the Cottrell Resolution, which calls for member nations to pool their information about possible cults and cult activity. In November 2001, Switzerland opened the Inter-Cantonal Centre for Information on Beliefs. The Swiss government formed this organization in response to the Solar Temple cult deaths (talked about in chapter 10), a number of which took place in Switzerland. The inter-Cantonal Centre provides information to Swiss citizens about possible dangerous groups.

"We don't want to infringe people's beliefs," said Gerald Ramseyer, Geneva's Cantonal Justice Minister, "but we do want people to be aware of the danger some of these groups pose."[16]

Often, despite the help offered by all the groups and agencies mentioned so far, families who believe that one of their members is in a cult choose to deal with the problem themselves. This is certainly their decision to make. However, the first thing they need to do before taking any action is to collect as much information as possible about destructive cults in general and about how to help the family member they suspect is in a cult. Most families know very little about destructive cults and how they operate. Fortunately, there are a number of groups and organizations that can provide families with this information and assistance. One of the largest informational groups dealing with cults is the American Family Foundation. Their Web address is http://www.csj.org. The American Family Foundation has many publications available about abusive cults and about recovery from the destructive effects of cults. Additional resources about cults and also information on cult support groups can be found at http://www. factnet.org. Along with this, a considerable amount of information about cults and former cult members can be found at http://www.excultworld.com.

Most families with a loved one who appears to have joined a cult and who appears to be thoroughly indoctrinated into the group's belief system naturally want to rescue that person. Frequently in the 1960s, to rescue a loved one from a cult, agents hired by concerned family members would kidnap the loved one from the cult, hold the person against his or her will at some secure location, and then put the cult member through a process called deprogramming. In deprogramming, an individual called a deprogrammer would attempt to force cult members to see that they had been duped by the cult leader. Although deprogramming was successful in about 65 percent of the cases,[17] the process could also be brutal because it was basically coercive. If a cult member fought deprogramming or the original kidnapping, physical injuries became possible. Potentially, the deprogramming could turn out to be as bad or worse psychologically as the alleged abuse within the cult. As discussed in chapter 2, The Way International discontinued its attempts to rescue members who had been grabbed by deprogrammers because, rather than wanting to return to the group, most "rescued" members just wanted to get away from both the deprogrammers and their "rescuers."

The Cult Awareness Network (CAN), which for years served as a source of information and referrals for the families of cult members, found itself in bankruptcy and out of business because of a lawsuit filed by a young man who had been kidnapped and forced to undergo an attempt at deprogramming by a deprogrammer referred to the family through an employee of CAN. According to news reports, the fall of CAN began in 1991 when the mother of an 18-year-old man named Jason Scott hired a deprogrammer referred to her through a counselor who worked for CAN. The mother wanted to get her son away from a Pentecostal group called the Life Tabernacle Church. The deprogrammer allegedly kidnapped Scott, held him handcuffed and gagged for five days in a secluded beach house, and forced him to watch videotapes about religious cults. To escape, Jason feigned conversion but, once released, immediately went to the police.

As a result of a lawsuit filed by Scott, a court ordered CAN to pay $1.08 million in damages, an award that the U.S. Supreme Court eventually upheld. Because of this, in June 1996, CAN filed for bankruptcy and had its assets, including its name, put up for sale. Readers, therefore, should be warned that the CAN organization still in existence is not the original organization.

An article in *Modern Maturity* magazine tells of another case in which a cult member forcibly underwent deprogramming. Although successful, the process left the former cult member with long-term detrimental effects. "One day my husband asked me to come home and pick up a package," the former cult member said. When she got to the house she found that her entire family, plus three deprogrammers, were waiting. "I was angry. I felt betrayed. It took several days of talking before I could simmer down and start to listen. Even though I was grateful to my family, it took a long time to get over that anger."[18]

Today, rather than deprogramming, most responsible professionals who want to help families extricate a loved one from a cult use a process called exit counseling. This is a much less physical approach in which the counselor uses logic and reason to show the cult member how deceptive the cult leader was. Unlike deprogramming, the cult member must voluntarily agree to take part in the process, although often this "voluntary agreement" is simply a reaction to severe pressure put on the cult member by his or her family, and is not what the cult member really wants to do. Consequently, exit counselors must be individuals who can establish almost instant rapport with cult members. They must be individuals to whom cult members will want to talk to. In addition, most successful exit counseling teams include a former member of the cult the family member belongs to. Having this person on the exit counseling team gives the cult member someone to talk to who can understand the dynamics and belief system of the cult, and it also allows the cult member to see that, contrary to what the cult leader has said, nothing terrible has happened to someone who left the cult.

"Exit counseling," says exit counselor Carol Giambalvo, "is a voluntary, intensive, time-limited, contractual educational process that emphasizes the respectful sharing of information with members of exploitatively manipulative groups, commonly called cults."[19]

Before considering exit counseling or any other attempt to persuade a family member to leave a cult, the family must, once it has obtained information on destructive cults in general, try to obtain as much information as possible about the specific group the loved one belongs to. If the family does decide to secure professional exit counseling, the counselors will need this information, and gathering it ahead of time can save the family both the time and expense of having the exit counselor do it. Fortunately, getting this information can often be done through the family member involved in the cult, because recruiting and proselytizing are a large part of almost every cult. Families should gather and read any pamphlets, books, or audiotapes the cult member can provide. Naturally, keep in mind that these are very slanted toward the cult viewpoint, but they should give the family an idea of the orientation of the group. Families may also want to contact the cult, without giving out too much personal data, and ask for information about the group. Many cults are glad to provide this since most are obsessed with bringing in new members. Such materials can often give families the cult's address, telephone number, names of the leaders, and so forth.

The Internal Revenue Service can be another source of information about a possible cult. If the investigation by the family shows that the group the loved one belongs to is a nonprofit organization, such groups are required to file an IRS form 990. Copies of these forms are available to the public through IRS, Ogden Service Center, P.O. Box 9941, Mail Stop 6716, Ogden, UT 84409.

As another source of information, concerned families should check the Internet to see if the group the loved one belongs to has a Web site—as many of them do. There are also Web sites that can provide families with information on specific cults; for example, http://www.csj.org, http://www.factnet.org, and http://www.rickross.com. Concerned families should also check for newsgroups on the Internet that focus on the cult they're interested in.

If family members can find the cult headquarters or a building used by the cult, they can check the tax records at the County Assessor's Office to see who owns the property. This information can be used to find where a cult is getting its financing and support from. Also, the owner of the property may have no idea what the group occupying the property is or what the group is using the property for. Families might also want to check with the local zoning commission to see if the property is zoned for the use the cult is making of it. If not, this can give the family some leverage.

One of the worst things family members can do though when they find that a loved one is in a possible cult is to confront the person in an argumentative, demeaning, or condescending manner. If anything, this type of behavior will only drive the loved one even deeper into the cult because it is exactly what the cult leader said would happen. Instead, this is a time for the family to try hard to be calm. It is a time, as previously mentioned, for family members to find out all the information available about the group. Keep in mind, however, that a loved one who belongs to what appears to be a strange or bizarre group may not belong to a cult at all but simply to a group whose ideals and aims seem foreign to the other family members. If the person doesn't display any of the symptoms I've talked about in this book, and the group doesn't exhibit the destructive traits of cults that I've talked about, family members should reexamine their opposition to the loved one belonging to the group. Perhaps it is simply that the family member's new religious or other beliefs run counter to those of the rest of the family, or simply that the rest of the family does not share this person's new goals. To decide if a person is in a cult, look at the group's behavior, not its beliefs. Also, parents should keep in mind that troubling behavior in children can be just the natural rebellious pattern many youths go through and may not have anything to do with belonging to a cult.

The experts on cults I have spoken with advise, however, that parents or family members who suspect that a child or other loved one actually is involved in a destructive cult should do the following:

1. Try not to panic or immediately jump to conclusions about the group.
2. Talk calmly with the cult member and listen to what he or she has to say about the group.
3. Show respect for the cult member's new beliefs.
4. Evaluate how committed the cult member appears to be to the group. Does he or she accept the group's philosophy totally and unconditionally? If so, keep in mind that the cult member will seem to have a totally different personality, one that will usually mimic the cult's leader. Family members should remember that this is not the person's real personality and avoid reacting angrily or harshly to it.
5. If, on the other hand, the cult member has doubts about the group, talk about them and have the person talk about and examine these doubts. This is why it is so important for the family to have gathered as much information as possible about the cult.
6. Family members should state their opinions, but do so in a calm and controlled manner, respecting the cult member's right to disagree.
7. Let the cult member know that you love and care about him or her.

8. Decide if you need to seek the help of a professional exit counselor. Some children are simply investigating these groups as a natural part of growing up and maturing. But in other cases, the cults may have already indoctrinated the cult member.

If it does appear that the family member indeed belongs to a destructive cult and that he or she has been thoroughly indoctrinated into the cult's belief system, it may be time to seek the assistance of a professional exit counselor. As with any business transaction, family members need to know what they're getting when they hire an exit counselor. The best way to do this is to seek referrals from competent agencies, ask for and check references, inquire about fees, and ask about experience and training in exit counseling.

As I mentioned earlier, the goal of exit counseling is to assist cult members in making informed judgments about cult membership by providing them with information the cult does not allow its members to access. Exit counselors don't force cult members to listen to or take part in any activities; rather, they simply offer them information. They engage the cult members in discussions, listen to their viewpoints, and then offer information and evidence about the true nature of the cult.

"You must understand what drew them to the cult, then show them how it really wasn't given to them," exit counselor Mitchell Mack, Jr., told me in an interview. "You must show them the contradictions between the teaching of the cult and its actions."[20]

Often, however, as I said earlier, cult members agree to talk to exit counselors only because of extreme pressure from family members. In such cases, during the exit counseling, cult members may resist the efforts of the exit counselors by praying, chanting, or using some other thought-stopping technique that the cult has taught them to use in such circumstances. This is usually something that the family alone is totally unprepared for, and this is when a trained, professional exit counselor becomes essential. It takes an exit counselor with a lot of patience, training, and experience to wade through this and overcome it. The ultimate goal of exit counseling is to make a cult member understand that he or she has been duped, and that there is a way out. But first the cult member must be willing to listen and discuss the issues.

To assist in accomplishing this goal, exit counselors will usually instruct family members about what to say or do, and the family then works as a team with the exit counselors to bring the cult member around to where he or she will stop the thought-stopping actions and begin listening and discussing issues. For example, there is usually one family member to whom the cult member is closest. Often this person is the one who, with help from the exit counselors, can break through the cult member's defenses.

"I can't do it by myself," exit counselor David Clark told me. "I must work with the family as a team."[21]

Sometimes just making the cult member aware of how much his or her cult involvement has hurt family members can bring about a breakthrough. This was the case with a member of a cult that called itself The Body, discussed in chapter 1. In this case, a counselor showed jailed cult member David Corneau pictures of his children, and looking at these photographs apparently made Corneau realize the harm he was doing to them and how, if he didn't change his behavior, he probably wouldn't see them for a long time. David subsequently broke down and began cooperating with the authorities.

"We were attempting to break through the 'cult David' to the real David, the David who loved his girls and missed them," Reverend Robert Pardon told me about the use of the pictures. "It worked not only with him, but we also used that strategy with Michelle Mingo [another member of The Body], and she also opened up."[22]

Along with using family members as part of the team, good exit counselors also know that they must be willing to listen patiently to the cult member's arguments and point of view, and then use various pieces of information to show the cult member how he or she was deceived. For example, an exit counselor tells of a case in which a cult member had repeatedly told family members to leave her alone because she was happy. She also told this to an exit counselor with whom she spoke after reluctantly giving in to her family's wishes. The exit counselor deflated her claim of happiness by showing her a videotape made by the members of the Heaven's Gate cult, talked about in chapter 8, in which they all said how happy they were. These individuals subsequently committed suicide. Good exit counselors want the cult members to talk about the cult and its beliefs, but also to question the accepted beliefs of the cult. In addition, it is important to let cult members know that their family members still love them, and to remind the cult members of all the fun things they used to do before joining the cult, things that they now likely miss.

As might be expected, often the difficulty of exit counseling depends on how deeply involved a person is in the cult. If a person has been to just a few meetings and seems intrigued by the group, presenting the person with the truth about the cult usually works much better than it does with someone who has been several years with the cult and has much more to lose by listening to the facts.

However, an article in the book *Recovery from Cults* states that regardless of the cult commitment or level of indoctrination, studies show that if exit counselors are given time to totally present their information without cult members stopping the process, about 90 percent of cult members exposed to exit counseling leave the group.[23] This high rate of success compared with deprogramming (65 percent) comes about because exit counselors present information to cult members in a way that shows respect for them, rather than in a pressured or argumentative manner. The information the counselors give cult members speaks for itself.

Despite the success rates though, experienced exit counselors say there is no formula that works for every person. Rather, each exit counseling is unique, and its format must be based on the individual involved, the cult he or she belongs to, and how committed the person is. There are some common features, however. According to a study of 80 former cult members, three factors stood out as most helpful to their decision to leave:

1. Learning about mind control (49 percent).
2. Having former cult members to talk to (47 percent).
3. Reading books on the subject of cults (40 percent).[24]

An excellent book for families wanting more in-depth information about exit counseling and how it works is the American Family Foundation book *Exit Counseling, A Family Intervention,* by Carol Giambalvo. This book gives readers step-by-step instructions on how family members can get a cult member into exit counseling and make it successful.

Families, however, should not believe that all of their efforts have been in vain if, after exit counseling, the loved one is one of the 10 percent who decides to return to the cult anyway. Keep in mind that the person has now been given a tremendous amount of previously unknown information to think about, and he or she likely will think about it and look at the cult with a different view from that point on. Exit counselors tell of many people (about 60 percent, according to one group of exit counselors) who have returned to a cult after exit counseling but then left on their own after they'd had time to think about what they were told during the exit counseling.[25]

"If it doesn't work," exit counselor David Clark told me, "at least I've given the cult member something to think about."[26]

On the other hand, if the cult member won't leave, or is frightened to leave, and it becomes impossible for the family to have exit counselors work with him or her, families might be able to get the cult to expel the family member or perhaps approve a short visit home. In a case reported in the article "Trying to Save Josh" in the July 1997 issue of *Good Housekeeping,* a woman whose son had joined the Moonies made so many telephone calls to the leadership of the Unification Church that they sent him home for a month to "straighten out family problems." It was during this time that she was able, with the help of exit counselors, to get her son out of the Moonies.[27]

Families might also want to consider threatening the cult with a civil suit or criminal charges, if such apply. This could possibly make the cult decide that the loved one is simply too big a liability to keep. *Caution:* Before attempting this, however, families need to take a long, hard, practical look at the cult the family member belongs to. Does the group have a history of violence? Do they reside so far outside accepted norms that it can't be predicted what they might do? Keep in mind what I've shown many times in this book: some cults can and will resort to deadly violence if threatened, so evaluate this possibility carefully before attempting to force the cult's hand. Also, it is possible that the cult, when threatened, might simply ship the family member somewhere outside the country. A better solution, if it is feasible, is to persuade the family member to voluntarily come home for a visit. In the book *Recovery from Cults*, Dr. Michael D. Langone tells of a study showing that only one-third of the people who were away from a cult for three or more weeks returned to the group.[28]

Along with family intervention, though, there are other ways of leaving a cult. First are the walk-aways—people who have finally come to see the cult for what it really is, or who have finally come to realize that the contradictions between what the leader preaches and practices are too great for them to ignore any longer. A study of former members of the Children of God, Hare Krishna, and the Unification Church found four factors that caused individuals to walk away from the cult:

1. A disruption of isolation from the outside world.
2. The development of an unauthorized romantic relationship that resulted in a conflict of loyalties.
3. The perception that the group had not and would not cause social change.
4. An experience of inconsistencies between the ideals and actions of movement leaders.[29]

Families should be warned, however, that there is always, as I have shown several times, the danger with walk-aways that the cult might send a gang to snatch the person back for reindoctrination. So, if a family member or friend in a cult walks away, it would be advisable to either keep the person's location secret for a while or to locate him or her somewhere out of the cult's reach.

Actually, the safety of a person who has walked away from a cult can depend on a number of factors:

1. How important was the person to the cult?
2. Does the person possess information that could be damaging to the cult?
3. Does the cult have a history of violent behavior?

Based on these factors, a person who has left a cult may need to take self-protective measures. These are described in a number of publications, including my books *The Complete Guide to Personal and Home Safety* and *Stopping a Stalker*. In addition, every state now has antistalking laws that prohibit harassing behavior. Investigate the laws in your state and use them if a cult constantly harasses a walk-away. Along with this, federal legislation now prohibits interstate stalking and provides that restraining and protective orders from any state or jurisdiction must be honored in all other states and jurisdictions. Incidentally, these laws can also be used against persistent cult recruiters.

Besides walking away, another way a member might leave a cult is by being thrown out. This often comes about because the member has been bucking authority or asking too many "inappropriate" questions about cult doctrine or practices. It can also come about because the cult member has suffered a physical or emotional breakdown from the stress of cult life, the member simply wouldn't conform to the rules of the cult, or the size of the cult has become unwieldy for the leader and he or she has decided to get rid of some of the less committed members.

A final method of leaving a cult is through family intervention, such as the exit counseling previously discussed. Deprogramming, although seldom used nowadays and not advised by most people involved in exit counseling, might still be considered under certain dire circumstances. These circumstances would include an underage child being held by a cult or a family member of any age about to be sent out of the country by a cult. Families, however, should retain competent legal assistance before pursuing deprogramming and have a court issue the necessary commitment papers prior to taking this action.

No matter how a person leaves a cult—by walking away, by being thrown out, or through a family intervention—former cult members often can't just simply return to society after cult life and begin functioning normally again. Keep in mind that even after successful exit counseling, the former cult member still has a lot of issues to deal with. While he or she may be out of the cult, the effects of the cult will likely linger for a long time.

"I left the group [Church Universal and Triumphant] after a family intervention," former cult member Cathleen Mann told me. "It took two years for me to actually stop reading cult materials and practicing decreeing (a cult ritual). Adjustment after the cult was very difficult. It took me many years to recover. I had nightmares and fears of retaliation from the group and the leader. I managed the adjustment by going to therapy, using a good resource system, educating myself about cults and mind control, and by becoming an anticult activist."[30]

Cult expert Carol Giambalvo told me, "The recovery process depends on the individual's experiences in the group, what kind of group it is, and the length of time spent in the group. There is no 'cookie-cutter' approach. The average recovery period is one to two years if the person has had some help getting out and access to information on thought reform programs and recovery. If they walk out of a group on their own, the recovery may take longer."[31]

As I have discussed here and in chapter 2, membership in a cult for a lengthy period can often leave the former cult member with serious psychological problems that must be dealt with. Former cult members can suffer from depression, panic attacks, guilt, low self-esteem, and a floating in and out of altered states. In addition, former cult members often feel overwhelmed at the prospect of having to readjust to normal society. While in a cult, a member's every decision, even the most minor, is usually made by cult leaders. When the individual leaves the cult, he or she must make decisions alone—a task that at times can seem impossible. A study of 350 former members of 48 different cults found that ex-members suffered from these effects for an average of 81.5 months.[32]

"An important study found that during the post cult adjustment period 95 percent of former [cult] members scored high enough on a psychological test to warrant a psychiatric diagnosis," says Dr. Michael D. Langone. "Their level of distress was higher than that of the average psychiatric inpatient."[33]

For individuals who have been involved in abusive and destructive cults for an extended period and need help readjusting, a number of mental health therapists around the country specialize in their treatment. "When people come to me," Erika Van Meir, a mental health therapist, told me, "it is usually to deal with the aftermath of the [cult] experience. I think people feel safe with me, feel understood, because I've been through something similar and do not react with astonishment to the pretty typical postcult personalities. I think that makes a big difference. [My clients] are often very scared and ask questions that might put the unprepared therapist on the defensive. I've had clients want to see my CV or try to find out if I'm working for their group as a spy. I don't write these people off as paranoid and delusional. I encourage them to ask questions."

Van Meir said that once former cult members feel comfortable with her, she can begin the healing process. "Once they come in," she said, "a lot of the work involves psychoeducation: providing them with information, resources about cultic groups, and Lifton's conditions for thought reform. Often people feel they are at fault because the group pressure was so compelling. Once they realize how they were manipulated, there are a lot of issues to deal with: anger for the time lost, money and other uncountable losses, job and health issues, and lots of unfinished business with former loved ones who may have been [ignored] due to the cult involvement. Eventually, it is good for them to get into a group with other members."[34]

This group therapy, however, doesn't have to be just in the formal therapeutic setting. There are a number of support groups around the country for former cult members. Like Alcoholics Anonymous and other groups, many people deal better with a problem if they can share their concerns with others who have suffered similar problems. One way to find such support groups is to contact reFOCUS, which stands for Recovering Former Cultists' Support Network. According to their Web site (http://www.refocus.org), "reFOCUS is not an organization, per se (it has no membership). It is rather a network, a nexus of connections between people in recovery, the lines of communication which link people up with available resources necessary to their recovery. Those resources include other former members, support groups and rehab facilities, mental health professionals, clergy, and other supportive organizations."

For former cult members who suffer after-effects too serious to be handled by group sessions or outpatient counseling, there is the Wellspring Retreat and Resource Center. This is a cult recovery treatment facility located 80 miles southeast of Columbus, Ohio, where former cult members can stay while undergoing the more intense psychotherapy needed to overcome the very serious detrimental effects they have suffered because of cult membership. According to their Web site (http://www.well springretreat.org), "The Wellspring Retreat and Resource Center residential treatment program for victims of cults and cult-like abuse is internationally known. We offer a two-week program that includes counseling, workshops, self-education opportunity, and personal, individual care.... Clients receive daily counseling and workshops from professionals who, themselves, have been hurt by cults."

Another cult recovery treatment center, named Meadow Haven, is located in Lakeville, Maine. Like Wellspring, it allows former cult members to live at the facility while receiving the counseling and treatment necessary to recover from their cult experience. For individuals who need intensive help such as this but can't afford it, Meadow Haven offers them the option of paying for their treatment through "work rendered to maintain the facility." Reverend Robert Pardon, the man who assisted in The Body cult situation discussed in chapter 1, manages this facility. The Web site of this facility is http://www.meadowhaven.org.

So far in this chapter, I have discussed different methods for striking back at cults, the various ways of getting someone out of a cult, and how to deal with the detrimental effects of the cult experience. But almost everyone would agree that it would be much better for all concerned if the family member or loved one had not become involved with a cult to begin with. Therefore, family members, friends, and others must make sure that impressionable and vulnerable youths, and, unfortunately, the elderly, are made aware of the signs that an organization is likely a cult. What are these signs? (Keep in mind, however, that some legitimate, benevolent groups may exhibit one or two of these traits, while cults will exhibit all or most of them.)

1. The group is focused around a living leader to whom the members show unquestioning obedience and commitment.
2. Group members are encouraged to associate only with other group members and to exclude anyone from their lives, including family members, who doesn't embrace the group's beliefs.
3. Group members are required to live in a facility with other group members.
4. Independent thought, dissension, or questioning of the group's values is discouraged through peer pressure or punishment.

5. The group leader makes every decision for group members, even the most minor.

6. The group is obsessed with recruiting and fund-raising.

7. Members are expected to give everything they own to the group, including property co-owned by nongroup members.

8. The group believes and preaches that it is an elite organization, has a world-saving mission, and anyone who disagrees with the group is the enemy. Many religious cults preach that nonmembers are not only the enemy but are also agents of Satan.

9. The group claims to have an answer for every question of life.

If, on the other hand, it is you, not a family member, who is being recruited into a group, ask direct questions and insist on answers. Who is the leader of the group? How do the members of the group view the leader? If you find that they see their leader as godlike, this is a good time to leave. Real benevolent groups worship God, an ideal, or a philosophy, not a person. If you're still interested in the group, do a little checking into the background of the group leader. What is the leader's lifestyle? Has the leader been in trouble? What public statements has he or she made? Ask about how the group raises its money. See if the group considers itself as special and elite. Ask who the other members of the group are, and check them out.

A universal warning that comes from many former cult members is that you should not walk but run away from any group that won't answer questions about their doctrine or purpose, about their leader, about their finances, and so forth. Evasiveness is a strong clue that the group is a cult. If you find your questions either put off or unanswered, there is something the group doesn't want you to know. You shouldn't be afraid to ask direct questions of anyone who invites you to a meeting or gathering. Don't allow evasiveness or changing the subject. If the recruiter tries to turn the tables by accusing you of being overly suspicious or untrusting, say thank you and leave. If the person wants to talk only in vague terms about the group or their purpose, leave.

But most important, never give out your personal information, such as an address or telephone number, to individuals who appear to be trying to recruit you; instead, ask for the recruiters' information and say you'll contact them. Individuals who have given out personal information to cult recruiters will testify that these individuals can become unbelievable pests, telephoning over and over or coming to a person's home over and over until the person agrees to attend a meeting. Also, *never, never* agree to go to a meeting or event at some out-of-the-way location from which there is no readily available form of transportation back. Incidentally, this caution applies not just to cult recruiters but to anyone who would make this kind of invitation. Instead of being a cult recruiter, the person could just as easily be a rapist or robber. Never surrender control to strangers.

If, however, you or a family member find that you are being contacted constantly by individuals attempting to recruit you into a cult, tell them, preferably in front of witnesses, that you don't wish any further contact with them. If they do contact you again, try to obtain proof of the contact, such as through voice-mail messages, handwritten notes, witnesses to the contact, or photographs. (In my book *Stopping a Stalker*, I advise stalking victims to carry a camera with them and use it to photograph their stalkers. Photos can be valuable evidence, as stalkers will almost certainly deny any claims of following someone.) Once you have done this, you can then petition a court for a restraining order or even have the cult recruiter arrested for stalking. Also, any threats made by cult members should be taken very seriously and should be recorded or witnessed if possible. Always report them to the police.

Children, it has been found, can be very vulnerable to cult recruiters. To decrease a child's chances of cult recruitment, parents should teach their children not to be too trusting. This is valuable not just for protection from cults but also from many other types of crime, such as drugs and sexual abuse. Children must also learn to ask questions of people and insist on answers, not evasive responses. Teach your children to distrust individuals who want to appear overly friendly but will not give direct answers to direct questions about their purpose. Again, this is good protection against sexual predators and drugs as well as cults.

Children and adults must also come to realize that unconditional love and acceptance doesn't occur immediately, as cults would have people believe. This is known as "love bombing." Real love and acceptance takes time to develop. Anyone who wants people to believe that they are being given instant love and acceptance almost always has unspoken motives. In addition, be concerned, and teach your children to be cautious, when a new acquaintance floods you or them with flattery.

Further, parents need to monitor their children's Internet use. This is no more intrusive than parents knowing where their children are at all times and with whom. Parents should be particularly concerned about which chat rooms their children visit. These can be recruiting arenas for cults, to say nothing of sexual predators. Parents may also want to consider installing software in their children's computers that can block Web sites and groups parents don't want their children having contact with. Just as responsible parents wouldn't allow their children to go to X-rated movies, they shouldn't allow them to visit Web sites containing even worse material.

The American Family Foundation's book *Cults and Psychological Abuse* offers some suggestions for keeping young people away from cults. Parents should teach their children to be wary of the following:

1. People who are excessively or inappropriately friendly.
2. People with simplistic answers or solutions to complex world problems.
3. People with invitations to free meals, lectures, and workshops.

4. People who are vague or evasive.

5. People who confidently claim that they can help you solve your problems, especially when they know little about you.

6. People who make grand claims about "saving mankind, achieving enlightenment, or following the road to happiness."[35]

As with many bad things that can befall children, such as drugs, sexual abuse, gangs, and cults, the best prevention against them is parents maintaining an open line of communication with their children. Young people must feel that they can talk with their parents about anything. The police, for example, often find that children will tell someone other than their parents about sexual abuse because they don't feel comfortable talking to their parents about it. The same can apply to the pressure children are receiving from someone trying to recruit them into a cult. If children feel comfortable talking to their parents about cults, parents have a much better chance of preventing their children's involvement in them.

Steve Wortham, a former federal agent, now operates Intellicon, an organization that provides seminars for government agencies. One of his seminars involves cults. When I asked him his thoughts about children and cults, he said, "Give them a reason to avoid them. Give children love, make them understand they are part of a family, make them feel important, listen to them, talk to them. Then they have no reason to join."[36]

The importance of open communication, however, never becomes more apparent than when parents find that their children are possibly involved in a satanic or occult cult. These parents almost certainly wish their children had come and talked to them first since these groups, as I have shown many times in this book, can be especially dangerous. For concerned parents, there are a number of signs that indicate a child has possibly become involved in one of these cults:

1. Collecting satanic material such as posters, books, patches, and so forth, or owning various occult materials, such as books on witchcraft and odd materials used for magic (items from graveyards, etc.)

2. Self-mutilation, such as razor cuts for sucking blood and excessive body piercing.

3. A sudden change in dress, with a strong tendency toward dark clothing.

4. New friends that also dress in dark clothing and sport signs of Satanism or the occult.

5. A sudden aversion to Christianity or other religious beliefs.

6. Dropping grades and sudden, uncharacteristic bad behavior.

7. A sudden fascination with death.[37]

Parents should keep in mind, however, that any of these signs could also be simply normal teenage rebellion. Parents shouldn't be alarmed right away, but instead investigate.

Parents also should be aware of the signs that a young person, while perhaps not yet belonging to a cult, could still be attracted to one. Research with former cult members has shown that a number of things make a youth more susceptible to cult recruitment. For example, families of young cult members have often set impossibly high standards for their children. These children feel attracted to a cult because many cults claim they will be able to help the children reach these high standards. Also, the worse the parent-child relationship is, the more likely cult membership is, as it is for children who have strong disagreements with their parents over values. Cult members, if asked to describe themselves before joining a cult, often say they felt lonely, rejected, and socially alienated.

Finally, young cult members often say that they didn't hold a devout belief in any religious theology before they joined the cult. Former members often say that a cult attracted them because they never had a real understanding of religion in their lives, that their religious belief system was fuzzy, and what the cult offered appeared clear and concise. Consequently, to guard against this attraction to cults, children should receive a solid education and grounding in whatever religion or belief system the family holds.

"Teach your children about religion and spirituality," exit counselor Mitchell Mack, Jr. told me. "Teach them to question anything they don't understand, and, most important, teach them to think independently."[38]

What else can individuals and family members do to combat cults or deal with the stress of having a family member or loved one involved in a destructive cult? Recently, I attended a talk given by The Roberts Group Parents Network (TRGPN). The members of this group all have children who have been recruited into an organization called the Brethren (also known as the Garbage Eaters). One rule of this organization is that its members can never contact their families. Of course, this can naturally cause severe distress to families who have a member that suddenly just disappears from college or some other location. Family members wonder, Has the loved one been kidnapped? Murdered? For some youths who join this organization, their families may never know what has happened to them.

The Brethren preaches that we are presently going through the "end times" talked about in the Bible, and as a consequence its members are trying to live pure lives in preparation for the end of the world. The group gets its nickname the Garbage Eaters because the members get their food by raiding garbage dumpsters.

TRGPN maintains a Web site at http://www.bigfoot.com/~trgpn. On this site, besides having information about the Brethren and this group's philosophy, they post photographs of unidentified members of the group so that parents might be able to locate a child that has disappeared. A number of TRGPN members travel around the country taking pictures of these group members in the hope of bringing some relief to the families of missing persons. Although the Brethren isn't a cult within the definition I have given, TRGPN stands as a model for family support groups of those who do have loved ones in a cult. Other support groups can be found through the Web sites listed earlier in this chapter.

While writing this book, I talked to many other police officers about cults and found that most knew practically nothing about them. This is totally unacceptable considering the many crimes that cults commit. Cults continue to thrive because police agencies know so little about them, and often feel reluctant to investigate them because they consider cults to be religious groups. Given the scope of the harm that cults do and the number of crimes they commit, police agencies must begin, from the recruit academy up through yearly in-service training, to make officers more aware of cults and how they operate. If cults knew the police were aware of and watching them, they would be less likely to commit some of the crimes they do.

During my research for this book, I also asked the people I interviewed what laws they believed should be enacted that, once in force, would be helpful in combating the destructiveness of cults. A few of the people I talked to felt that states should pass laws making it easier for the families of cult members to gain conservatorships. These conservatorships would not give families access to the cult member's assets, but would instead temporarily stop the transfer of these assets to the cult while the family attempts to provide exit counseling to the cult member. However, attorney Lawrence Levy, who has been involved in many cases concerning cults, doesn't think conservatorships are worth the high legal cost of pursuing them.

"Conservatorships are usually a waste of time," Levy told me, "because the cults usually have members so programmed that when they come to court they know the right things to say and how to sound rational and normal. The only way it may work is when the person is so far off center that he or she sounds that way to the judge."[39]

Exit counselor Steven Hassan, however, had a suggestion that I thought certainly merited mentioning. He pointed out to me that while a number of cults are recognized as nonprofit organizations by the Internal Revenue Service, there is no mechanism to investigate whether these groups continue to abide by the regulations that establish them as nonprofit.

"We need to establish a mechanism for investigating groups to see if they really are nonprofit or simply defrauding the American public," Steven Hassan told me. "If it can be shown that an organization is defrauding people, they should lose their nonprofit status. There must be some agency authorized to look into citizen complaints of fraud by these groups."[40]

Many of the people I spoke with, however, said that the criminal justice system, rather than passing any new laws, instead just needs to enforce the laws already on the books against sexual and physical abuse, confinement, kidnapping, child molestation, financial fraud, and other crimes that cults regularly commit.

"The main way that cults become 'dangerous cults' is when they break the law," cult expert Nori Muster told me. "They set up drug-dealing scams to raise money. They beat up members or murder members or critics. Laws already exist to cover the destructive behavior that cults exhibit."[41]

Attorney Lawrence Levy agreed: "I don't think any new legislation needs to be passed. There are a lot of laws on the books that are not enforced against cults. Ninety-nine percent of the cult cases I've been involved in I've used existing tort law violations."[42]

However, what many cult victims and the families of cult victims find when they report cult crimes is that police departments and prosecutors are often reluctant to investigate and prosecute these offenses. Many police officers and prosecutors claim they fear infringement of First Amendment rights.

"Many police departments and district attorneys are hesitant to apply all the laws on the books to groups that call themselves churches," Professor Margaret Thaler Singer told me. "They feel very reluctant, but they don't know how much fraud and deception is involved."[43]

This reluctance is, of course, totally unacceptable. The First Amendment right of religious expression does not give people the right to commit crimes in the name of religion. Courts have ruled on this many times. However, the solution to this problem is not that difficult, as I will explain.

When I first became a police officer in the late 1960s, the criminal justice system did not involve itself in family quarrels. Unless someone died or received severe injuries during a family fight, the police and the court system simply did not become involved, holding that this was a "personal family problem" that needed to be worked out within the family. When called to a "domestic disturbance," the police would separate the couple and then either tell them to knock it off because if officers came back that night, both parties would go to jail, or, if someone had received a non-life-threatening injury (such as a black eye, broken tooth, etc.), the police would send the assaulting party away for the night. And that was it. No report was even made.

However, in the last few decades, advocates for the victims of domestic violence have been involved in a very intensive public relations campaign that I'm sure every reader has seen at some time. They have worked tirelessly, using television, radio, and the print media, in an effort to make the public aware of the extent of domestic violence and its damaging effects. Their goal is to make the American public see domestic violence as the crime it really is. This publicity campaign has worked marvelously. Not only is domestic violence now seen as wrong by most of the general public, but the view of it by the criminal justice system has also changed. Today in Indiana and many other states, for example, if a police officer goes to a domestic disturbance and finds evidence that someone has been assaulted, the officer is mandated to make an arrest. In addition, the prosecutor will try the case, even if the complaining witness changes his or her mind and later doesn't want to prosecute, which, because of the dynamics of domestic abuse, occurs frequently.

These types of publicity campaigns aren't limited to only domestic violence however. Similar successful publicity campaigns have also been launched against the crimes of driving while intoxicated (previously often simply winked at by the criminal justice system) and child molestation (another crime previously considered a "private family matter"). It can also work for cults. Groups such as the American Family Foundation and others need to follow the lead of the successful publicity campaigns above and institute a similar campaign to make the public, and consequently the criminal justice system, aware of the dangers of destructive cults and how much of cult behavior is a crime. This would be a major step in breaking the secrecy that surrounds and protects cults, much as it did with domestic violence and child abuse. A successful publicity campaign that would increase the public's awareness of the workings of destructive cults could be the key to eventually bringing such cults under control.

"There's a lot of research that shows that when people are aware of the factors that lead to mind control, they're less likely to succumb," says Jim Maas, a professor of psychology at Cornell University. "It [cult tragedies] keeps happening, and I think that's because people keep forgetting."[44]

As I have shown throughout this book, cults can have devastating effects on their members, crippling them physically, financially, emotionally, and psychologically. But this doesn't have to happen. I hope I have been able to show that the families and loved ones of cult members are not powerless. Membership in destructive cults can be broken. A public that is aware of what cults are, how they recruit, and how they operate is also well armed to stop them.

Notes

CHAPTER 1

1. "5 'Vampire Clan' Members Held in Brutal Slaying," *St. Louis Post-Dispatch* (November 30, 1996), Internet edition.

2. "Teens Linked to Cult Held in Slaying of Girl's Parents," *Miami Herald* (November 30, 1996), p. 6B.

3. Lesley Clark and Jerry Fallstrom, "Captured 'Vampire' Teen Talked of Killing Parents, Woman Claims," *Houston Chronicle* (November 30, 1996), p. 12.

4. Martin Merzer, "Trial of 'Teenage Vampire' Transfixes a Florida Town," *Miami Herald* (February 5, 1998), p. 1A.

5. "Cult Leader, 17, Pleads Guilty in Slaying," *St. Louis Post-Dispatch* (February 6, 1998), Internet edition.

6. "Leader of Vampire Cult Pleads Guilty in Slayings," *Houston Chronicle* (February 6, 1998), p. 20.

7. Mike Schneider, "'Vampire' Leader Sexually Abused, Expert Testifies," *Miami Herald* (February 18, 1998), p. 5B.

8. Mike Schneider, "Man Who Initiated 'Vampire' Teen Testifies," *Miami Herald* (February 20, 1998), p. 2B.

9. Donald P. Baker, "'Vampire' Murderer Is Sentenced to Death in Florida's Electric Chair," *Houston Chronicle* (February 28, 1998), p. 20.

10. "Vampire Cult Leader Receives Death Sentence," *Kansas City Star* (February 28, 1998), Internet edition.

11. David Royse, "Town Is Frightened of Teens' Involvement with Vampire Rituals," *Houston Chronicle* (December 2, 1996), p. 7.

12. "Bill for 4 Teenagers' Rampage Comes to $300,000," *St. Louis Post-Dispatch* (March 8, 1998), Internet edition.

13. Ibid.

14. Interview by author, July 1, 2002.

15. Ken McCarthy, "On Cults, Computers, and Cash," *Rewired* (March 31, 1997), posted on Internet at http://www.rewired.com/97/0331.html

16. Michael D. Langone, Ph.D., "Cults: Questions & Answers," *Cultic Studies* (June 7, 2002), posted on Internet at http://www.csj.org/studyindex/study cult/cultqa.htm

17. Ibid.

18. Don Lattin, "The End to Innocent Acceptance of Sects," *San Francisco Chronicle* (November 13, 1998), p. A1.

19. Terrence Monmaney, "Free Will, or Thought Control?" *Los Angeles Times* (April 4, 1997), p. A1.

20. Janja Lalich, "Repairing the Soul After a Cult Experience," *Cult Recovery* (May 31, 1999), posted on Internet at http://www.csj.org/studyindex/study recovery/study_repairsoul.htm

21. Chris Bader and Alfred Demaris, "A Test of the Stark-Bainbridge Theory of Affiliation with Religious Cults and Sects," *Journal for the Scientific Study of Religion* (September 1996), p. 19.

22. Michael D. Langone, Ph.D., foreword in *Captive Hearts, Captive Minds*, by Madeleine Landau Tobias and Janja Lalich (Alameda, California: Hunter House, 1994), p. xii.

23. Jan Groenveld, "Totalism & Group Dynamics," *Cult Awareness and Information Centre* (May 7, 1999), posted on Internet at http://www.ex-cult.org/General/totalism-group-dynamics.htm

24. Sonja Barisic, "P&G Bedeviled Once Again by Satanism Rumors," *Detroit News* (September 5, 1995), Internet edition.

25. "Yoga Leads to Devil Worship!" *Freedom Writer* (September/October 1990), posted on Internet at http://berkshire.net/~ifas/fw/9009/yoga.html

26. "The Sect," *Boston Globe* (November 26, 2000), p A1.

27. Dave Wedge, "Cultists Convinced Only God Will Provide," *Boston Herald* (September 3, 2000), p. A1.

28. "Cult Expert Explains Attleboro Sect," *MSNBC* (September 1, 2000), posted on Internet at http://www.rickross.com/reference/attleboro/attleboro22.html

29. Dave Wedge, "Cultists Indicted in 'Chilling' Murder of Infant," *Boston Herald* (November 14, 2000), p. A1.

30. Dave Wedge, "Cult Tries Secession to Avoid Charges," *Boston Herald* (June 5, 2000), Internet edition.

31. Interview by author, July 12, 2002.

32. Paul Edward Parker, "Sect Case Jurors Say Religion Didn't Play into Verdict," *Providence Journal* (June 29, 2002), Internet edition.

33. Paul Edward Parker, "Attleboro Sect Member Asks for Delay in Start of Murder Trial," *Providence Journal* (August 21, 2002), Internet edition.

34. Dave Wedge, "Attleboro Mom Said to Be Cutting Ties to Cult," *Boston Herald* (October 12, 2002), p. A1.

CHAPTER 2

1. T.R. Reid, "Suspect Held in Gassing of Tokyo Trains," *San Francisco Chronicle* (March 21, 1995), p. A1.

2. T. R. Reid, "Japan Cult's Strange Scene," *San Francisco Chronicle* (March 23, 1995), p. A10.

3. Irene M. Kunii, "Engineer of Doom," *Time* (June 12, 1995), p. 45.

4. Nicholas D. Kristof, "Japanese Cult Said to Have Planned Nerve-Gas Attacks in U.S.," *New York Times* (March 23, 1997), p. 14.

5. "Surveillance Extension Sought," *Japan Times* (November 24, 2002), Internet edition.

6. Mari Yamaguchi, "Japan Grapples with Resilient Doomsday Cult," *Raleigh News & Observer* (September 11, 2002), p. 1.

7. Ibid.

8. Gail Russell Chaddock, "Rise of New Faiths Jolts Old Order to Red Alert," *Christian Science Monitor* (January 24, 1996), p. 8.

9. Kathryn Knight, "Millennium Cults Pose Bigger Threat Than Terrorists," *London Times* (August 20, 1996), p. 1.

10. Michael D'Antonio, "The New 'Hidden' Cults Want You," *Redbook* (April 1995), p. 93.

11. Matthew Forney, "Jesus Is Back, and She's Chinese," *Time Asia* (November 5, 2001), Internet edition.

12. Benjamin Zablocki, Paper presented at Cults: Theory and Treatment Issues conference in Philadelphia on May 31, 1997, quoted by Michael D. Langone, Ph.D., and Herbert L. Rosedale in "On Using the Term 'Cult,'" *American Family Foundation* (May 31, 1999), posted on Internet at http://www.csj.org/infoserv_cult101/essay_cult.htm

13. Robert D. Hare, *Without Conscience: The Disturbing World of the Psychopaths Among Us,* quoted by Madeleine Landau Tobias and Janja Lalich in *Captive Hearts, Captive Minds* (Alameda, California: Hunter House, 1994), p. 69.

14. Paula Dranov, "The Frightening Lure of the Cult," *Cosmopolitan* (December 1994), p. 190.

15. Bill Osinski, "Putnam Grand Jury Reindicts Top Nuwaubian," *Atlanta Journal-Constitution* (October 4, 2002), p. 1.

16. Rob Peecher, "York's Accusers Describe Years of Sexual Abuse," *Macon Telegraph* (September 1, 2002), p. 1.

17. Don Lattin, "Escaping a Free Love Legacy," *San Francisco Chronicle* (February 14, 2001), p. A1.

18. Ibid.

19. David Halperin, M.D., "Cults and Children: The Role of the Psychotherapist," *Cultic Studies Journal,* vol. 6, no. 1 (1989), p. 76.

20. M. J. Gaines et al., "The Effects of Cult Membership on the Health Status of Adults and Children," in *Health Values: Achieving High Level Wellness,* quoted by Michael D. Langone, Ph.D., in *Recovery from Cults,* ed. by Michael D. Langone, Ph.D. (New York: Norton, 1993), p. 330.

21. Christine J. Gardner, "Remembering Jonestown," *Christianity Today* (January 11, 1999), p. 31.

22. Kenneth Wooden, *The Children of Jonestown,* quoted in *Recovery from Cults,* p. 332.

23. Philip Zimbardo, Ph.D., "What Messages Are Behind Today's Cults?" *APA Monitor* (May 1997), p. 14.

24. Maria Karen Zerby, "An Answer to Him That Asketh Us!" in *The New Good News!*, quoted by Stephen A. Kent and Deana Hall in "Brainwashing and Re-Indoctrination Programs in the Children of God/The Family," *Cultic Studies Journal*, vol. 17, no. 1 (2000), p. 62.

25. Interview by author, July 12, 2002.

26. Seth M. Asser and Rita Swan, "Child Fatalities from Religion-Motivated Medical Neglect," *Cultic Studies Journal*, vol. 17, no. 1 (2000), p. 1.

27. Louis Jolyon West, M.D., "Persuasive Techniques in Contemporary Cults: A Public Health Approach," *Cultic Studies Journal*, vol. 7, no. 2 (1990), p. 131.

28. Dianne Casoni, "The Relation of Group Philosophy to Different Types of Dangerous Conduct in Cultic Groups," *Cultic Studies Journal*, vol. 17, no. 1 (2000), p. 155.

29. Barbara Grizzuti Harrison, "Children and the Cult," *New England Monthly* (December 1984), p. 51.

30. Interview by author, August 18, 2002.

31. Interviews by author, November 1, 2002.

32. *Cults and Psychological Abuse* (Naples, Florida: American Family Foundation, 1999), p. 8.

33. Gunrun Swartling, O.T., and Per G. Swartling, M.D., "Psychiatric Problems in Ex-Members of Word of Life," *Cultic Studies Journal*, vol. 9, no. 1 (1992), p. 78.

34. F. Conway et al., "Information Disease: Effects of Covert Induction and Deprogramming," in *Update: A Journal of New Religious Movements*, quoted by Paul R. Martin, Ph.D., et al., in "Post-Cult Symptoms," *Cultic Studies Journal*, vol. 9, no. 2 (1992), p. 220.

35. Michael D. Langone, Ph.D., *Recovery from Cults*, quoted by Martin et al. in "Post-Cult Symptoms," p. 221.

36. Interview by author, August 11, 2002.

CHAPTER 3

1. Mary McCormick Maaga, *Hearing the Voices of Jonestown* (Syracuse, New York: Syracuse University Press, 1998), posted on Internet at http:// www.und. nodak.edu/dept/philrel/jonestown/suicide.html

2. Ibid.

3. Martin Merzer, "Cultists Commit Mass Suicide in Guyana," *Associated Press* (November 20, 1978).

4. Mary McCormick Maaga, *Hearing the Voices of Jonestown*.

5. Ibid.

6. Rebecca Moore, *A Sympathetic History of Jonestown: The Moore Family Involvement in Peoples Temple*, quoted by Catherine Wessinger in *Alternate Considerations of Jonestown and Peoples Temple* (July 19, 1999), posted on Internet at http://www.und.nodak.edu/dept/philrel/jonestown/jt1978.html

7. David Chidester, *Salvation and Suicide: An Interpretation of Jim Jones, the Peoples Temple, and Jonestown*, quoted by Wessinger in *Alternate Considerations of Jonestown and Peoples Temple*.

8. Michael Taylor, "Jones Captivated S.F.'s Liberal Elite," *San Francisco Chronicle* (November 12, 1998), p. A1.

9. Rebecca Moore, *A Sympathetic History of Jonestown: The Moore Family Involvement in Peoples Temple* (Lewiston, New York: Edwin Mellen Press, 1985), p. 305.

10. Maitland Zane, "Surviving the Heart of Darkness," *San Francisco Chronicle* (November 13, 1998), p. A1.

11. Ibid.

12. Ibid.

13. Tara Shioya, "Pair Sentenced to 3 Years in Ritual Beating Death," *San Francisco Chronicle* (August 3, 1996), p. A20.

14. Interview by author, October 3, 2002.

15. David Crumm, "Krishna Unity Grows in Detroit," *Detroit Free Press* (August 1, 1998), p. 1A.

16. Don Lattin, "A Test of Faith," *San Francisco Chronicle* (February 13, 2001), p. A1.

17. Don Lattin, "Krishna's Honesty in Scandal Could Prove Costly," *San Francisco Chronicle* (June 15, 2002), p. A1.

18. Ibid.

19. Daniel Shaw, C.S.W., "Traumatic Abuse in Cults," (May 10, 1999), posted on Internet at http://www.cyberpass.net/truth/essay.htm

20. Interview by author, June 19, 2002.

21. Interview by author, May 30, 2002.

22. Don Lattin, "Experts Warn of Small Sects' Dangers," *San Francisco Chronicle* (March 17, 1995), p. A19.

23. "The Unification Church," (May 20, 1999), posted on Internet at http://www.netcentral.co.uk/steveb/cults/moon.html

24. Don Lattin, "In Oakland, Moon Stresses Family," *San Francisco Chronicle* (March 13, 2001), p. A28.

25. Jane Lampman, "Rev. Moon Raising His Profile," *Christian Science Monitor* (April 19, 2001), Internet edition.

26. Steven Hassan, *Combatting Cult Mind Control* (Rochester, Vermont: Park Street Press, 1990), p. 22.

27. Ibid., p.9.

28. Peter Fimrite, "Unification Church Spokesman," *San Francisco Chronicle* (September 18, 1995), p. A13.

29. Jim Mitzelfeld, "House of Judah Leader Gets 3 Years for Enslavement, Death," *Detroit Free Press* (December 20, 1986), p. A1.

30. "Police Seek Cult Leader," *New York Times* (November 23, 1984), p. A19.

31. James Pinkerton, "Sect's Leader Says God Will Come to Garland Next Year," *Houston Chronicle* (December 24, 1997), p. 13.

32. Rick Miller, "Religious Sect Travels to God's 'Landing Site,'" *Houston Chronicle* (January 11, 1998), p. 9.

33. Don Lattin, "Apocalypse Meets Millennium in Texas Sect," *San Francisco Chronicle* (March 7, 1998), p. A1.

34. Jim Henderson, "Heaven Can Wait," *Houston Chronicle* (March 26, 1998), p. 1.

35. Ibid.

CHAPTER 4

1. Frank Newport and Maura Strausberg, "Americans' Belief in Psychic and Paranormal Phenomena Is Up over Last Decade," *Gallup Organization* (June 8, 2001), posted on Internet at http://www.gallup.com/poll/releases/pr010608.asp

2. Ruth Rendon, "Kilroys Say a Prayer for Kids on Break," *Houston Chronicle* (March 21, 1999), p. 37.

3. David A. Halperin, M.D., "The Appeal of the Impossible and the Efflorescence of the Unbelievable: A Psychoanalytic Perspective on Cults and Occultism," *Cultic Studies Journal,* vol. 9, no. 2 (1992), p. 190.

4. Wiccan, a fast-growing belief system based on witchcraft, has gained many adherents in the United States and has even been recognized as a new religion in some quarters. However, its activities thus far have not involved criminal behavior except where offshoot groups, like the one Natasha belonged to, twist beliefs and practices into something devious and dangerous.

5. Steven James, "It Happened to Me," *Campus Life* (May/June 2000), posted on Internet at http://www.christianitytoday.com/cl/2000/003/3.32.html

6. "6 Arrested in Slayings Near Tennessee Rest Area," *CNN Interactive* (April 8, 1997), posted on Internet at http://www.cnn.com

7. Randy Furst, "Victim's Rich Life, Link to Occult Spiraled into Mysterious Death," *Minneapolis-St. Paul Star Tribune* (August 29, 1997), p. 1A.

8. Ibid.

9. Randy Furst and Paul McEnroe, "Pharmacist Killed by Fellow Voodoo Adherents, Cop Says," *Minneapolis-St. Paul Star Tribune* (August 1, 1997), p. 1A.

CHAPTER 5

1. Jay Hughes, "Pathologist Details Mother's Many Wounds," *Biloxi Sun Herald* (June 4, 1998), p. A1.

2. Tom Wilemon and Brad Branan, "Pearl Struggles to Heal," *Biloxi Sun Herald* (October 12, 1997), p. A1.

3. Martha Mendoza, "Talk of Death, Cults Follow Shootings," *Detroit News* (October 12, 1997), Internet edition.

4. James Malone et al., "A Community and Its Shooter," *Louisville Courier-Journal* (December 8, 1998), Internet edition.

5. Carol Morello, "Teen Defendants Hinted at Dark Side," *Detroit News* (October 22, 1997), Internet edition.

6. Mendoza, "Talk of Death."

7. J.R. Moehringer, "Killings Linked to Satan-Loving Teen," *Indianapolis Star* (October 15, 1997), p. A8.

8. Jay Hughes, "Teen Blames Demons, Friends in Slayings," *Seattle Times* (June 4, 1998), Internet edition.

9. Kevin Sack, "Grim Details Emerge in Teen-Age Slaying Case," *New York Times* (October 15, 1997), p. A10.

10. Malone et al., "A Community and Its Shooter."

11. Susan Schramm, "Man Admits Church Arsons," *Indianapolis Star* (February 24, 1999), p. A1.

12. Susan Schramm, "Plea Solves 26 Church Fires," *Indianapolis Star* (July 12, 2000), p. A1.

13. Vic Ryckaert, "Church Arsonist Gets 42-1/2 Years," *Indianapolis Star* (November 15, 2000), p. B1.

14. "Satanic Worship Services Suspended at Prison in Kentucky," *Indianapolis Star* (September 1, 2002), p. A18.

15. Suzanne Klotz, "Teenage 'Satanists' Dreamed of Killing," *The Age* (September 4, 1999), posted on Internet at http://www.rickross.com/reference/satanism/satanism60.html

16. Christian Caryl, "Church Arson in Norway: The Devil Made Them Do It," *Wall Street Journal* (August 27, 1996), p. A10.

17. Kate Connolly, "German Sect Accused of Rape and Cannibalism," *Telegraph* (January 16, 2003), p. 1.

18. Cathy Stapells, "When Teens Venture to the Dark Side," *Toronto Sun* (May 16, 1999), p. A1.

19. "Suspect Ties Miss. Deaths to Satan," *Washington Post* (November 12, 1997), p. A2.

20. "Church of Satan Founder Anton LaVey Claimed 10,000 Followers Worldwide," *Toronto Star* (November 9, 1997), p. A11.

21. Kenneth V. Lanning, "Investigator's Guide to Allegations of 'Ritual' Child Abuse" (January 1992), posted on Internet at http://web.mit.edu/harris/www/lanning.html

22. Ibid.

23. Susan J. Kelley, Ph.D., R.N., "Ritualistic Abuse of Children in Day-Care Centers," in *Recovery from Cults*, ed. by Michael D. Langone, Ph.D. (New York: Norton, 1993), p. 344.

CHAPTER 6

1. Hanna Rosin, "Cult Leader with Violent Leanings May Have Led Followers to Israel," *Houston Chronicle* (October 18, 1998), p. A10.

2. Ibid.

3. "Millennial Madness, Jerusalem Jitters," *U.S. News & World Report* (January 18, 1999), p. 32.

4. Margie Mason, "Cult's Local Ties a Concern," *Jacksonville Times-Union* (February 7, 1999), Internet edition.

5. Rosin, "Cult Leader with Violent Leanings."

6. Don Lattin, "The End to Innocent Acceptance of Sects," *San Francisco Chronicle* (November 13, 1998), p. A1.

7. Don Lattin, "Cult Experts Say Arrests May Bolster Sect Leader," *San Francisco Chronicle* (January 6, 1999), p. A1.

8. Mike McPhee, "Relatives Fear for Group's Members," *Denver Post* (October 8, 1998), Internet edition.

9. John C. Ensslin, "38 in Cult Leave Denver, Upset Families," *Rocky Mountain News* (October 8, 1998), posted on Internet at http://insidedenver.com/news/1008doom1.shmtl

10. Peggy Lowe, "Denver Cultists Arrested in Israel," *Denver Post* (January 4, 1999), Internet edition.

11. Lattin, "Cult Experts Say Arrests May Bolster Sect Leader."

12. Ibid.

13. Kirk Mitchell, "Doomsday-Cult Leader's Words Reappear on Web," *Denver Post* (May 11, 2001), Internet edition.

14. "Cult Leader Prophesies End of World," *Montreal Gazette* (February 16, 2002), p. 1.

15. "Cult Leader Prophecies Doom, Vanishes with Followers," *St. Louis Post-Dispatch* (October 16, 1998), Internet edition.

16. Interview by author, July 12, 2002.

17. Lowe, "Denver Cultists Arrested in Israel."

18. Hanna Rosin, "Apocalypse Doomsayers Change Their Story," *Washington Post* (January 1, 2000), p. A1.

19. Ibid.

20. Ibid.

21. Don Lattin, "The Day After Doomsday in the Holy City," *San Francisco Chronicle* (January 30, 2000), p. A6.

22. Richard Erdoes, *A.D. 1000: Living on the Brink of Apocalypse* (San Francisco: Harper & Row, 1988), p. vii.

23. E.C. Krupp, "In the Wake of Heaven's Gate," *Sky & Telescope* (September 1997), p. 80.

24. Ann LoLordo, "The Jerusalem Syndrome," *Baltimore Sun* (April 8, 1999), p. 1F.

25. Philip Lamy, *Millennium Rage* (New York: Plenum Press, 1996), p. 4.

26. Bob Von Sternberg, "Millennial Musings," *Minneapolis-St. Paul Star Tribune* (October 25, 1997), p. 5B.

27. Ibid.

28. "41 Failed End-of-the-World Predictions for 1999" (July 3, 2002), posted on Internet at http://www.religioustolerance.org/end_wr19.htm

29. Jeff Coen, "Some Christians Fear Y2K Signals the End," *Chicago Tribune* (March 1, 1999), Internet edition.

30. Gerald Renner, "Computer Bug Is Stuff of Prophecy to Fundamentalist Faithful," *Hartford Courant* (January 2, 1999), p. 1.

31. David Neiwert, "An Interview with John Trochmann/Randy Trochmann," *Militia Watchdog* (February 14, 1996), posted on Internet at http://www.militia-watchdog.org/dn-troch.htm

32. Michael Kelly, "The Road to Paranoia," *The New Yorker* (June 19, 1995), p. 60.

33. Tom Post and Melinda Liu, "Doomsday Cults: 'Only the Beginning,'" *Newsweek* (April 3, 1995), p. 40.

34. Ibid.

35. Henri E. Cauvin, "Fateful Meeting Led to Founding of Cult in Uganda," *New York Times* (March 27, 2000), p. A3.

36. Ibid.

37. Karl Vick, "Prophecy's Price," *Washington Post* (April 1, 2000), p. A1.

38. Ian Fisher, "Yet Another Mass Grave Is Uncovered in Uganda," *New York Times* (March 31, 2000), p. A10.

39. Craig Nelson, "Journey into a Heart of Darkness," *Seattle Times* (April 2, 2000), p. A1.

40. Dean E. Murphy, "Ugandan Cult's New Death Site—153 Bodies," *San Francisco Chronicle* (March 25, 2000), p. A1.

41. Adrian Blomfield, "Ugandan Mass Murder Baffles Investigators," *Detroit News* (March 31, 2000), Internet edition.

42. Sheila MacVicar, "Uganda Hunts Cult Leaders," *ABC News* (April 4, 2000), posted on Internet at http://abcnews.go.com/sections/world/DailyNews/chat_uganda0404.html

43. Henry Wasswa, "Uganda Cult Deaths Remain a Mystery," *Associated Press* (March 16, 2002).

44. Craig Nelson, "Kibwetere's Wife Says He Did Not Run Uganda Cult," *Seattle Times* (March 31, 2000), p. A1.

CHAPTER 7

1. John Gallagher, "Diving to Conscience Bay," *Psychology Today* (December 1998), p. 54.

2. Pamela Abramson and Bill Barol, "Who Is This Rama?" *Newsweek* (February 1, 1988), p. 58.

3. Debra West, "Late Guru's Detractors Lay Claim to His Millions," *Seattle Times* (March 28, 1999), Internet edition.

4. Abramson and Barol, "Who Is This Rama?", p. 58.

5. Gallagher, "Diving to Conscience Bay," p. 76.

6. Ibid., p. 78.

7. Ibid., p. 78.

8. West, "Late Guru's Detractors Lay Claim to His Millions."

9. Gallagher, "Diving to Conscience Bay," p. 56.

10. Debra West, "2 Claims Complicate Tussle over New Age Guru's Estate," *New York Times* (June 13, 1999), p. A1.

11. Michael D. Langone, Ph.D., "What Is 'New Age?'" in *Cults and Psychological Abuse* (Naples, Florida: American Family Foundation, 1999), p. 33.

12. Peter Steinfels, "Beliefs," *New York Times* (July 13, 1996), p. 10.

13. Arthur A. Dole, Ph.D., et al., "Is the New Age Movement Harmless?" *Cultic Studies Journal*, vol. 10, no. 1 (1993), p. 54.

14. Erica Goode, "The Eternal Quest for a New Age," *U.S. News & World Report* (April 7, 1997), p. 32.

15. Lawrence Sartorius and Michael Sartorius, "The New Earth" (June 7, 1999), posted on Internet at http://www.islandnet.com/~arton/newearth.html

16. Ray Clancy, "Professionals Fall Prey to New Age Gurus," *London Times* (July 21, 1992), p. 1.

17. Posted on Internet (May 21, 1999) at http://www.miu.edu

18. "Guru Rajneesh Dead at 58," *Watchman Expositor* (July 24, 2002), posted on Internet at http://www.watchman.org/na/rajneesh.htm

19. Lewis F. Carter, *Charisma and Control in Rajneeshpuram* (Cambridge: Cambridge University Press, 1990), p. 1.

20. Lawrence K. Grossman, "The Story of a Truly Contaminated Election," *Columbia Journalism Review* (January/February 2001), posted on Internet at http://www.cjr.org

21. Gillian Flaccus, "Oregon Town Has Never Gotten over Its 1984 Bioterrorism Scare," *San Francisco Chronicle* (October 19, 2001), p. A1.

22. Rachel Graham, "The Saffron Swami," *Willamette Week—25 Years* (July 24, 2002), posted on Internet at http://www.wweek.com/html/25–1983.html

23. Langone, "What Is 'New Age?'" p. 34.

24. Frank Newport and Maura Strausberg, "Americans' Belief in Psychic and Paranormal Phenomena Is Up over Last Decade," *Gallup Organization* (June 8, 2001), posted on Internet at http://www.gallup.com/poll/releases/pr010608.asp.

25. Abramson and Barol, "Who Is This Rama?" p. 59.

CHAPTER 8

1. Jacques Steinberg, "From Religious Childhood to Reins of a U.F.O. Cult," *New York Times* (March 29, 1997), p. 9.

2. Howard Chua-Eoan, "The Faithful Among Us," *Time* (April 14, 1997), p. 44.

3. "Techno-Religious Order Members Died Using Drugs, Bags over Heads," *Detroit News* (March 28, 1997), Internet edition.

4. Barry Bearak, "Eyes on Glory: Pied Pipers of Heaven's Gate," *New York Times* (April 28, 1997), p. B9.

5. "Group May Have Roots in '70s 'UFO Cult,'" *Detroit News* (March 28, 1997), Internet edition.

6. Bearak, "Eyes on Glory."

7. Mark Miller, "Secrets of the Cult," *Newsweek* (April 14, 1997), p. 28.

8. Bearak, "Eyes on Glory."

9. "The Comet: Bad Astronomy, Radio Hype Added to UFO Belief," *Detroit News* (March 28, 1997), Internet edition.

10. Marshall Wilson, "Last 2 Cult Members' Names Released," *San Francisco Chronicle* (April 1, 1997), p. A3.

11. Timothy Ferris, "De-Programming Heaven's Gate," *The New Yorker* (April 14, 1997), p. 31.

12. B. Drummond Ayres, Jr., "Families Learning of 39 Cultists Who Died Willingly," *New York Times* (March 29, 1997), p. 1.

13. Todd S. Purdum, "Videotapes Left by 39 Who Died Described Cult's Suicide Goal," *New York Times* (March 28, 1997), p. A19.

14. Marshall Wilson, "Cult Left Arsenal Behind," *San Francisco Chronicle* (April 2, 1997), p. A1.

15. Elizabeth Gleick, "The Marker We've Been…Waiting For," *Time* (April 7, 1997), p. 14.

16. Seth Hettena, "Heaven's Gate Survivor Keeps Faith," *Associated Press* (March 26, 2002).

17. "Unarius Perspective on the September 11 Terrorist Attack" (July, 29, 2002), posted on Internet at http://www.unarius.org/sept11.html

18. Joe Mozingo, "On Top of Old Baldy, Prayers Go Out for the World," *Los Angeles Times* (October 4, 1998), p. B2.

19. "Cosmic Activities" (July 29, 2002), posted on Internet at http://www.aetherius.org/NewFiles/current_cosmic_activities.html

20. Information posted on Internet at http://religiousmovements.lib.virginia.edu/nrms/rael.html

21. Tom Abate, "Leader Emerges for Disciples of Human Cloning," *San Francisco Chronicle* (October 12, 2000), p. A1.

22. "Korean Cloning Out of this World," *CNN* (July 25, 2002), posted on Internet at http://europe.cnn.com

23. Luke Coppen, "Nightmare in Embryo?" *London Times* (August 17, 2002), p. 1.

24. Jane Gross, "In the Hunt for Answers, Only Questions Arise," *New York Times* (March 28, 1997), p. A21.

25. Stephen O'Leary, "Seeds of Apocalypse Are Among Us," *Los Angeles Times* (April 22, 1997), p. B7.

26. Joel Achenbach, "The CEO from Cyberspace," *Washington Post* (March 31, 1999), p. A1.

27. Tom Rhodes, "UFOs: It's a Coverup," *Ottawa Citizen* (October 11, 1998), p. 1.

28. Howie Paul Hartnett, "UFO Group: Truth Will Land in 2003," *Charlotte Observer* (November 4, 2002), p. 1.

CHAPTER 9

1. Philip Lamy, *Millennium Rage* (New York: Plenum Press, 1996), p. 3.

2. "Church Universal and Triumphant Unifying World Religions" (December 11, 2002), posted on Internet at http://www.tsl.org/AboutUs/TheMysticalPath.asp

3. Interview by author, August 18, 2002.

4. Scott McMillion, "CUT's Theology Hasn't Changed," *Bozeman Chronicle* (March 18, 1998), p. 1.

5. Karin Ronnow, "CUT Leaders Admit Group Living Beyond Its Means," *Bozeman Chronicle* (March 17, 1998), p. 1.

6. "Church Universal & Triumphant Leader Retires," *Associated Press* (January 2, 1999).

7. Interview by author, August 18, 2002.

8. Peter Klebnikov, "Times of Troubles: Heaven's Gate Isn't the Only One," *Newsweek* (April 7, 1997), p. 48.

9. Bob Anez, "Apocalyptic Church Struggling after Armageddon Didn't Happen," *Detroit News* (April 4, 1998), Internet edition.

10. McMillion, "CUT's Theology Hasn't Changed."

11. Ibid.

12. "The Little Pebble Press Releases" (June 27, 2002), posted on Internet at http://www.shoal.net.au/~mwoa/press_releases/press_release_27_june_2002.html

13. "The Little Pebble Press Releases" (July 10, 2002), posted on Internet at http://www.shoal.net.au/~mwoa/press_releases/press_release_10_july_2002.html

14. "Vatican Outlaws South Coast Religious Sect," *ABC News Online* (June 18, 2002), posted on Internet at http://abc.net.au/news/newsitems/s584603.htm

15. "Indonesia Cultists Killed Amid Doomsday No-Show," *Reuters* (September 13, 1999).

CHAPTER 10

1. Richard Lacayo, "Cults: In the Reign of Fire," *Time* (October 17, 1994), Internet edition.

2. "3 Teens Say They Skipped Parents' Suicide Offer," *Detroit Free Press* (March 25, 1997), p. 10A.

3. Patrick White, "Solar Temple Cult Worries Rise As Millennium Nears," *Reuters* (April 26, 1999).

4. "Close-Up: How Do Cults Convince People It's Time to Die?" *Seattle Times* (March 27, 1997), p. 1.

5. Robert Marquand and Daniel B. Woods, "Rise in Cults as Millennium Approaches," *Christian Science Monitor* (March 28, 1997), p. 1C.

6. Posted on Internet (August 5, 2002) at http://www.elia777.com/uk/main-Top.asp

7. Ibid.

8. "End of the World Again Postponed," *De Telegraaf* (December 22, 2001), p. 1.

9. "Dutch Prosecutors Investigate Cult," *Associated Press* (November 1, 2001).

10. "Three Die in Cambodia Cult Suicide," *CNN* (October 1, 2002), posted on Internet at http://europe.cnn.com

11. Ibid.

CHAPTER 11

1. Jenifer Warren, "Trouble Taints a Cerebral Sanctuary," *Los Angeles Times* (November 4, 1996), p. A1.

2. Katherine Seligman, "Yuba Church or Cult?" *San Francisco Examiner* (October 12, 1997), p. 1A.

3. Ibid.

4. Warren, "Trouble Taints a Cerebral Sanctuary."

5. Ibid.

6. Gordon Smith, "Wave of Resignations and Expulsions Following Open Letter," *San Diego Union-Tribune* (March 16, 1995), p. 1.

7. Gordon Smith, "In the Name of Religion," *San Diego Union-Tribune* (March 15, 1995), p. 1.

8. Seligman, "Yuba Church or Cult?"

9. Smith, "Wave of Resignations and Expulsions Following Open Letter."

10. Seligman, "Yuba Church or Cult?"

11. Smith, "In the Name of Religion."

12. Jonathan Rabinovitz, "College Idealism Was Fertile Soil for Fringe Group," *New York Times* (November 15, 1996), p. A1.

13. John Kifner, "Drawn by Child's Cries, Police Uncover Arsenal," *New York Times* (November 13, 1996), p. B4.

14. Ibid.

15. Anne McAndrews, "I Lost My Husband to a Cult," *Redbook* (May 1994), p. 60.

16. Ted Rohrlich, "After Synanon," *Los Angeles Times Magazine* (March 29, 1998), p. 16.

17. Jounice L. Nealy, "Robberies' Planner Sentenced," *St. Petersburg Times* (August 10, 2000), p. 1B.

18. Mike Brassfield and Jounice L. Nealy, "'Queen' Accused of Ordering Thefts," *St. Petersburg Times* (January 19, 2000), p. 1B.

CHAPTER 12

1. Laura Ziv, "Heaven's Gate Hell," *Cosmopolitan* (July 1997), p. 130.

2. Philip G. Zimbardo, Ph.D., "What Messages Are Behind Today's Cults?" *APA Monitor* (May 1997), p. 14.

3. David Holmstrom, "Parents Can Reduce Lure of Cults for Children," *Christian Science Monitor* (April 3, 1997), p. 14.

4. Tom Greenwood, "History: Group Deaths March Across the Pages of Time," *Detroit News* (March 28, 1997), Internet edition.

5. Paula Dranov, "The Frightening Lure of the Cult," *Cosmopolitan* (December 1994), p. 190.

6. Michael D. Langone, Ph.D., "Cults: Questions and Answers," (December 12, 2002), posted on Internet at http://www.csj.org/studyindex/studycult/cultqa.htm

7. Margaret W. Long, Ph.D., "The Cult Appeal: Susceptibilities of the Missionary Kid," *Cultic Studies Journal*, vol. 4, no. 1 (1987), p. 40.

8. Interview by author, August 11, 2002.

9. Interview by author, May 30, 2002.

10. Langone, "Cults: Questions and Answers," quoted by Madeleine Landau Tobias and Janja Lalich in *Captive Hearts, Captive Minds* (Alameda, California: Hunter House, 1994), p. 27.

11. Steven Hassan, *Combatting Cult Mind Control* (Rochester, Vermont: Park Street Press, 1990), p. 12.

12. Ibid., p. 13.

13. Chris Bader and Alfred Demaris, "A Test of the Stark-Bainbridge Theory of Affiliation with Religious Cults and Sects," *Journal for the Scientific Study of Religion*, vol. 35, no. 3 (September 1996), p. 285.

14. Ellie Brenner, "Trying to Save Josh," *Good Housekeeping* (July 1997), p. 67.

15. Ibid.

16. Eagan Hunter, "Adolescent Attraction to Cults," *Adolescence,* vol. 33 (Fall 1998), p. 709.

17. James Rudin and Marcia Rudin, *Prison or Paradise*, quoted by Hassan in *Combatting Cult Mind Control*, p. 49.

18. "Colorado Cult Leader Once Railed against Such Groups," *St. Louis Post-Dispatch* (January 10, 1999), p. 1A.

19. Interview by author, June 19, 2002.

20. Julia Campbell, "Apocalyptic Cult Members Deported from Israel," *Fox News* (December 21, 1999).

21. Lorna Goldberg, M.S.W., A.C.S.W., "Guidelines for Therapists," in *Recovery from Cults,* ed. by Michael D. Langone, Ph.D. (New York: Norton, 1993), p. 238.

22. Adam Sage, "Lured by the Cult," *London Times* (April 18, 2001), p. 1.

23. Dena S. Davis, "Joining a Cult: Religious Choice or Psychological Aberration?" *Journal of Law and Health,* vol. 11, no. 1 (Spring/Summer 1996), p. 145.

24. Hassan, *Combatting Cult Mind Control,* p. 76.

25. Madeleine Landau Tobias and Janja Lalich, *Captive Hearts, Captive Minds* (Alameda, California: Hunter House, 1994), p. 11.

26. Margaret Thaler Singer, Ph.D., *Cults in Our Midst* (San Francisco: Jossey-Bass Publishers, 1995), p. xxiii.

27. Howard Chua-Eoan, "The Faithful Among Us," *Time* (April 14, 1997), p. 44.

28. Ted Byfield and Virginia Byfield, "Extraterrestrial Cultism May Be New; the Phenomenon of the False Prophet Isn't," *Alberta Report* (April 28, 1997), p. 35.

29. Interview by author, August 18, 2002.

30. Rob Tucker, M.Ed., "Teen Satanism," in *Recovery from Cults*, p. 358.

31. Ibid., p. 386.

32. Hassan, *Combatting Cult Mind Control*, 77.

33. Goldberg, "Guidelines for Therapists," p. 242.

34. Zimbardo, "What Messages Are Behind Today's Cults?"

35. James Rudin and Marcia Rudin, "The Effect of Religious Cults on Western Mainstream Religion," *Cultic Studies Journal*, vol. 8, no. 1 (1991), p. 12.

36. "Jesus of Siberia," *The Guardian* (May 24, 2002), p. 1.

37. Tom Whitehouse, "'Messiah' or Cult Leader?" *Detroit News* (June 4, 1999), Internet edition.

38. Ibid.

CHAPTER 13

1. Paula Dranov, "The Frightening Lure of the Cult,"*Cosmopolitan* (December 1994), p. 192.

2. Nadine W. Craig, M.A., and Robert Weathers, Ph.D., "The False Transformational Promise of Bible-Based Cults: Archetypal Dynamics," *Cultic Studies Journal*, vol. 7, no. 2 (1990), p. 164.

3. Madeleine Landau Tobias and Janja Lalich, *Captive Hearts, Captive Minds* (Alameda, California: Hunter House, 1994), p. 25.

4. Interview by author, August 9, 2002.

5. Steven Hassan, *Combatting Cult Mind Control* (Rochester, Vermont: Park Street Press, 1990), p. 13.

6. Kristin Kloberdanz, "Cult Attraction," *Book* (May/June 2001), p. 16.

7. Andrew J. Pulskamp, "Are Cults Working Your College Campus?" *CPNet* (April 17, 2000), posted on Internet at http://www.rickross.com/reference/icc/ICC252.html

8. Margaret Thaler Singer, Ph.D., *Cults in Our Midst* (San Francisco: Jossey-Bass Publishers, 1995), p. 24.

9. "Close-up: How Do Cults Convince People It's Time to Die?" *Seattle Times* (March 27, 1997), p. 1.

10. Interview by author, June 19, 2002.

11. Interview by author, August 20, 2002.

12. Interview by author, June 10, 2002.

13. Interview by author, November 19, 2002.

14. Philip Zimbardo, Ph.D., "What Messages Are Behind Today's Cults?" *APA Monitor* (May 1997), p. 14.

15. Interview by author, August 26, 2002.

16. Gregory S. Blimling, Ph.D., "The Involvement of College Students in Totalist Groups: Causes, Concerns, Legal Issues, and Policy Considerations," *Cultic Studies Journal*, vol. 7, no. 1 (1990), p. 48.

17. James Rudin and Marcia Rudin, "The Effect of Religious Cults on Western Mainstream Religion," *Cultic Studies Journal,* vol. 8, no. 1 (1991), p. 8.

18. Janja Lalich, "Repairing the Soul after a Cult Experience," *Cult Recovery* (May 31, 1999), posted on Internet at http://www.csj.org/studyindex/ studyrecovery/study_repairsoul.htm

19. Pulskamp, "Are Cults Working Your College Campus?"

20. Russell K. Elleven, Ed.D. et al., "Residence Halls and Cults: Fact or Fiction?" *Cultic Studies Journal,* vol. 15, no. 1 (1998), p. 69.

21. Greg Lefevre, "The Internet as a God and Propaganda Tool for Cults," *CNN* (March 27, 1997), posted on Internet at http://www.cnn.com/TECH/ 9703/27/techno.pagans/index.html

22. Jane R. Lindley, "Cult Recruitment of International Students on American Campuses," in *Cults on Campus: Continuing Challenge,* ed. by Marcia R. Rudin (New York: International Cult Education Program, 1996), p. 20.

23. Catherine Collins and Douglas Franz, "Let Us Prey," *Modern Maturity* (June 1994), quoted by Loretta J. Bradley and Beth Robinson in "Adaptation to Transition: Implications for Working with Cult Members," *Journal of Humanistic Education & Development,* vol. 36, no. 4 (1998), p. 212.

24. Catherine Collins and Douglas Franz, "Let Us Prey," *Modern Maturity* (June 1994), p. 22.

25. Ibid.

26. Becky Beaupre, "'Net Creates 'Community' for Those on Fringe," *Detroit News* (March 28, 1997), Internet edition.

27. William M. Alnor, *UFO Cults and the New Millennium* (Grand Rapids, Michigan: Baker Books, 1998), p. 31.

28. John Markoff, "To Gullible, Net Offers Many Traps," *New York Times* (March 28, 1997), p. A20.

29. Terence Monmaney and Doug Smith, "Cult Targeted Web Sites for Abuse, Depression Victims," *Los Angeles Times* (March 28, 1997), p. A15.

30. Robert B. Cialdini, Ph.D., *Influence, Science and Practice* (New York: Scott, Foresman, 1985), p. 50.

31. Singer, *Cults in Our Midst,* p. 105.

32. Interview by author, August 18, 2002.

33. Interview by author, August 27, 2002.

34. From an undated pamphlet titled *Who Are They?* Published by the Cult Awareness Network.

CHAPTER 14

1. Carolyn Gard, "The Power and Peril of Cults," *Current Health,* vol. 23, no. 9 (May 1997), p. 18.

2. Ibid.

3. Ken McCarthy, "On Cults, Computers, and Cash," *Rewired* (March 31, 1997), posted on Internet at http://www.rewired.com/97/0331.html

4. Zay N. Smith, "The Way—40,000 and Still Growing," *Chicago Sun-Times* (August 17, 1980), quoted by Karl Kahler in *The Cult That Snapped* (Los Gatos, California: Ex-Way.Com, 1999), p. 126.

5. Geri-Ann Galanti, Ph.D., "Reflections on 'Brainwashing,'" in *Recovery from Cults,* ed. by Michael D. Langone, Ph.D. (New York: Norton, 1993), p. 100.

6. Interview by author, July 1, 2002.

7. Robert Jay Lifton. M.D., *Thought Reform and the Psychology of Totalism* (Chapel Hill: University of North Carolina Press, 1989), p. 420.

8. Margaret Thaler Singer, Ph.D., *Cults in Our Midst* (San Francisco: Jossey-Bass Publishers, 1995), p. 8.

9. Adam Sage, "Lured by the Cult," *London Times* (April 18, 2001), p. 1.

10. Tom Fennell, "Doom Sects: False Prophets Attract the Vulnerable," *Maclean's* (April 7, 1997), p. 48.

11. Leon Festinger et al., *When Prophecy Fails* (New York: Harper & Row, 1964), p. 105.

12. Rich McGee, "Cults," *Leadership University* (April 16, 1997), posted on Internet at http://www.leaderu.com/common/cults.html

13. Michael D. Langone, Ph.D., *Recovery from Cults* (New York: Norton, 1993), p. 8.

14. Jere Hester, "In Cults, Leader's Charisma Takes Over," *New York Daily News* (March 27, 1997), p. 1.

15. Interview by author, August 18, 2002.

16. Steven Hassan, *Combatting Cult Mind Control* (Rochester, Vermont: Park Street Press, 1990), p. 25.

17. Jenifer Warren, "Trouble Taints a Cerebral Sanctuary," *Los Angeles Times* (November 4, 1996), p. A12.

18. Frank Rich, "Journal," *New York Times* (April 17, 1997), p. A1.

19. Margaret Thaler Singer, Ph.D., and Louis J. West, M.D., "Cults, Quacks, and Nonprofessional Therapies," in *Comprehensive Textbook of Psychiatry*, III, ed. by Harold I. Kaplan et al. (Baltimore: Williams & Wilkins, 1980), p. 3284.

20. Richard Ofshe, Ph.D., and Margaret Thaler Singer, Ph.D., "Thought Reform Programs and the Production of Psychiatric Casualties," *Psychiatric Annals*, vol. 20, no. 4 (1990), posted on Internet at http://www.rickross.com/-reference/ brainwashing/brainwashing21.html

21. Ibid.

22. Edgar H. Schein, Ph.D., et al., *Coercive Persuasion* (New York: Norton, 1961), p. 67.

23. Harriet Chiang et al., "Victims Left Home Without Looking Back," *San Francisco Chronicle* (March 29, 1997), p. A1.

24. Jean-Louis Valatx, M.D., "Sleep Deprivation," *Cultic Studies Journal*, vol. 11, no. 2 (1994), p. 215.

25. Langone, *Recovery from Cults*, p. 7.

26. Richard Ofshe, Ph.D., and Margaret Thaler Singer, Ph.D., "Attacks on Peripheral Versus Central Elements of Self and the Impact of Thought Reforming Techniques," quoted by Madeleine Landau Tobias and Janja Lalich in *Captive Hearts, Captive Minds* (Alameda, California: Hunter House, 1994), p. 37.

27. Elena S. Whiteside, *The Way: Living in Love*, quoted by Karl Kahler in *The Cult That Snapped* (Los Gatos, California: Ex-Way.Com, 1999), p. 38.

28. Interview by author, August 20, 2002.

29. Interview by author, June 19, 2002.

30. Karl Kahler, *The Cult That Snapped* (Los Gatos, California: Ex-Way.Com, 1999), p. 71.

31. Ibid., p. 137.

32. Interview by author, December 6, 2002.

33. Interview by author, November 1, 2002.

34. Stanley Milgram, *Obedience to Authority* (New York: Harper & Row, 1974), p. xii.

35. "Archbishop's Book Confesses All on Moon Marriage," *New York Times* (September 8, 2002), Internet edition.

36. Irving L. Janis, *Groupthink,* quoted by Mark N. Wexler, Ph.D., in "Expanding the Groupthink Explanation to the Study of Contemporary Cults," *Cultic Studies Journal,* vol. 12, no. 1 (1995), p.49.

37. Ibid.

38. Wexler, "Expanding the Groupthink Explanation to the Study of Contemporary Cults."

39. Thomas Strentz, *The Stockholm Syndrome,* quoted by Robert L. Snow in *SWAT Teams* (Cambridge: Perseus Publishing, 1996), p. 167.

40. Mark Simon, "Survivor Recalls Guyana," *San Francisco Chronicle* (March 28, 1997), p. A19.

CHAPTER 15

1. Benjamin Pimentel, "'Guru Hunters' Take on Palo Alto Swami," *San Francisco Chronicle* (February 9, 1998), p. A16.

2. Ibid.

3. Lawrence Levy, "Prosecuting an Ex-Cult Member's Undue Influence Suit," *Cultic Studies Journal,* vol. 7, no. 1 (1990), p. 15.

4. Interview by author, August 26, 2002.

5. Lawrence Levy, "Prosecuting an Ex-Cult Member's Undue Influence Suit," *Cultic Studies Journal,* vol. 7, no. 1 (1990), p. 15.

6. Interview by author, August 26, 2002.

7. Sara Van Hoey, "Cults in Court," *Cultic Studies Journal,* vol. 8, no. 1 (1991), p. 61.

8. William Laney, "The Way International Reaches Settlement with Couple," *Wapakoneta Daily News* (November 7, 2000), p. 1.

9. Randy Frances Kandel, J.D., Ph.D., "Litigating the Cult-Related Child Custody Case," *Cult Observer,* posted on Internet at http://www.csj.org/pubs_co/guestcolumn/cultismandlaw.htm

10. Katie N. Johannes, "Attorney Argues Abuse Defendant Is Mentally Ill," *Great Falls Tribune* (September 25, 2002), Internet edition.

11. Brendan McGinty, "Cult Held Me Captive for Six Months," *Sunday Mail-England* (March 9, 2002), p. 1.

12. Kevin Sullivan, "Japanese Villagers Lay Siege to House Bought by Doomsday Cult," *Washington Post* (January 1, 1999), p. A23.

13. Tony Keim, "Police Block Drive-In Protest Against Guru," *Courier-Mail* (September 4, 2002), p. 1.

14. Justin Gillis and Caryle Murphy, "Concerned about Campus Cults, Colleges Arm Students with Facts," *Washington Post* (December 9, 1997), p. B1.

15. William Goldberg, M.S.W., A.C.S.W., "Cults on Campus: How Can You Help?" in *Cults on Campus: Continuing Challenge,* ed. by Marcia Rudin (New York: International Cult Education Foundation, 1996), p. 18.

16. Roy Probert, "Geneva Seeks to Temper Influence of Cults," *Swiss Info* (November 3, 2001), p. 1.

17. Michael D. Langone, Ph.D., "Deprogramming: An Analysis of Parental Questionnaires," quoted by Carol Giambalvo et al. in "Ethical Standards for Thought Reform Consultants," *Cultic Studies Journal,* vol. 13, no. 1 (1996), p. 97.

18. Catherine Collins and Douglas Franz, "Let Us Prey," *Modern Maturity* (June 1994), p. 22.

19. Carol Giambalvo, *Exit Counseling: A Family Intervention* (Bonita Springs, Florida: American Family Foundation, 1995), p. 35.

20. Interview by author, May 30, 2002.

21. Interview by author, October 17, 2002.

22. Interview by author, July 12, 2002.

23. David Clark et al., "Exit Counseling: A Practical Overview," in *Recovery from Cults,* ed. by Michael D. Langone, Ph.D. (New York: Norton, 1993), p. 163.

24. Patricia Goski, R.N., "Grief, Loss, and the Former Cult Member," in *Cults and Psychological Abuse* (Naples, Florida: American Family Foundation, 1999), p. 46.

25. Clark, "Exit Counseling: A Practical Overview."

26. Interview by author, October 17, 2002.

27. Ellie Brenner, "Trying to Save Josh," *Good Housekeeping* (July 1997), p. 67.

28. Langone, *Recovery from Cults,* p. 9.

29. E.S. Piper and S.A. Wright, "Families and Cults: Familial Factors Related to Youth Leaving or Remaining in Deviant Religious Groups," *Journal of Marriage and the Family,* vol. 48 (1986), p. 15.

30. Interview by author, August 18, 2002.

31. Interview by author, June 10, 2002.

32. Paul Martin, Ph.D., "Study Indicates Rehab's Benefits," *American Family Foundation,* posted on Internet at http://www.csj.org/rg/rgessays/rgessay_studyrehab.htm

33. Madeleine Landau Tobias and Janja Lalich, *Captive Hearts, Captive Minds* (Alameda, California: Hunter House, 1994), p. x.

34. Interview by author, August 11, 2002.

35. *Cults and Psychological Abuse* (Naples, Florida: American Family Foundation, 1999), p. 67.

36. Interview by author, October 17, 2002.

37. "The Red Flag List," January 7, 2003, posted on Internet at http://www.tunnellight.org/redflag.htm

38. Interview by author, May 30, 2002.

39. Interview by author, November 4, 2002.

40. Interview by author, November 19, 2002.

41. Interview by author, October 29, 2002.

42. Interview by author, November 4, 2002.

43. Interview by author, November 4, 2002.

44. Gillis and Murphy, "Concerned about Campus Cults, Colleges Arm Students with Facts," p. B1.

Bibliography

Abate, Tom. "Leader Emerges for Disciples of Human Cloning," *San Francisco Chronicle,* October 12, 2000, p. A1.

Abramson, Pamela, and Barol, Bill. "Who Is This Rama?" *Newsweek,* February 1, 1988, p. 58–59.

Achenbach, Joel. "The CEO from Cyberspace," *Washington Post,* March 31, 1999, p. A1.

Alnor, William M. *UFO Cults and the New Millennium,* Grand Rapids, Michigan: Baker Books, 1998.

Anez, Bob. "Apocalyptic Church Struggling after Armageddon Didn't Happen," *Detroit News,* April 4, 1998, Internet edition.

"Archbishop's Book Confesses All on Moon Marriage," *New York Times,* September 8, 2002, Internet edition.

Asahara, Shoko. *Declaring Myself the Christ,* Self-published, 1992.

Asser, Seth M., and Swan, Rita. "Child Fatalities from Religion-Motivated Medical Neglect," *Cultic Studies Journal,* vol. 17, no. 1, 2000, p. 1.

Ayres, B. Drummond, Jr. "Families Learning of 39 Cultists Who Died Willingly," *New York Times,* March 29, 1997, p. 1.

Bader, Chris, and Demaris, Alfred. "A Test of the Stark-Bainbridge Theory of Affiliation with Religious Cults and Sects," *Journal for the Scientific Study of Religion,* vol. 35, no. 3, September 1996, p. 295.

Baker, Donald P. "'Vampire' Murderer Is Sentenced to Death in Florida's Electric Chair," *Houston Chronicle,* February 28, 1998, p. 20.

Balizer, Carol. *Born in Zion,* Evless, Texas: Christ Center Publications International, 1992.

Barisic, Sonja. "P&G Bedeviled Once Again by Satanism Rumors," *Detroit News,* September 5, 1995, Internet edition.

Bearak, Barry. "Eyes on Glory: Pied Pipers of Heaven's Gate," *New York Times,* April 28, 1997, p. B9.

Beaupre, Becky. "'Net Creates 'Community' for Those on Fringe," *Detroit News*, March 28, 1997, Internet edition.

"Bill for 4 Teenagers' Rampage Comes to $300,000," *St. Louis Post-Dispatch*, March 8, 1998, Internet edition.

Blimling, Gregory S., Ph.D. "The Involvement of College Students in Totalist Groups: Causes, Concerns, Legal Issues, and Policy Considerations," *Cultic Studies Journal*, vol. 7, no. 1, 1990, p. 48.

Blomfield, Adrian. "Ugandan Mass Murder Baffles Investigators," *Detroit News*, March 31, 2000, Internet edition.

Boyle, James J. *Killer Cults*, New York: St. Martin's Press, 1995.

Bradley, Loretta J., and Robinson, Beth. "Adaptation to Transition: Implications for Working with Cult Members," *Journal of Humanistic Education and Development*, vol. 36, no. 4, 1998, p. 212.

Brassfield, Mike, and Nealy, Jounice L. "'Queen' Accused of Ordering Thefts," *St. Petersburg Times*, January 19, 2000, p. 1B.

Brenner, Ellie. "Trying to Save Josh," *Good Housekeeping*, July 1997, p. 67.

Burton, Robert. *Self-Remembering*, Boston: Red Wheel/Weiser, 1995.

Byfield, Ted, and Byfield, Virginia. "Extraterrestrial Cultism May Be New; The Phenomenon of the False Prophet Isn't," *Alberta Report*, April 28, 1997, p. 35.

Campbell, Julia. "Apocalyptic Cult Members Deported from Israel," *Fox News*, December 21, 1999.

Carter, Lewis F. *Charisma and Control in Rajneeshpuram*, Cambridge: Cambridge University Press, 1990.

Caryl, Christian. "Church Arson in Norway: The Devil Made Them Do It," *Wall Street Journal*, August 27, 1996, p. A10.

Casoni, Dianne. "The Relation of Group Philosophy to Different Types of Dangerous Conduct in Cultic Groups," *Cultic Studies Journal*, vol. 17, no. 1, 2000, p. 155.

Cauvin, Henri E. "Fateful Meeting Led to Founding of Cult in Uganda," *New York Times*, March 27, 2000, p. A3.

Chaddock, Gail Russell. "Rise of New Faiths Jolts Old Order to Red Alert," *Christian Science Monitor*, January 24, 1996, p. 8.

Chiang, Harriet, et al. "Victims Left Home Without Looking Back," *San Francisco Chronicle*, March 29, 1997, p. A1.

Chua-Eoan, Howard. "The Faithful Among Us," *Time*, April 14, 1997, p. 44.

"Church of Satan Founder Anton LaVey Claimed 10,000 Followers Worldwide," *Toronto Star*, November 9, 1997, p. A11.

"Church Universal and Triumphant Unifying World Religions," December 11, 2002, posted on Internet at http://www.tsl.org/AboutUs/TheMystical-Path.asp.

"Church Universal and Triumphant Leader Retires," *Associated Press*, January 2, 1999.

Cialdini, Robert B., Ph.D. *Influence, Science and Practice*, New York: Scott, Foresman, 1985.

Clancy, Ray. "Professionals Fall Prey to New Age Gurus," *London Times*, July 21, 1992, p. 1.

Clark, David, et al. "Exit Counseling: A Practical Overview," in *Recovery from Cults*, ed. by Michael D. Langone, Ph.D., New York: Norton, 1993, p. 158–80.

———. Interviewed by Robert L. Snow, November 17, 2002.

Clark, Lesley, and Fallstrom, Jerry. "Captured 'Vampire' Teen Talked of Killing Parents, Woman Claims," *Houston Chronicle,* November 30, 1996, p. 12.

"Close-Up: How Do Cults Convince People It's Time to Die?" *Seattle Times,* March 27, 1997, p. 1.

Coen, Jeff. "Some Christians Fear Y2K Signals the End," *Chicago Tribune,* March 1, 1999, Internet edition.

Collins, Catherine, and Franz, Douglas. "Let Us Prey," *Modern Maturity,* June 1994, p. 22.

"Colorado Cult Leader Once Railed against Such Groups," *St. Louis Post-Dispatch,* January 10, 1999, p. 1A.

"The Comet: Bad Astronomy, Radio Hype Added to UFO Belief," *Detroit News,* March 28, 1997, Internet edition.

Conway, F., et al. "Information Disease: Effects of Covert Induction and Deprogramming," *Update: A Journal of New Religious Movements,* vol. 10, 1986, p. 45.

Coppen, Luke. "Nightmare in Embryo?" *London Times,* April 17, 2002, p. 1.

"Cosmic Activities," July 29, 2002, posted on Internet at http://www.aetherius. org/NewFile/current_cosmic_ activities.html.

Craig, Nadine W., M.A.; and Weathers, Robert, Ph.D. "The False Transformational Promise of Bible-Based Cults: Archetypal Dynamics," *Cultic Studies Journal,* vol. 7, no. 2, 1990, p. 164.

Crumm, David. "Krishna Unity Grows in Detroit," *Detroit Free Press,* August 1, 1998, p. 1A.

Cult Awareness Network. *Who Are They?* Undated pamphlet.

"Cult Expert Explains Attleboro Sect," *MSNBC,* September 1, 2000, posted on Internet at http://www.rickross.com/reference/attleboro/attleboro22. html.

"Cult Leader Prophesies Doom, Vanishes with Followers," *St. Louis Post-Dispatch,* October 16, 1998, Internet edition.

"Cult Leader Prophesies End of World," *Montreal Gazette,* February 16, 2002, p. 1.

"Cult Leader, 17, Pleads Guilty in Slaying," *St. Louis Post-Dispatch,* February 6, 1998, p. 20.

Cults and Psychological Abuse, Naples, Florida: American Family Foundation, 1999.

D'Antonio, Michael. "The New 'Hidden' Cults Want You," *Redbook,* April 1995, p. 93.

Davis, Dena S. "Joining a Cult: Religious Choice or Psychological Aberration?" *Journal of Law and Health,* vol. 11, no. 1, Spring/Summer 1996, p. 145.

Dilley, Maureen. Interviewed by Robert L. Snow, August 18, 2002.

Dole, Arthur A., Ph.D., et al. "Is the New Age Movement Harmless?" *Cultic Studies Journal,* vol. 10, no. 1, 1993, p. 54.

Dranov, Paula. "The Frightening Lure of the Cult," *Cosmopolitan,* December 1994, p. 190.

"Dutch Prosecutors Investigate Cult," *Associated Press,* November 1, 2001.

Elleven, Russell K., Ph.D., et al. "Residential Halls and Cults: Fact or Fiction?" *Cultic Studies Journal,* vol. 15, no. 1, 1998, p. 69.

"End of the World Again Postponed," *De Telegraaf,* December 22, 2001, p. 1.

Ensslin, John C. "38 in Cult Leave Denver, Upset Families," *Rocky Mountain News,* October 8, 1998, posted on Internet at http://insidedenver.com/news/1008doom1.shtml.

Erdoes, Richard. *A.D. 1000: Living on the Brink of Apocalypse,* San Francisco: Harper & Row, 1988.

Fennell, Tom. "Doom Sects: False Prophets Attract the Vulnerable," *Maclean's,* April 7, 1997, p. 48.

Ferris, Timothy. "De-Programming Heaven's Gate," *The New Yorker,* April 14, 1997, p. 31.

Festinger, Leon, et al. *When Prophecy Fails,* New York: Harper & Row, 1964.

Fimrite, Peter. "Unification Church Spokesman," *San Francisco Chronicle,* September 18, 1995, p. A13.

Fisher, Ian. "Yet Another Mass Grave Is Uncovered in Uganda," *New York Times,* March 31, 2000, p. A10.

"5 'Vampire Clan' Members Held in Brutal Slaying," *St. Louis Post-Dispatch,* November 30, 1996, Internet edition.

Flaccus, Gillian. "Oregon Town Has Never Gotten over Its 1984 Bioterrorism Scare," *San Francisco Chronicle,* October 19, 2001, p. A1.

Forney, Matthew. "Jesus Is Back, and She's Chinese," *Time Asia,* November 5, 2001, Internet edition.

"41 Failed End-of-the-World Predictions for 1999," July 3, 2002, posted on Internet at http://www. religioustolerance.org/end_wr19.htm.

Furst, Randy. "Victim's Rich Life, Link to Occult Spiraled into Mysterious Death," *Minneapolis-St. Paul Star Tribune,* August 29, 1997, p. 1A.

Furst, Randy, and McEnroe, Paul. "Pharmacist Killed by Fellow Voodoo Adherents, Cop Says," *Minneapolis-St. Paul Star Tribune,* August 1, 1997, p. 1A.

Gaines, M. J., et al. "The Effects of Cult Membership on the Health Status of Adults and Children," *Health Values: Achieving High Level Wellness,* vol. 8, no. 2, 1984, p. 13.

Galanti, Geri-Ann, Ph.D. "Reflections on 'Brainwashing,'" in *Recovery from Cults,* ed. by Michael D. Langone, Ph.D., New York: Norton, 1993, pp. 85–103.

Gallagher, John. "Diving to Conscience Bay," *Psychology Today,* December 1998, p. 54.

Gard, Carolyn. "The Power and Peril of Cults," *Current Health,* vol. 23, no. 9, May 1997, p. 18.

Gardner, Christine J. "Remembering Jonestown," *Christianity Today,* January 11, 1999, p. 31.

Giambalvo, Carol. *Exit Counseling: A Family Intervention,* Bonita Springs, Florida: American Family Foundation, 1995.

———. Interviewed by Robert L. Snow, June 10, 2002.

Giambalvo, Carol, et al. "Ethical Standards for Thought Reform Consultants," *Cultic Studies Journal,* vol. 13, no. 1 (1996), p. 97.

Gillis, Justin, and Murphy, Caryle. "Concerned about Campus Cults, Colleges Arm Students with Facts," *Washington Post,* December 9, 1997, p. B1.

Gleick, Elizabeth. "The Marker We've Been…Waiting For," *Time,* April 7, 1997, p. 14.

Goldberg, Lorna, M.S.W., A.C.S.W. "Guidelines for Therapists," in *Recovery from Cults,* ed. by Michael D. Langone, Ph.D., New York: Norton, 1993, pp. 232–50.

Goldberg, William, M.S.W., A.C.S.W. "Cults on Campus: How Can You Help?" in *Cults on Campus: Continuing Challenge,* ed. by Marcia Rudin, New York: International Cult Education Foundation, 1996, p. 11–18.

Goode, Erica. "The Eternal Quest for a New Age," *U.S. News & World Report,* April 7, 1997, p. 32.

Goski, Patricia, R.N. "Grief, Loss, and the Former Cult Member," in *Cults and Psychological Abuse,* Naples, Florida: American Family Foundation, 1999, pp. 46–48.

Graham, Rachel. "The Saffron Swami," *Willamette Week – 25 Years,* July 24, 2002, posted on Internet at http://www.wweek.com/html/25–1983.html.

Greenwood, Tom. "History: Group Deaths March Across the Pages of Time," *Detroit News,* March 28, 1997, Internet edition.

Groenveld, Jan. "Totalism and Group Dynamics," *Cult Awareness and Information Centre,* May 7, 1999, posted on Internet at http://www.ex-cult.org/General/totalist-group-dynamics.htm.

Gross, Jane. "In the Hunt for Answers, Only Questions Arise," *New York Times,* March 28, 1997, p. A21.

Grossman, Lawrence K. "The Story of a Truly Contaminated Election," *Columbia Journalism Review,* January/February 2001, posted on Internet at http://www.cjr.org.

"Group May Have Roots in '70s 'UFO Cult'" *Detroit News,* March 28, 1997, Internet edition.

"Guru Rajneesh Dead at 58," *Watchman Expositor,* July 24, 2002, posted on Internet at http://www.watchman.org/na/rajneesh.htm.

Halperin, David A., M.D. "The Appeal of the Impossible and the Efflorescence of the Unbelievable: A Psychoanalytic Perspective on Cults and Occultism," *Cultic Studies Journal,* vol. 9, no. 2, 1992, p. 190.

———. "Cults and Children: The Role of the Psychotherapist," *Cultic Studies Journal,* vol. 6, no. 1, 1989, p. 76.

Hare, Robert D. *Without Conscience: The Disturbing World of the Psychopaths Among Us,* New York: Pocket Books, 1993.

Harrison, Barbara Grizzuti. "Children and the Cult," *New England Monthly,* December 1984, p. 51.

Hartnett, Howie Paul. "UFO Group: Truth Will Land in 2003," *Charlotte Observer,* November 4, 2002, p. 1.

Hassan, Steven. *Combatting Cult Mind Control,* Rochester, Vermont: Park Street Press, 1990, pp. 9, 12–13, 22, 25, 49, 77.

———. Interviewed by Robert L. Snow, November 19, 2002.

———. *Releasing the Bonds: Empowering People to Think for Themselves,* Somerville, Mass.: Freedom of Mind Press, 2000.

Henderson, Jim. "Heaven Can Wait," *Houston Chronicle,* March 26, 1998, p. 1.

Hester, Jere. "In Cults, Leader's Charisma Takes Over," *New York Daily News,* March 27, 1997, p. 1.

Hettena, Seth. "Heaven's Gate Survivor Keeps Faith," *Associated Press,* March 26, 2002.

Hewes, Hayden. *UFO Missionaries Extraordinary,* New York: Pocket Books: 1976.

Holmstrom, David. "Parents Can Reduce Lure of Cults for Children," *Christian Science Monitor,* April 3, 1997, p. 14.

Hughes, Jay. "Pathologist Details Mother's Many Wounds," *Biloxi Sun Herald,* June 4, 1998, p. A1.

———. "Teen Blames Demons, Friends in Slayings," *Seattle Times,* June 4, 1998, Internet edition.

Hunter, Eagan. "Adolescent Attraction to Cults," *Adolescence,* vol. 33, Fall 1998, p. 709.

"Indonesia Cultists Killed Amid Doomsday No-Show," *Reuters,* September 13, 1999.

James, Steven. "It Happened to Me," *Campus Life,* May/June 2000, posted on Internet at http://www.christianitytoday.com/cl/2000/003/3.32.html.

Janis, Irving L. *Groupthink,* Boston: Houghton Mifflin, 1982.

"Jesus of Siberia," *The Guardian,* May 24, 2002, p. 1.

Johannes, Katie N. "Attorney Argues Abuse Defendant Is Mentally Ill," *Great Falls Tribune,* September 25, 2002, Internet edition."

Kahler, Karl. *The Cult That Snapped,* Los Gatos, California: Ex-Way.Com, 1999.

———. Interviewed by Robert L. Snow, August 20, 2002.

Kandel, Randy Frances, J.D., Ph.D. "Litigating the Cult-Related Child Custody Case," *Cult Observer,* July 12, 1999, posted on Internet at http://www. csj.org/pubs_co/guestcolumn/cultismandlaw.htm.

Keim, Tony. "Police Block Drive-In Protest Against Guru," *Courier-Mail,* September 4, 2002, p. 1.

Kelley, Susan J., Ph.D., R.N. "Ritualistic Abuse of Children in Day-Care Centers," in *Recovery from Cults,* ed. by Michael D. Langone, Ph.D., New York: Norton, 1993, p. 344.

Kelly, Michael. "The Road to Paranoia," *The New Yorker,* June 19, 1995, p. 60.

Kifner, John. "Drawn by Child's Cries, Police Uncover Arsenal," *New York Times,* November 13, 1996, p. B4.

Klebnikov, Peter. "Time of Troubles: Heaven's Gate Isn't the Only One," *Newsweek,* April 7, 1997, p. 48.

Klee, Robi. Interviewed by Robert L. Snow, August 27, 2002.

Kloberdanz, Kristin. "Cult Attraction," *Book,* May/June 2001, p. 16.

Klotz, Suzanne. "Teenage 'Satanists' Dreamed of Killing," *The Age,* September 4, 1999, posted on Internet at http://www.rickross.com/reference/satanism/satanism60. html.

Knight, Kathryn. "Millennium Cults Pose Bigger Threat Than Terrorists," *London Times,* August 20, 1996, p. 1.

"Korean Cloning Out of this World," *CNN,* July 25, 2002, posted on Internet at http://europe.cnn.com.

Kristof, Nicholas D. "Japanese Cult Said to Have Planned Nerve-Gas Attacks in U.S.," *New York Times,* March 23, 1997, p. 14.

Krupp, E.C. "In the Wake of Heaven's Gate," *Sky & Telescope,* September 1997, p. 80.

Kunii, Irene M. "Engineer of Doom," *Time,* June 12, 1995, p. 45.

Lacayo, Richard. "Cults: In the Reign of Fire," *Time,* October 17, 1994, Internet edition.

Lalich, Janja. "Repairing the Soul after a Cult Experience," *Cult Recovery,* May 31, 1999, posted on Internet at http://www.csj.org/studyindex/study recovery/study_repairsoul.htm.

Lampman, Jane. "Rev. Moon Raising His Profile," *Christian Science Monitor,* April 19, 2001, Internet edition.

Lamy, Phillip. *Millennium Rage,* New York: Plenum Press, 1996.

Laney, William. "The Way International Reaches Settlement with Couple," *Wapakoneta Daily News,* November 7, 2000, p. 1.

Langone, Michael D., Ph.D. "Cults: Questions & Answers," *Cultic Studies,* June 7, 2002, posted on Internet at http://www.csj.org/studyindex/studycult/cultqa.htm.

———. Foreword in *Captive Hearts, Captive Minds,* by Madeleine Landau Tobias and Janja Lalich, Alameda, California: Hunter House, 1994, p. ix–xiii.

———. *Recovery from Cults,* New York: Norton, 1993.

———. "What is 'New Age?'" in *Cults and Psychological Abuse,* Naples, Florida: American Family Foundation, 1999, pp. 33–36.

Langone, Michael D., Ph.D., and Rosedale, Herbert L. "On Using the Term 'Cult,'"*American Family Foundation* (May 31, 1999), Posted on Internet at http://www.csj.org/infoserv_cult101/essay_cult.htm.

Lanning, Kenneth V. "Investigator's Guide to Allegations of 'Ritual' Child Abuse," January 1992, posted on Internet at http://web.mit.edu/harris/ www/lanning.htm.

Lattin, Don. "Apocalypse Meets Millennium in Texas Sect," *San Francisco Chronicle,* March 7, 1998, p. A1.

———. "Cult Experts Say Arrests May Bolster Sect Leader," *San Francisco Chronicle,* January 6, 1999, p. A1.

———. "The Day After Doomsday in the Holy City," *San Francisco Chronicle,* January 30, 2000, p. A6.

———. "The End to Innocent Acceptance of Sects," *San Francisco Chronicle,* November 13, 1998, p. A1.

———. "Escaping a Free Love Legacy," *San Francisco Chronicle,* February 14, 2001, p. A1.

———. "Experts Warn of Small Sects' Dangers," *San Francisco Chronicle,* March 17, 1995, p. A19.

———. "In Oakland, Moon Stresses Family," *San Francisco Chronicle,* March 13, 2001, p. A28.

———. "Krishna's Honesty in Scandal Could Prove Costly," *San Francisco Chronicle,* June 15, 2002, p. A1.

———. "A Test of Faith," *San Francisco Chronicle,* February 13, 2001, p. A1.

"Leader of Vampire Cult Pleads Guilty in Slayings," *Houston Chronicle,* February 6, 1998, p. 20

Lefevre, Greg. "The Internet as a God and Propaganda Tool for Cults," *CNN,* March 27, 1997, posted on Internet at http://cnn.com/TECH/9703/27/techno.pagans/index.html.

Levy, Lawrence. Interviewed by Robert L. Snow, August 26, 2002 and November 4, 2002.

———. "Prosecuting an Ex-Cult Member's Undue Influence Suit," *Cultic Studies Journal,* vol. 7, no. 1, 1990, p. 15.

Lifton, Robert Jay, M.D. *Thought Reform and the Psychology of Totalism,* Chapel Hill: University of North Carolina Press, 1989.

Lindley, Jane R. "Cult Recruitment of International Students on American Campuses," in *Cults on Campus: Continuing Challenge,* ed. by Marcia R. Rudin, New York: International Cult Education Program, 1996, pp. 19–24.

"The Little Pebble Press Releases," June 27, 2002, posted on Internet at http://www.shoal.net.au/~mwoa/press_releases/press_release_27_june_2002.html.

"The Little Pebble Press Releases," July 10, 2002, posted on Internet at http://www.shoal.net.au/~mwoa/press_releases/press_release_10_July_2002.html.

LoLordo, Ann. "The Jerusalem Syndrome," *Baltimore Sun,* April 8, 1999, p. 1F.

Long, Margaret W. "The Cult Appeal: Susceptibilities of the Missionary Kid," *Cultic Studies Journal,* vol. 4, no. 1, 1987, p. 40.

Lowe, Peggy. "Denver Cultists Arrested in Israel," *Denver Post,* January 4, 1999, Internet edition.

Maaga, Mary McCormick. *Hearing the Voices of Jonestown,* Syracuse, New York: Syracuse University Press, 1998, posted on Internet at http://www.und.nodak.edu/dept/philrel/jonestown/suicide.html.

Mack, Mitchell, Jr. Interviewed by Robert L. Snow, May 30, 2002.

MacVicar, Sheila. "Uganda Hunts Cult Leaders," *ABC News,* April 4, 2000, posted on Internet at http://abcnews.go.com/sections/world/DailyNews/chat_uganda0404.html.

Malone, James, et al. "A Community and Its Shooter," *Louisville Courier-Journal,* December 8, 1998, Internet edition.

Mann, Cathleen. Interviewed by Robert L. Snow, August 18, 2002.

Markoff, John. "To Gullible, Net Offers Many Traps," *New York Times,* March 28, 1997, p. A20.

Marquand, Robert, and Woods, Daniel B. "Rise in Cults as Millennium Approaches," *Christian Science Monitor,* March 28, 1997, p. 1C.

Martin, Jim. Interviewed by Robert L. Snow, June 19, 2002 and November 1, 2002.

Martin, Paul R., Ph.D., et al. "Post-Cult Symptoms," *Cultic Studies Journal,* vol. 9, no. 2, 1992, p. 220.

———. "Study Indicates Rehab's Benefits," *American Family Foundation,* posted on Internet at http://www.csj.org/rg/rgessays/rgessay_studyrehab.htm.

Mason, Margie. "Cult's Local Ties a Concern," *Jacksonville Times-Union,* February 7, 1999, Internet edition.

McAndrews, Anne. "I Lost My Husband to a Cult," *Redbook,* May 1994, p. 60.

McCarthy, Ken. "On Cults, Computers, and Cash," *Rewired,* March 31, 1997, posted on Internet at http://www.rewired.com/97/0331.html.

McGee, Rich. "Cults," *Leadership University,* April 16, 1997, posted on Internet at http://www.leaderu.com/common/cults.html.

McGinty, Brendan. "Cult Held Me Captive for Six Months," *Sunday Mail-England,* March 9, 2002, p. 1.

McMillion, Scott. "CUT's Theology Hasn't Changed," *Bozeman Chronicle,* March 18, 1998, p. 1.

McPhee, Mike. "Relatives Fear for Group's Members," *Denver Post,* October 8, 1998, Internet edition.

Mendoza, Martha. "Talk of Death, Cults Follow Shootings," *Detroit News*, October 12, 1997, Internet edition.

Merzer, Martin. "Cultists Commit Mass Suicide in Guyana," Associated Press, November 20, 1978.

———. "Trial of 'Teenage Vampire' Transfixes a Florida Town," *Miami Herald*, February 5, 1998, p. 1A.

Milgram, Stanley. *Obedience to Authority*, New York: Harper & Row, 1974.

"Millennial Madness, Jerusalem Jitters," *U.S. News & World Report*, January 18, 1999, p. 32.

Miller, Mark. "Secrets of the Cult," *Newsweek*, April 14, 1997, p. 28.

Miller, Rick. "Religious Sect Travels to God's 'Landing Site,'" *Houston Chronicle*, January 11, 1998, p. 9.

Mitchell, Kirk. "Doomsday-Cult Leader's Words Reappear on Web," *Denver Post*, May 11, 2001, Internet edition.

Mitzelfeld, Jim. "House of Judah Chief Gets 3 Years for Enslavement, Death," December 20, 1986, p. A1.

Moehringer, J. R. "Killings Linked to Satan-Loving Teen," *Indianapolis Star*, October 15, 1997, p. A8.

Monmaney, Terrence. "Free Will, or Thought Control?" *Los Angeles Times*, April 4, 1997, p. A1.

Monmaney, Terrence, and Smith, Doug. "Cult Targeted Web Sites for Abuse, Depression Victims," *Los Angeles Times*, March 28, 1997, p. A15.

Moore, Rebecca. *A Sympathetic History of Jonestown: The Moore Family Involvement in Peoples Temple*, Lewiston, New York: Edwin Mellen Press, 1985.

Morello, Carol. "Teen Defendants Hinted at Dark Side," *Detroit News*, October 22, 1997, Internet edition.

Mozingo, Joe. "On Top of Old Baldy, Prayers Go Out for the World," *Los Angeles Times*, October 4, 1998, p. B2.

Murphy, Dean E. "Ugandan Cult's New Death Site—153 Bodies," *San Francisco Chronicle*, March 25, 2000, p. A1.

Muster, Nori. Interviewed by Robert L. Snow, June 10, 2002.

Nealy, Jounice L. "Robberies' Planner Sentenced," *St. Petersburg Times*, August 10, 2000, p. 1B.

Neiwert, David. "An Interview with John Trochmann/Randy Trochmann," *Militia Watchdog*, February 14, 1996, posted on Internet at http://www.militia watchdog.org/dn-troch.htm.

Nelson, Craig. "Journey into a Heart of Darkness," *Seattle Times*, April 2, 2000, p. A1.

———. "Kibwetere's Wife Says He Did Not Run Uganda Cult," *Seattle Times*, March 31, 2000, p. A1.

Newport, Frank, and Strausberg, Maura. "Americans' Belief in Psychic and Paranormal Phenomenon Is Up over Last Decade," *Gallup Organization*, June 8, 2001, posted on Internet at http://www.gallup.com/poll/releases/pr010608.asp.

Ofshe, Richard, Ph.D., and Singer, Margaret Thaler, Ph.D. "Attacks on Peripheral Versus Central Elements of Self and the Impact of Thought Reforming Techniques," *Cultic Studies Journal*, vol. 3, no. 1, 1986, p. 3.

———. "Thought Reform Programs and the Production of Psychiatric Casualties," *Psychiatric Annals,* vol. 20, no. 4, 1990, posted on Internet at http://www.rickross. com/reference/brainwashing/brainwashing21.html.

O'Leary, Stephen. "Seeds of Apocalypse Are Among Us," *Los Angeles Times,* April 22, 1997, p. B7.

Osinski, Bill. "Putnam Grand Jury Reindicts Top Nuwaubian," *Atlanta Journal-Constitution,* October 4, 2002, p. 1.

Pardon, Robert. Interviewed by Robert L. Snow, July 12, 2002.

Parker, Paul Edward. "Attleboro Sect Member Asks for Delay in Start of Murder Trial," *Providence Journal,* August 21, 2002, Internet edition.

———. "Sect Case Jurors Say Religion Didn't Play into Verdict," *Providence Journal,* June 29, 2002, Internet edition.

Peecher, Rob. "York's Accusers Describe Years of Sexual Abuse," *Macon Telegraph,* September 1, 2002, p. 1.

Pimentel, Benjamin. "'Guru Hunters' Take on Palo Alto Swami," *San Francisco Chronicle,* February 9, 1998, p. A16.

Pinkerton, James. "Sect's Leader Says God Will Come to Garland Next Year," *Houston Chronicle,* December 24, 1997, p. 13.

Piper, E.S., and Wright, S.A. "Families and Cults: Familial Factors Related to Youth Leaving or Remaining in Deviant Religious Groups," *Journal of Marriage and the Family,* vol. 48, 1986, p. 15.

"Police Seek Cult Leader," *New York Times,* November 23, 1984, p. A19.

Polly, Jim. Interviewed by Robert L. Snow, October 3, 2002.

Post, Tom, and Liu, Melinda. "Doomsday Cults: 'Only the Beginning,'" *Newsweek,* April 3, 1995, p. 40.

Probert, Roy. "Geneva Seeks to Temper Influence of Cults," *Swiss Info,* November 3, 2001, p. 1.

Pulskamp, Andrew J. "Are Cults Working Your College Campus?" *CPNet,* April 17, 2000, posted on Internet at http://www.rickross.com/reference/icc/ICC252.html.

Purdum, Todd S. "Videotapes Left by 39 Who Died Described Cult's Suicide Goal," *New York Times,* March 28, 1997, p. A19.

Rabinovitz, Jonathan. "College Idealism Was Fertile Soil for Fringe Group," *New York Times,* November 15, 1996, p. A1.

"The Red Flag List," January 7, 2003, posted on Internet at http://www.tunnellight.org/redflag.htm.

Reid, T.R. "Japan Cult's Strange Scene," *San Francisco Chronicle,* March 23, 1995, p. A10.

———. "Suspect Held in Gassing of Tokyo Trains," *San Francisco Chronicle,* March 21, 1995, p. A1.

Rendon, Ruth. "Kilroys Say a Prayer for Kids on Break," *Houston Chronicle,* March 21, 1999, p. 37.

Renner, Gerald. "Computer Bug Is Stuff of Prophecy to Fundamentalist Faithful," *Hartford Courant,* January 2, 1999, p. 1.

Rhodes, Tom. "UFOs: It's a Coverup," *Ottawa Citizen,* October 11, 1998, p. 1.

Rich, Frank. "Journal," *New York Times,* April 17, 1997, p. A1.

Roberge, Pat. Interviewed by Robert L. Snow, December 6, 2002.

Rohrlich, Ted. "After Synanon," *Los Angeles Times Magazine,* March 29, 1998, p. 16.

Ronnow, Karin. "CUT Leaders Admit Group Living Beyond Its Means," *Bozeman Chronicle,* March 17, 1998, p. 1.

Rosin, Hanna. "Apocalypse Doomsayers Change Their Story," *Washington Post,* January 1, 2000, p. A1.

———. "Cult Leader with Violent Leanings May Have Led Followers to Israel," *Houston Chronicle,* October 18, 1998, p. A10.

Ross, Jackie. "Religious Group Still Affecting Students, Soliciting on Campus," *Vanderbilt Hustler,* November 13, 1998, p. 1.

Royse, David. "Town Is Frightened of Teens' Involvement with Vampire Rituals," *Houston Chronicle,* December 2, 1996, p. 7.

Rudin, James, and Rudin, Marcia. "The Effect of Religious Cults on Western Mainstream Religion," *Cultic Studies Journal,* vol. 8, no. 1, 1991, pp. 7–36.

———. *Prison or Paradise,* Philadelphia: Fortress Press, 1980.

Rudin, Marcia. *Cults on Campus: Continuing Challenge,* New York: International Cult Education Program, 1999.

Ryckaert, Vic. "Church Arsonist Gets 421/2 Years," *Indianapolis Star,* November 15, 2000, p. B1.

Sack, Kevin. "Grim Details Emerge in Teen-Age Slaying Case," *New York Times,* October 15, 1997, p. A10.

Sage, Adam. "Lured by the Cult," *London Times,* April 18, 2001, p. 1.

Sartorius, Lawrence, and Sartorius, Michael. "The New Earth," June 7, 1999, posted on Internet at http://www.islandnet.com/~arton/newearth.html.

"Satanic Worship Services Suspended at Prison in Kentucky," *Indianapolis Star,* September 1, 2002, p. A18.

Schein, Edgar H., Ph.D., et al. *Coercive Persuasion,* New York: Norton, 1961.

Schneider, Mike. "Man Who Initiated 'Vampire' Teen Testifies," *Miami Herald,* February 20, 1998, p. 2B.

———. "'Vampire' Leader Sexually Abused, Expert Testifies," *Miami Herald,* February 18, 1998, p. 5B.

Schramm, Susan. "Man Admits Church Arsons," *Indianapolis Star,* February 24, 1999, p. A1.

———. "Plea Solves 26 Church Fires," *Indianapolis Star,* July 12, 2000, p. A1.

"The Sect," *Boston Globe,* November 26, 2000, p. A1.

Seligman, Katherine. "Yuba Church or Cult?" *San Francisco Examiner,* October 12, 1997, p. 1A.

Shaw, Daniel, C.S.W. "Traumatic Abuse in Cults," May 10, 1999, posted on Internet at http://www.cyberpass.net/truth/essay.htm.

Shioya, Tara. "Pair Sentenced to 3 Years in Ritual Beating Death," *San Francisco Chronicle,* August 3, 1996, p. A20.

Simon, Mark. "Survivor Recalls Guyana," *San Francisco Chronicle,* March 28, 1997, p. A19.

Singer, Margaret Thaler, Ph.D. *Cults in Our Midst,* San Francisco: Jossey-Bass Publishers, 1995.

———. Interviewed by Robert L. Snow, July 1, 2002, and November 4, 2002.

Singer, Margaret Thaler, Ph.D., and West, Louis J., M.D. "Cults, Quacks, and Nonprofessional Therapies," in *Comprehensive Textbook of Psychiatry,* III, ed. by Harold I. Kaplan et al., Baltimore: Williams & Wilkins, 1980, p. 3284.

"6 Arrested in Slayings near Tennessee Rest Area," *CNN Interactive,* April 8, 1997, posted on Internet at http://www.cnn.com.

Smith, Gordon. "In the Name of Religion," *San Diego Union-Tribune,* March 15, 1995, p. 1.

———. "Wave of Resignations and Expulsions Following Open Letter," *San Diego Union-Tribune,* March 16, 1995, p. 1.

Smith, Zay N. "The Way—40,000 and Still Growing," *Chicago Sun-Times,* August 17, 1980, p. 1.

Snow, Robert L. *The Complete Guide to Personal and Home Safety,* Cambridge: Perseus Publishing, 2002.

———. *Family Abuse,* New York: Plenum Press, 1997.

———. *Stopping a Stalker,* Cambridge: Perseus Publishing, 1998.

———. *SWAT Teams,* Cambridge: Perseus Publishing, 1996.

———. *Terrorists Among Us: The Militia Threat,* Cambridge: Perseus Publishing, 1999.

Spargimino, Larry. *Y2K-666?,* Oklahoma City: Hearthstone publishers, 1998.

Steinberg, Jacques. "From Religious Childhood to Reins of a U.F.O. Cult," *New York Times,* March 29, 1997, p. 9.

Steinfels, Peter. "Beliefs," *New York Times,* July 13, 1996, p. 10.

Strentz, Thomas. *The Stockholm Syndrome,* undated, report from Special Operations and Research Unit, FBI Academy, Quantico, Virginia.

Sullivan, Kevin. "Japanese Villagers Lay Siege to House Bought by Doomsday Cult," *Washington Post,* January 1, 1999, p. A23.

"Surveillance Extension Sought," *Japan Times,* November 24, 2002, Internet edition.

"Suspect Ties Miss. Deaths to Satan," *Washington Post,* November 12, 1997, p. A2.

Swartling, Gunrun, O.T., and Swartling, Per G., M.D. "Psychiatric Problems in Ex-Members of Word of Life," *Cultic Studies Journal,* vol. 9, no. 1, 1992, p. 78.

Taylor, Michael. "Jones Captivated S.F.'s Liberal Elite," *San Francisco Chronicle,* November 12, 1998, p. A1.

"Techno-Religious Order Members Died Using Drugs, Bags over Heads," *Detroit News,* March 28, 1997, Internet edition.

"Teens Linked to Cult Held in Slaying of Girl's Parents," *Miami Herald,* November 30, 1996, p. 6B.

"Three Die in Cambodia Cult Suicide," *CNN,* October 1, 2002, posted on Internet at http://europe.cnn.com.

"3 Teens Say They Skipped Parents' Suicide Offer," *Detroit Free Press,* March 25, 1997, p. 10A.

Tobias, Madeleine Landau, and Lalich, Janja. *Captive Hearts, Captive Minds,* Alameda, California: Hunter House, 1994.

Tucker, Rob, M.Ed. "Teen Satanism," in *Recovery from Cults,* ed. by Michael D. Langone, Ph.D., New York: Norton, 1993, pp. 356–81.

Tuhuirwe, Chris. *The Kanungu Cult Saga: Suicide, Murder, or Salvation?,* Makerere University Press, Uganda, 2000.

"Unarius Perspective on the September 11 Terrorist Attack," July 29, 2002, posted on Internet at http://www.unarius.org/sept11.html.

Valatx, Jean-Louis, M.D. "Sleep Deprivation," *Cultic Studies Journal,* vol. 11, no. 2, 1994, p. 215.

"Vampire Cult Leader Receives Death Sentence," *Kansas City Star,* February 28, 1998, Internet edition.

Van Hoey, Sara. "Cults in Court," *Cultic Studies Journal,* vol. 8, no. 1, 1991, p. 61.

Van Meir, Erika. Interviewed by Robert L. Snow, August 9, 2002, and August 11, 2002.

"Vatican Outlaws South Coast Religious Sect," *ABC News Online,* June 18, 2002, posted on Internet at http://abc.net.au/news/newsitems/s584603.htm.

Vick, Karl. "Prophecy's Price," *Washington Post,* April 1, 2000, p. A1.

Von Sternberg, Bob. "Millennial Musings," *Minneapolis-St. Paul Star Tribune,* October 25, 1997, p. 5B.

Warren, Jenifer. "Trouble Taints a Cerebral Sanctuary," *Los Angeles Times,* November 4, 1996, p. A1.

Wasswa, Henry. "Uganda Cult Deaths Remain a Mystery," *Associated Press,* March 16, 2002.

Wedge, Dave. "Attleboro Mom Said to Be Cutting Ties to Cult," *Boston Herald,* October 12, 2002, p. A1.

———. "Cultists Convinced Only God Will Provide," *Boston Herald,* September 3, 2000, p. A1.

———. "Cultists Indicted in 'Chilling' Murder of Infant," *Boston Herald,* November 14, 2000, p. A1.

———. "Cult Tries Secession to Avoid Charges," *Boston Herald,* June 5, 2000, Internet edition.

Wessinger, Catherine. "1978—Jonestown," *Alternate Considerations of Jonestown and Peoples Temple,* July 19, 1999, posted on Internet at http://www.und.nodak.edu/dept/philrel/jonestown/jt1978.html.

———. *How the Millennium Comes Violently,* New York: Chatham House Publishers, 2000.

West, Debra. "Late Guru's Detractors Lay Claim to His Millions," *Seattle Times,* March 28, 1999, Internet edition.

———. "2 Claims Complicate Tussle over New Age Guru's Estate," *New York Times,* June 13, 1999, p. A1.

West, Louis Jolyon, M.D. "Persuasive Techniques in Contemporary Cults: A Public Health Approach," *Cultic Studies Journal,* vol. 7, no. 2, 1990, p. 131.

Wexler, Mark N., Ph.D. "Expanding the Groupthink Explanation to the Study of Contemporary Cults," *Cultic Studies Journal,* vol. 12, no. 1, 1995, p. 49.

White, Patrick. "Solar Temple Cult Worries Rise as Millennium Nears," *Reuters,* April 26, 1999.

Whitehouse, Tom. "'Messiah' or Cult Leader?" *Detroit News,* June 4, 1999, Internet edition.

Whiteside, Elena S. *The Way: Living in Love,* New Knoxville, Ohio: American Christian Press, 1971.

Wilemon, Tom, and Branan, Brad. "Pearl Struggles to Heal," *Biloxi Sun Herald,* October 12, 1997, p. A1.

Wilson, Marshall. "Cult Left Arsenal Behind," *San Francisco Chronicle,* April 2, 1997, p. A1.

———. "Last 2 Cult Members' Names Released," *San Francisco Chronicle,* April 1, 1997, p. A3.

Wooden, Kenneth. *The Children of Jonestown,* New York: McGraw-Hill, 1981.

Worthan, Steve. Interviewed by Robert L. Snow, October 17, 2002.

Yamaguchi, Mari. "Japan Grabbles with Resilient Doomsday Cult," *Raleigh News & Observer,* September 11, 2002, p. 1.

"Yoga Leads to Devil Worship!" *Freedom Writer,* September/October 1990, posted on Internet at http://berkshire.net/~ifas/fw/9009/yoga.html.

Zablocki, Benjamin. Paper presented to Cults: Theory and Treatment Issues Conference in Philadelphia on May 31, 1997.

Zane, Maitland. "Surviving the Heart of Darkness," *San Francisco Chronicle,* November 13, 1998, p. A1.

Zerby, Maria Karen. "An Answer to Him That Asketh Us!" *The New Good News!,* no. 3016 GN 653 DFO, 1995, p. 6.

Zimbardo, Philip G., Ph.D. "What Messages Are Behind Today's Cults?" *APA Monitor,* May 1997, p. 14.

Ziv, Laura. "Heaven's Gate Hell," *Cosmopolitan,* July 1997, p. 130.

Index

About the Author

ROBERT L. SNOW has been a police officer with the Indianapolis Police for 34 years and is currently a captain and commander of the Homicide Branch. He is the author of *The Militia Threat* (1999), and *Looking for Carol Beckwith* (1999).